CHILTON'S REPAIR & TUNE-UP GUIDE
HONDA 1973-78

Civic 1973-78 • Civic CVCC 1975-78 • Accord CVCC 1975-78

Managing Editor KERRY A. FREEMAN, S.A.E.
Senior Editor RICHARD J. RIVELE
Editor ROBERT F. KING JR.

President WILLIAM A. BARBOUR
Executive Vice President RICHARD H. GROVES
Vice President and General Manager JOHN P. KUSHNERICK

CHILTON BOOK COMPANY
Radnor, Pennsylvania
19089

The Chilton Book Company expresses its appreciation to the Honda
Training Center, Moorestown, New Jersey for its assistance in the
preparation of this book.

SAFETY NOTICE

Proper service and repair procedures are vital to the safe, reliable
operation of all motor vehicles, as well as the personal safety of those
performing repairs. This book outlines procedures for servicing and
repairing vehicles using safe, effective methods. The procedures
contain many NOTES, CAUTIONS and WARNINGS which should be
followed along with standard safety procedures to eliminate the
possibility of personal injury or improper service which could damage
the vehicle or compromise its safety.

It is important to note that repair procedures and techniques, tools
and parts for servicing motor vehicles, as well as the skill and experience
of the individual performing the work vary widely. It is not possible to
anticipate all of the conceivable ways or conditions under which vehicles
may be serviced, or to provide cautions as to all of the possible hazards
that may result. Standard and accepted safety precautions and equipment should be used when handling toxic or flammable fluids, and safety
goggles or other protection should be used during cutting, grinding,
chiseling, prying, or any other process that can cause material removal
or projectiles.

Some procedures require the use of tools specially designed for a
specific purpose. Before substituting another tool or procedure, you
must be completely satisfied that neither your personal safety, nor the
performance of the vehicle will be endangered.

Contents

Quick Reference Specifications

For quick and easy reference, complete this page with the most commonly used specifications for your vehicle. The specifications can be found in Chapters 1 through 3 or on the tune-up decal under the hood of the vehicle.

TUNE-UP

Firing Order _____

Spark Plugs:

    Type _____

    Gap (in.) _____

Point Gap (in.) _____

Dwell Angle (°) _____

Ignition Timing (°) _____

    Vacuum (Connected/Disconnected) _____

Valve Clearance (in.)

    Intake _____   **Exhaust** _____

CAPACITIES

Engine Oil (qts)

    With Filter Change _____

    Without Filter Change _____

Cooling System (qts) _____

Manual Transmission (pts) _____

    Type _____

Automatic Transmission (pts) _____

    Type _____

Differential (pts) _____

    Type _____

COMMONLY FORGOTTEN PART NUMBERS

Use these spaces to record the part numbers of frequently replaced parts.

PCV VALVE   **OIL FILTER**   **AIR FILTER**

Manufacturer _____   **Manufacturer** _____   **Manufacturer** _____

Part No. _____   **Part No.** _____   **Part No.** _____

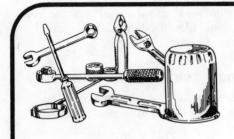

General Information and Maintenance

HOW TO USE THIS BOOK

Chilton's Repair and Tune-up Guide for the Honda is designed for the Honda owner who desires to do much of the tune-ups, repair, and servicing on his vehicle. The instructions are easy to follow and include both simple *and* complex operations, making the book essential for both the inexperienced and those familiar with auto repairing.

Before applying the information in this book to your automobile, be sure that you have a set of metric tools, as all Hondas use metric nuts, bolts, and fittings. The wrong tool could damage a nut or bolt, turning a simple procedure into a frustrating and difficult one. In addition to standard hand tools, certain factory special tools may be necessary. Wherever possible, a standard or makeshift tool has been substituted. However, for those jobs requiring special tools, it will be necessary to acquire the tool from a Honda dealer.

Before starting, you should become as familiar as possible with the area you intend to repair by reading the entire section dealing with that particular area. This book was designed to give simple but detailed information and you should be able to learn rapidly and effectively if you take your time and concentrate on the procedures detailed in this book.

One final note before you begin: all references to the left side of the car apply to the driver's side while, conversely, the right side specifies the passenger side of the vehicle.

TOOLS AND EQUIPMENT

Now that you have purchased this book and committed yourself to maintaining your car, a small set of basic tools and equipment will prove handy. The first group of items should be adequate for most maintenance and light repair procedures:

Sliding T-bar handle or ratchet wrench;

⅜ in. drive socket wrench set (with breaker bar) (metric);

Universal adapter for socket wrench set;

Flat blade and phillips head screwdrivers;

Pliers;

Adjustable wrench;

Locking pliers;

Open-end wrench set (metric);

Feeler gauge set;

Oil filter strap wrench;

Brake adjusting spoon;

Drift pin;

Torque wrench;

and, of course, a hammer.

Along with the above mentioned tools, the following equipment should be on hand:

Scissors jack or hydraulic jack of sufficient capacity;

Wheel blocks;

Grease gun (hand-operated type);

Drip pan (low and wide);

Drop light;

Tire pressure gauge;

Penetrating oil (spray lubricant)

and a can of waterless hand cleaner.

In this age of emission controls and high priced gasoline, it is important to keep your car in proper tune. The following items, though they will represent an investment equal or greater to that of the first group, will tell you everything you might need to know about a car's state of tune:

12-volt test light;

Compression gauge;

Manifold vacuum gauge;

Power timing light;

Dwell-tachometer.

SERIAL NUMBER IDENTIFICATION

Vehicle Identification (Chassis) Number

Vehicle identification numbers are mounted on the top edge of the instrument panel and are visible from the outside. In addition, there is a Vehicle/Engine Identification plate under the hood on the hood mounting bracket.

The chassis number and engine number are both stamped on the tag under the hood

Engine Serial Number

The engine serial number is stamped into the clutch casing. The first three digits indicate engine model identification. The remaining numbers refer to production sequence. This same number is also stamped onto the Vehicle/Engine Identification plate mounted on the hood bracket.

Transmission Serial Number

The transmission serial number is stamped on the top of the transmission/clutch case.

ROUTINE MAINTENANCE

Air Cleaner

A conventional circular air cleaner element, housed above the carburetor, must be replaced every 12,000 miles (1973–74 models) or 15,000 (1975 and later models). To remove, unscrew the wing nut from the container top, then remove the top and the air cleaner element. Be sure to clean out the container before installing a new element.

NOTE: *Accord and Civic air cleaner elements are not interchangeable, although they appear to be.*

Air cleaner element replacement

Positive Crankcase Ventilation (PCV)

The Honda is equipped with a "Dual Return" PCV system in which blow-by gas is returned to the combustion chamber through the intake manifold and the air cleaner.

Maintenance on the system is relatively

MODEL IDENTIFICATION

Honda Civic sedan

Honda Civic CVCC sedan

Honda Civic wagon

Honda Accord

simple and can be conducted by observing the following steps:

1. On 1973–75 models, squeeze the lower end of the drain tube and drain any oil or water which may have collected. On 1976 and later models, remove the tube, invert and drain it.

After all condensation has drained out, install it.

2. Make sure that the intake manifold T-joint is clear. You first have to remove the air cleaner to where the joint is located. To clear the joint, pass the shank end of the appropriate size drill through both ends (both orifices) of the joint.

3. Check for loose, disconnected, or deteriorated tubes and replace if necessary.

For further information on the servicing of

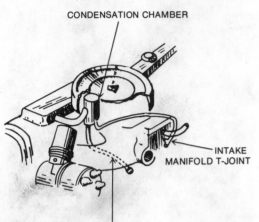

Typical PCV system component location. 1973 model shown

Remove this Phillips head screw to disconnect the condensation chamber from the air cleaner

Removing the air cleaner housing bolts from the engine

1976 and later drain tube location. Disconnect the tube from the condensation chamber and invert it to drain

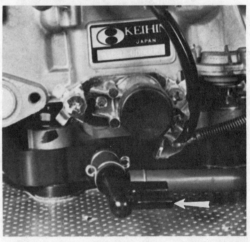

1975 and later CVCC PCV system orifice location

Honda emission control components. check the "Emission Controls" section of Chapter 4.

Evaporative Charcoal Canister

The charcoal canister is part of the Evaporative Emission Control System. This system prevents the escape of raw gasoline vapors from the fuel tank and carburetor.

The charcoal canister is designed to absorb fuel vapors under certain conditions (for a more detailed description, see the "Evapora-

Check the belt tension midway between the two pulleys

Evaporative canister

tive Emission Control System" section in Chapter 4). Maintenance on the canister consists of testing and inspection at 12,000 mile intervals (1973–74 models), or 15,000 mile intervals (1975 and later models), and replacement at 24,000 miles (1973–74 models), or 30,000 miles (1975 and later models). See Chapter 4 for testing procedures.

The canister is a coffee can-sized object located in the engine compartment. Label the hoses leading to the canister before disconnecting them. Then, simply remove the old canister from its mounting bracket and discard it. Install the new canister and connect the hoses as before.

Belts

CHECKING AND ADJUSTING TENSION

The initial inspection and adjustment to the alternator drive belt should be performed after the first 3,000 miles or if the alternator has been moved for any reason. Afterwards, you should inspect the belt tension every 12,000 miles. Before adjusting, inspect the belt to see that it is not cracked or worn. Be sure that its surfaces are free of grease and oil.

Loosen the pivot bolt before loosening the adjusting bolt

1. Push down on the belt halfway between pulleys with moderate force. The belt should deflect approximately ½ inch.

2. If the belt tension requires adjustment, loosen the adjusting link bolt and move the alternator with a pry bar positioned against the front of the alternator housing.

CAUTION: *Do not apply pressure to any other part of the alternator.*

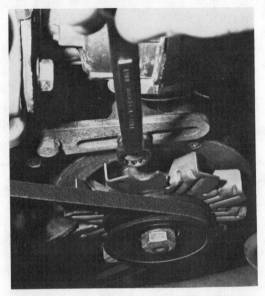

Loosen the adjusting bolt and pry the alternator outward

3. After obtaining the proper tension, tighten the adjusting link bolt.

CAUTION: *Do not overtighten the belt; damage to the alternator bearings could result.*

Air Conditioning

This book contains no repair or maintenance procedures for the air conditioning system. It is recommended that any such repairs be left to trained technicians who are well aware of the hazards and who have the proper equipment.

CAUTION: *The compressed refrigerant used in the air conditioning system expands into the atmosphere at a temperature of −21.7°F or lower. This will freeze any surface, including your eyes, that it contacts. In addition, the refrigerant decomposes into a poisonous gas in the presence of flame. Do not open or disconnect any part of the air conditioning system.*

When placing the unit in service at the

The sight glass is located on top of the receiver-drier

beginning of the summer season, make the following checks:

1. Operate the engine at approximately 1,500 rpm. Locate the sight glass, located on top of the receiver-drier, a small, black cylinder which is in the engine compartment.

2. Have someone turn the blower to high speed and switch the AIR lever to A/C position while you watch the sight glass. The glass should first become clouded with bubbles, and then clear up. Operate the unit for five minutes while watching the glass. If outside temperature is 68°F or above, the glass should be perfectly clear. If there is a continuous stream of bubbles, it indicates that the system has a slight leak and will require additional refrigerant. If the system starts and runs and no bubbles appear, the entire refrigerant charge has been lost. *Stop the system and do not operate it until it has been repaired.*

3. Inspect all lines for signs of oil accumulation, which would indicate leakage. If leaks are indicated, have the leak repaired by a professional mechanic. Do not attempt to tighten fittings or otherwise repair the system unless you have been trained in refrigeration repair as the system contains high pressure. Do not operate the system if it seems to have leaks as this can aggravate possible damage to the system.

4. Check the tension and condition of the compressor drive belt and adjust its tension or replace as necessary.

5. Test the blower to make sure that it operates at all speeds and have it repaired if it does not.

In winter, operate the air conditioner for 10 minutes with the engine at 1,500 rpm once a month to circulate oil to the compressor seal, thus preventing leakage.

Fluid Level Checks

ENGINE OIL LEVEL

Checking the oil level is one of the simplest and most important checks and it should be done FREQUENTLY.

NOTE: *If the engine has been running, let it sit for a few minutes until all the oil accumulates in the sump, before checking the oil level.*

To check the oil level, simply raise the hood, pull the oil dipstick from the engine and wipe it clean. Insert the dipstick into the engine until it is fully seated, then remove it and check the reading. The oil level on all Hondas should register within the crosshatch design on the dipstick. Do not add oil if this is the case. If the level is below the crosshatch, ADD oil but do not overfill. The length covered by the crosshatching on the dipstick is roughly equivalent to one quart of oil.

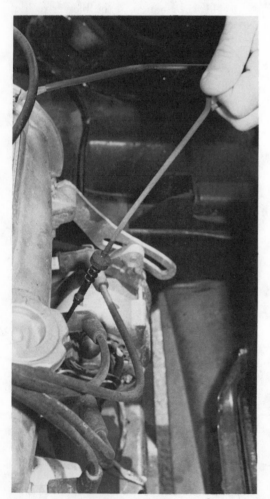

Removing dipstick to check oil

TRANSMISSION FLUID LEVEL

The transmission fluid should be checked about once a month and replaced after the first 3,000 miles (every 24,000 miles thereafter). Both the 4-speed manual transmission and the Hondamatic automatic transmission use a threaded dipstick with a crosshatch pattern. The dipstick is located beneath the battery. Approximately ¾ qt. will bring the fluid level from the ADD (lower) to the FULL (upper) line.

This is the oil filler plug on the five-speed. The four-speed and the Hondamatic have a dipstick located here instead of a simple filler plug

On automatic transmission equipped cars, the fluid is checked with the engine running. It is also necessary to warm up the transmission by driving the car a few miles, starting and stopping frequently. Then park the car on level ground and let the engine idle with the transmission in park. Unscrew the dipstick, wipe it clean, and insert it. DO NOT SCREW IT IN, as this would result in an erroneous reading. Top up, as necessary, with DEXRON® type automatic transmission fluid. Add the fluid, if necessary, in small amounts, taking care not to overfill.

Five-speed oil level checking bolt location

On the 5-speed transmission, a dipstick is not used. Instead, there is an oil level checking bolt on the side of the case. To check the oil level, loosen the bolt until transmission oil begins to run out, then quickly tighten it. If oil runs out, the level is OK, but if oil does not run out, you'll have to add some through the oil cap bolt (directly beneath the battery).

COOLANT LEVEL

To check the coolant level, simply discern whether the coolant is up to the "FULL" line on the expansion tank. Add coolant to the expansion tank if the level is low, being sure to replenish with clean water. Be sure to use a high quality coolant, designed for use in aluminum engines. Never add cold water to a hot engine as damage to both the cooling system and the engine could result.

The radiator cap should be removed only for the purpose of cleaning or draining the system.

CAUTION: *The cooling system is under pressure when hot. Removing the radiator cap when the engine is warm or overheated will cause coolant to spill or shoot out, possibly causing serious burns. The system should be allowed to cool before attempting removal of the radiator cap or hoses. If any coolant spills on painted portions of the body, rinse it off immediately.*

COOLANT CHANGE AND BLEEDING

The radiator coolant should be changed every 24,000 miles (1973–74 models) or 30,000 miles (1975 and later models). When following this procedure, be sure to follow the same precautions as detailed in the above "Coolant Level" section.

1. Remove the radiator cap.

2. Slide a drip pan underneath the radiator. Then loosen the drain bolt at the base of the radiator and drain the radiator.

3. Drain the coolant in the reservoir tank.

4. Mix a solution of 50% ethylene glycol (designed for use in aluminum engines) and 50% clean water. Tighten the drain bolt and fill the radiator all the way to the filler mouth. The radiator coolant capacity is about 4.2 qts.

5. Loosen the cooling system bleed bolt to purge air from the system. When coolant

Coolant system bleed bolt (arrow). The bleed bolt is always located in the vicinity of the thermostat housing

Coolant reserve tank located next to windshield washer reservoir

flows out of the bleed port, close the bolt and refill the radiator with coolant up to the mouth.

6. To purge any air trapped in other parts of the cooling system, start the engine, set it to fast idle and allow it to warm up. Do not tighten down the radiator cap, and leave the heater control in the "hot" position.

When the engine reaches normal operating temperature, top up the radiator and keep checking until the level stabilizes.

Then fill the coolant reservoir to the "full" mark and make sure that the radiator cap is properly tightened.

BRAKE AND CLUTCH MASTER CYLINDER FLUID LEVEL

Brake and clutch master cylinder fluid level should be checked every few weeks for indication of leaks or low fluid level due to normal wear. Infrequent topping-off will be required in normal use due to brake pad wear.

On all Hondas there is a fill line on the brake fluid reservoir(s) as well as an arrow on the reservoir cap(s) which should face forward when installed. When adding brake fluid, the following precautions should be observed:

1. Use only recommended brake fluid—DOT 3 or DOT 4; SAE J 1703b HD type.

2. Never reuse brake fluid and never use fluid that is dirty, cloudy, or has air bubbles.

3. Store brake fluid in a clean dry place in the original container. Cap tightly and do not puncture a breather hole in the container.

4. Carefully remove any dirt from around the master cylinder reservoir cap before opening.

5. Take special care not to spill the fluid. The painted surface of the vehicle will be damaged by brake fluid.

BATTERY LEVEL

The battery electrolyte level should be checked at least once a month to see if the fluid level is between the "Lower" and "Upper Level" lines on the outside of the battery. Should the level be low, you can fill it with ordinary tap water.

NOTE: *If you live in an area having exceptionally hard water, use only distilled water.*

Be sure not to overfill the battery, or the elctrolyte may run out giving you a useless battery filled with water.

CAUTION: *The battery gives off highly explosive hydrogen gas. Never hold an open flame, such as a lighted match, near the top of the battery.*

Checking the battery electrolyte level

POWER STEERING RESERVOIR

The fluid in the power steering reservoir should be checked every few weeks for indications of leaks or low fluid level.

NOTE: *Only genuine Honda power steering fluid may be used when adding fluid. The use of any other fluid will cause the seals to swell and create leaks.*

Power steering fluid reservoir. Use only genuine Honda power steering fluid

Tires and Wheels

When buying or changing tires, you should remember two things:

1. Do not mix tires of different sizes on the same axle.

2. Never mix radial and bias-ply tires. Not only is it a potentially dangerous practice, but many states prohibit the mixing of the two tire types.

CAUTION: *In no case should you ever mix tires of different construction (bias and radial) on the same axle. Handling will deteriorate dangerously.*

Tires must also be checked regularly for damage and signs of uneven wear. The tire tread should wear evenly across the width of the tire. If an uneven wear pattern is evident (such as cupping or severe wear on only one side of the tire) then front end alignment or wheel balance is out of adjustment. Steering wheel vibration is usually an indication of front-end tire imbalance or misalignment. "Straying" from the direction of travel, when the steering wheel is released, is also a clue to alignment problems. The cause of irregular tire wear should always be investigated and corrected.

And if you want to get the *maximum* life out of your tires, you can rotate them every 5,000 miles (except snow tires, of course) according to the diagram.

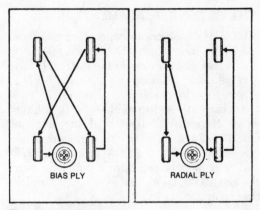

BIAS PLY   RADIAL PLY

Tire rotation diagrams

Tire life will also be increased if the tires are kept properly inflated. Excessive wear on the outer edges is an indication of underinflation, while too much center wear is usually a sign of overinflation. The air pressure in your tires should be checked at least once a month. Do this when the tires are cold; since tire pressure increases with temperature, an improper reading will result if you measure the pressure when the tires are hot.

NOTE: *When measuring tire pressure, always use a tire pressure gauge. Use the gauge even when adding air, as gas station air pumps are often inaccurate.*

A plate located on the left door will tell you the proper pressure for your tires.

Capacities

Year	Model	Engine Displacement (cc)	Engine Crankcase (qts) w/filter	Transmission (pts) Manual 4-sp	5-sp	Automatic	Gasoline Tank (gals)	Cooling System (qts)
1973	Civic	1170	3.2	2.6	—	2.6	10.0	4.2
1974	Civic	1237	3.2	2.6	—	2.6	10.0	4.2
1975–78	Civic	1237	3.2	2.6	—	2.6	10.6	4.2
1975–78	CVCC Sedan	1487	3.2	2.6	2.6	2.6	10.6	4.2
1975–78	CVCC Wagon	1487	3.2	2.6	—	2.6	11.0	4.2
1975–78	Accord CVCC	1600	3.2	2.6	2.6	2.6	13.2	4.2

FUEL FILTER REPLACEMENT

CAUTION: *Before disconnecting any fuel lines, be sure to open the gas tank filler cap to relieve any pressure in the system. If this is not done, you may run the risk of being squirted with gasoline.*

All cars use a disposable-type fuel filter which cannot be disassembled for cleaning. On 1973–74 models, the recommended replacement interval is 24,000 miles. On 1975 and later models, the filter is replaced after the first 15,000 miles, and every 30,000 miles thereafter.

On all 1973–74 Civics, as well as 1975 and later Civics with the air-injection 1237 cc (AIR) engine, the filter is located in the engine compartment, inline between the fuel pump and carburetor. Replacement is a simple matter of pinching the lines closed, loosening the hose clamps and discarding the old filter.

On all CVCC Sedan models, the filter is located beneath a special access cover under the rear seat on the driver's side. The rear

Fuel filter—non-CVCC Civic (arrow)

CVCC sedan fuel filter location .1 is the fuel pump, 2 is the fuel filter

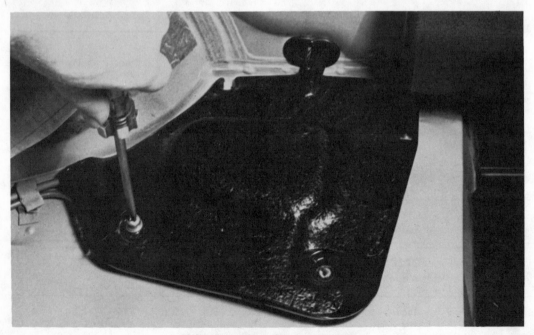

CVCC sedan fuel filter access plate

seat can be removed after removing the bolt at the rear center of the cushion and then pivoting the seat forward from the rear. Then, remove the four screws retaining the access cover to the floor and remove the cover. The filter, together with the electric fuel pump, are located in the recess. Pinch the lines shut, loosen the hose clamps and remove the filter.

Accord fuel filter location (arrow); wagon similar

On all 1975 and later wagon and Accord models, the filter is located under the car, in front of the spare tire, together with the electrical fuel pump. To replace the fuel filter, you must raise the rear of the car, support it with jackstands, and clamp off the fuel lines leading to and from the filter. Then, loosen the hose clamps and, taking note of which hose is the inlet and which is the outlet, remove the filter. Some replacement filters have an arrow embossed or printed on the filter body, in which case you want to install the new filter with the arrow pointing in the direction of fuel flow. After installing the new filter, remember to unclamp the fuel lines. Check for leaks.

LUBRICATION

Oil and Fuel Recommendations

FUEL

All Hondas are designed to run on regular gasoline; high-octane (premium) gasoline is not required. The octane number is used as a measure of the anti-knock properties of a gasoline and the use of a higher octane gasoline than that which is necessary to prevent engine knock is simply a waste of money. If your Honda does knock (usually heard as a pinging noise), it is probably a matter of improper ignition timing, in which case you

should check Chapter 2 for the proper adjustment procedure.

OIL

As far as engine oil is concerned, there are two types of ratings with which you should be familiar: viscosity and service (quality). There are several service ratings, resulting from tests established by the American resulting Institute. For your Honda, use only SE rated oil. No other service rating is acceptable.

Typical oil rating location on can

You can buy oil in two different types of viscosity ratings, single and multi-viscosity. Single viscosity oil, designated by only one number (SAE 30), maintains the same viscosity, or thickness, over a wide range of temperatures. A multi-viscosity oil rating is given in two numbers (SAE 10W-40) and changes viscosity, within the range of the rating, according to various engine temperature conditions, such as cold starts and eventual engine warm-up and operation. Because of its versatility, a multi-viscosity oil would be the most likely choice.

When you add oil, try to use the same brand since all oils are not completely compatible with each other. Refer to the "Lubrication" chart in this chapter for service and viscosity rating information.

Oil Changes

ENGINE OIL CHANGE

After the initial 600 miles oil and filter change, the oil should mile changed every 3,000 miles or every 3 months, whichever comes first. The oil filter should be changed at every oil change.

1. Before changing the oil, see that the car is situated on a flat surface with the engine warmed up. Warm oil will flow more freely from the oil pan.

2. Shut the engine off, open the hood, and remove the oil filler cap from the top of the engine valve cover.

Lubricant Specifications

Engine Oil	6000 mile motor oil (MS or SE sequence tested)

Single Viscosity Oils

When outside tempera- ture is consistently	Use SAE Viscosity Number
— 4° F to + 32° F	10W
+ 32° F to + 59° F	20W-20
+ 59° F to + 86° F	30
Above 86° F	40

Multiviscosity Oils

Above 5° F	10W/40
+ 5° F to + 86° F	10W/30
Above 32° F	20W/40
	20W/50

Manual Transmission and Differential Gear Oil	Use engine oil according to the above specifications

Automatic Transmission	Automatic Transmission Fluid—Dexron® type

CAUTION: *Hot oil can burn you. Keep an inward pressure on the plug until the last thread is cleared. Then quickly remove it.*

3. Place a container underneath the oil pan large enough to catch the oil. A large, flat drain pan is the most desirable.

4. Using a proper-size wrench, remove the oil drain plug and allow the oil to drain completely. When the oil has finished draining, install the drain plug tight enough to prevent oil leakage. Remove the drain pan from under the engine.

5. Add the correct amount of recommended oil into the oil filler hole on top of the valve cover. Be sure that the oil level registers near the full line on the oil dipstick.

6. Replace the filler cap, start the engine, and allow it to idle. The oil pressure light on the instrument panel should go out after a few seconds of running.

7. Shut the engine off after a few minutes of running and recheck the oil level. Add oil if necessary. Be sure to check for oil leaks, as this is a common problem on early production models using the Japanese filter.

OIL AND FILTER CHANGE

A conventional spin-on oil filter is used.

NOTE: *Only oil filters which have an integral by-pass should be used.*

1. Before removing the filter it is advisable to have an oil filter wrench which is inexpensive and makes the job much easier. Follow Steps 1–4 of the above oil change procedure before removing the filter.

2. Place the oil drain pan underneath the filter. The filter retains some oil which will drain when removed.

Oil pan drain plug location

3. Loosen the oil filter with the oil filter wrench. Unscrew it by hand.

4. Clean the filter mounting surface of the cylinder block with a clean cloth. Apply a thin coat of oil to the new filter gasket and install the filter.

NOTE: *Hand-tighten the filter only. Do not use a wrench for tightening.*

5. Fill the engine with oil and replace the filler cap.

6. Run the engine for a few minutes and check for leakage. Be sure to recheck the oil level.

TRANSMISSION FLUID CHANGE

Both the manual and automatic transmission models have drain plugs located on the bottom of the transmission for draining. To change the fluid, remove the drain plug and drain the fluid into a drain pan. Refit the plug and fill the transmission with the specified fluid (MT—API service SE or SD; AT—DEXRON®) through the transmission fluid dipstick hole.

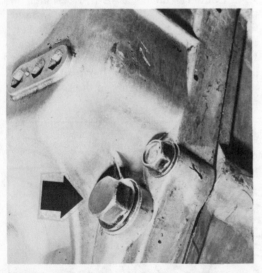

Manual transmission drain plug location—automatic similar

NOTE: *Although the specified quantity of fluid in both the manual and automatic transmissions is 2.5 liters, or 2.6 quarts, be sure that the required quantity of fluid is always slightly less than the specified quantity, due to the remaining fluid left in the transmission housing recesses. While changing fluid, always check the level with the dipstick as you are pouring the fluid to see that you do not overfill the transmission.*

WHEEL BEARINGS

Refer to the appropriate section in Chapter 9 for procedures on wheel bearing assembly and repacking. The front wheel bearings should be inspected and repacked (or replaced) every 30,000 miles. To check the wheel bearings for any play, jack up each wheel to clear the ground. Hold the wheel and shake it to check the bearings for any play. If any play is felt, tighten the castellated spindle nut to the specified torque (87–130 ft lbs) and reinspect. If play is still present, replace the bearing.

Checking wheel bearings for excessive play

NOTE: *Overtightening the spindle nuts will cause excessive bearing friction and will result in rough wheel rotation and eventual bearing failure.*

BODY LUBRICATION

Lubricate all locks and hinges with multi-purpose grease every 6000 miles or 6 months.

PUSHING, TOWING, AND JUMP STARTING

Pushing

Hondas equipped with a standard transmission can be push-started. Make sure that the bumpers match as a damaged bumper and/or fender could result from push-starting. To push-start your Honda, turn the ignition switch ON, push the clutch in, and select Second or Third gear. As the car picks up speed (10–15 mph), slowly release the clutch pedal until the engine fires up.

If your Honda is equipped with an automatic transmission, it cannot be push-started.

Towing

If your Honda's rear axle is operable, then you can tow your car with the rear wheels on the ground. Due to its front wheel drive, the Honda is a relatively easy vehicle to tow with the front wheels up. Before doing so, you should release the parking brake.

If the rear axle is defective, the car must then be towed with the rear wheels off the ground. Before attempting this, a dolly should be placed under the front wheels. If a dolly is not available, and you still have to tow it with the rear wheels up, then you should first shift the transmission into Neutral and then lock the steering wheel so that the front wheels are pointing straight ahead. In such a position, the car must not be towed at speeds above 20 mph or for more than short distances (5–10 miles).

Jump Starting

When jump starting a car, be sure to observe the proper polarity of the battery connections.

CAUTION: *Always hook up the positive (+) terminal of the booster battery to the positive terminal of the discharged battery and the negative terminal (−) to a good ground.*

If the battery terminals are unmarked, the correct polarity of each battery may be determined by examining the battery cables. The negative (ground) cable will run to the chassis and the positive (hot) cable will run to the starter motor. A 12 volt fully charged battery should be used for jump starting.

To jump start the car, proceed in the following manner:

1. Put the transmission in Park (P) or Neutral (N) and set the parking brake. Make sure that all electrical loads are turned off (lights, wipers, etc.).

2. Remove the vent caps from both batteries. Cover the opened vents of both batteries with a clean cloth. These two steps help reduce the hazard of an explosion.

3. Connect the positive (+) terminals of both batteries first. Be sure that the cars are not touching or the ground circuit may be completed accidentally.

4. Connect the negative (−) terminal of the booster battery to a suitable ground (engine lifting bracket, alternator bracket, etc.) on the engine of the car with the dead battery. Do not connect the negative jumper cable to the ground post of the dead battery.

5. Start the car's engine in the usual manner.

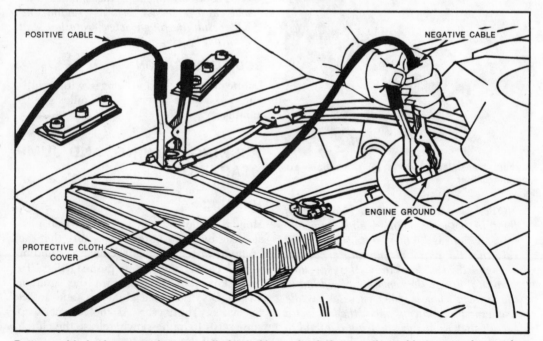

Battery cable hookup procedure on stalled car. Always hook the negative cable to a good ground on the engine block, *not* the battery negative terminal

6. Remove the jumper cables in *exactly* the reverse order used to hook them up.

JACKING AND HOISTING

Your Honda came equipped with a scissors jack. This jack is fine for changing a flat tire or other operations where you do not have to go beneath the car. There are four lifting points where this jack may be used; one behind each front wheel well and one in front of each rear wheel well in reinforced sheet metal brackets beneath the rocker panels (see illustration).

A more convenient way of jacking is the use of a garage or floor jack. You may use the floor jack beneath any of the four scissors jacking points, or you can raise either the entire front or entire rear of the car using the special jacking brackets beneath the front center or rear center of the car. On station wagon models, the rear of the car may be jacked beneath the center of the rear axle beam.

CAUTION: *The following safety points cannot be overemphasized;*
. . always block the opposite wheel or wheels to keep the car from rolling off the jack.
. . when raising the front of the car, firmly apply the parking brake.

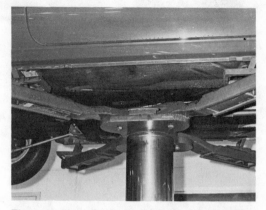

The correct method of raising the Honda with a garage hoist

. . when raising the rear of the car, place the transmission in low or reverse gear.
. . always use jack stands to support the car when you are working underneath. Place the stands beneath the scissors jacking brackets. Before climbing underneath, rock the car a bit to make sure it is firmly supported.

If you are going to have your Honda serviced on a garage hoist, make sure the four hoist platform pads are placed beneath the scissors jacking brackets. These brackets are reinforced and will support the weight of the entire vehicle.

Reinforced lifting point on the side of the Honda (arrow)

2

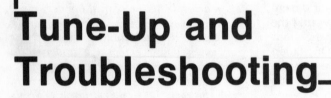

Tune-Up and Troubleshooting

TUNE-UP PROCEDURES

The procedures in this section are specifically intended for your Honda and intended to be as basic and complete as possible. For those already familiar with engine tune-ups, there is a generalized tune-up section, to be used with the "Tune-Up Specifications" chart, at the end of this chapter.

Underhood emissions control sticker containing tune-up information

Spark Plugs

Most people know that the spark plug ignites the air/fuel mixture in the cylinder, which in turn forces the piston downward, turning the crankshaft. This action turns the drivetrain (clutch, transmission, drive axles) and moves the car. What many people do not know, however, is that spark plugs should be chosen according to the type of driving done. The plug with a long insulator nose retains heat long enough to burn off oil and combustion deposits under light engine load conditions. A short-nosed plug dissipates heat rapidly and prevents pre-ignition and detonation under heavy loaded conditions. Under normal driving conditions, a standard plug is just fine. However, for continuous use above 70 mph, a colder plug will perform better. Conversely, for continuous around-town use below 30 mph, a hotter plug is recommended.

Spark plug life is largely governed by operating conditions and varies accordingly. To ensure peak performance, inspect the plugs at least every 6,000 miles. Faulty or excessively worn plugs should be replaced immediately. It is also helpful to check plugs for types of deposit and degree of electrode wear, as an indication of engine operating condition. Excessive or oily deposits could be

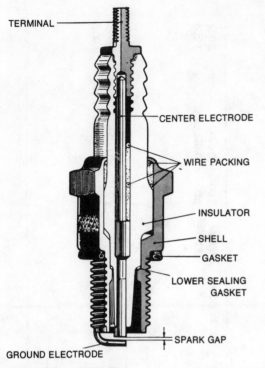

TERMINAL

CENTER ELECTRODE

WIRE PACKING

INSULATOR

SHELL

GASKET

LOWER SEALING GASKET

SPARK GAP

GROUND ELECTRODE

Spark plug cross-section

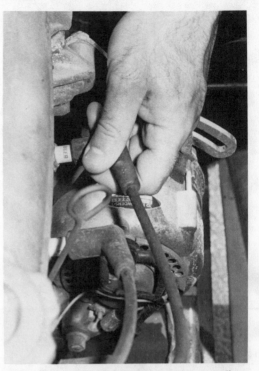

When removing spark plug wires, always pull on the plug boot, never on the wire itself

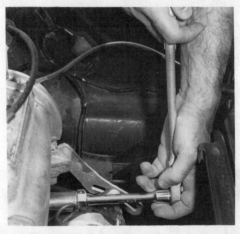

Keep the socket straight on the plug to avoid breaking the insulator. A ratchet with a flexible head is helpful

an indication of real engine trouble, and it would be wise to investigate the problem thoroughly until the cause is found and corrected.

Check the "Troubleshooting" section at the end of this chapter for diagnosing spark plug condition.

REMOVAL

1. Place a piece of masking tape around each spark plug wire and number it according to its corresponding cylinder.

2. Pull the wires from the spark plugs, grasping the wire by the end of the rubber boot and twisting off.

NOTE: *Avoid spark plug removal while the engine is hot. Since the cylinder head spark plug threads are aluminum, the spark plug becomes tight due to the different coefficients of heat expansion. If a plug is too tight to be removed even while the engine is cold, apply a solvent around the plug followed with an application of oil once the solvent has penetrated the threads. Do this only when the engine is cold.*

3. Loosen each spark plug with a $^{13}/_{16}$ in. spark plug socket. When the plug has been loosened a few turns, stop to clean any material from around the spark plug holes. Com-

pressed air is preferred; however, if air is not available, simply use a rag to clean the area.

NOTE: *In no case should foreign matter be allowed to enter the cylinders. Severe damage could result.*

4. Finish unscrewing the plugs and remove them from the engine.

INSPECTION AND CLEANING

Before attempting to clean and re-gap plugs, be sure that the electrode ends aren't worn

Tune-Up Specifications

When analyzing compression test results, look for uniformity among cylinders, rather than specific pressures.

Year	Model	Engine Displacement (cc)	Original Equipment Spark Plugs ° Type	Gap (in.)	Distributor Point Dwell (deg)	Point Gap (in.)	Basic Ignition Timing (deg) MT	AT	Intake Valve Opens (deg)	Fuel Pump Pressure (psi)	Idle Speed (rpm) MT	AT	Valve Clearance (in.) Intake (cold)	Auxiliary (cold)	Exhaust (cold)
1973	Civic	1170	NGK B-6ES or Nippon Denso W-20EP ①	0.028–0.031	49–55	0.018–0.022	TDC ③⑧	TDC ③⑧	32B	2.56	750–850 ④	700–800 ⑤	0.005–0.007	—	0.005–0.007
1974	Civic	1237	NGK B-6ES or Nippon Denso W-20EP ①	0.028–0.031	49–55	0.018–0.022	5B ⑧	5B ⑧	31B	2.56	750–850 ④	700–800 ⑤	0.004–0.006	—	0.004–0.006
1975–78	Civic AIR	1237	NGK B-6ES or Nippon Denso W-20EP ①	0.028–0.032	49–55	0.018–0.022	7B ⑧	7B ⑧	31B	2.56	750–850 ④	700–800 ⑤	0.004–0.006	—	0.004–0.006
1975	Civic CVCC	1487	NGK B-6ES or Nippon Denso W-20ES ②	0.028–0.032	49–55	0.018–0.022	TDC ⑨	3A ⑨	—	1.85–2.56	800–900 ④	700–800 ⑤	0.005–0.007	0.005–0.007	0.005–0.007

| 1976–78 | Civic and Accord CVCC | 1487, 1600 | NGK B-6ES or Nippon Denso W-20ES ② | 0.028–0.032 | 49–55 | 0.018–0.022 | 2B ⑥ ⑨ | 2B ⑦ ⑨ | — | 1.85–2.56 | 800–900 ④ | 700–800 ⑤ | 0.005–0.007 | 0.005–0.007 | 0.005–0.007 | 0.005–0.007 |

NOTE: The underhood specifications sticker often reflects tune-up specification changes made in production. Sticker figures must be used if they disagree with those in this chart.

* Similar characteristic spark plugs of different manufacture may be used without damage to the engine

① For continuous highway use over 70 mph, use cooler NGK B-7ES, Nippon Denso W-22EP or equivalent
② For continuous low-speed use under 30 mph, use hotter NGK B-5ES, Nippon Denso W-16ES or equivalent
③ Static ignition timing—5B
④ In neutral, with headlights on
⑤ In drive range, with headlights on
⑥ 5-speed sedan (hatchback) from engine number 2500001-up—6B; Accord—6B
⑦ Station wagon—TDC
⑧ Aim timing light at red notch on crankshaft pulley with distributor vacuum hose(s) connected at specified idle speed
⑨ Aim timing light at red mark on flywheel or torque converter drive plate with distributor vacuum hose connected at specified idle speed

TDC—Top Dead Center
B—Before Top Dead Center
A—After Top Dead Center

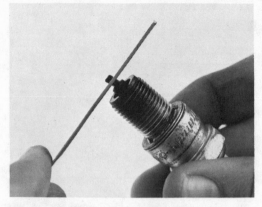

Use a small file to clean and square up the electrode if the plug is still usable

Always start the plugs by hand to avoid crossthreading them

or damaged and that the insulators (the white porcelain covering) are not cracked. Replace the plug if this condition exists.

Clean reusable plugs with a small file or a wire brush. The plug gap should be checked and readjusted, if necessary, by bending the ground electrode with a spark plug gapping tool.

NOTE: *Do not use a flat gauge to check plug gap; an incorrect reading will result. Use a wire gauge only.*

When gapping plugs, new or used, make sure the wire gauge passes through the gap with just a slight drag. Don't use a flat feeler gauge

Bend the side electrode carefully using a spark plug gapping tool

INSTALLATION

1. Lightly oil the spark plug threads and hand tighten them into the engine.

2. Tighten the plugs securely with a spark plug wrench (about 10 ft lbs of torque).

CAUTION: *Do not overtighten because of the aluminum threads.*

3. Connect the wires to the plugs, making sure that each is securely fitted.

Breaker Points and Condenser

The points and condenser function as a circuit breaker for the primary circuit of the ignition system. The ignition coil must boost the 12 volts (V) of electrical pressure supplied to it by the battery to about 20,000 V in order to fire the spark plugs. To do this, the coil depends on the points and condenser for assistance.

The coil has a primary and a secondary circuit. When the ignition key is turned to the "on" position, the battery supplies voltage to the primary side of the coil which passes the voltage on to the points. The points are connected to ground to complete the primary circuit. As the cam in the distributor turns, the points open and the primary circuit collapses. The magnetic force in the primary circuit of the coil cuts through the secondary circuit and increases the voltage in the secondary circuit to a level that is sufficient to fire the spark plugs. When the points open, the electrical charge contained in the primary circuit jumps the gap that is created between the two open contacts of the points. If this

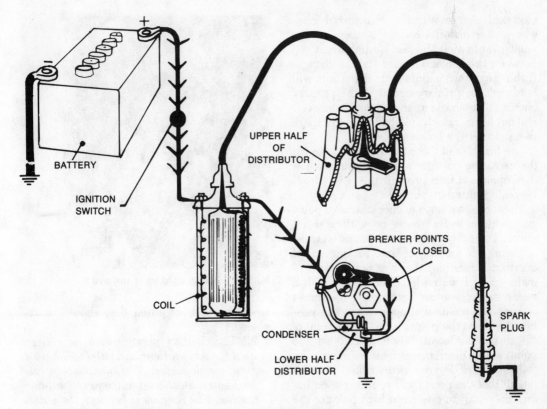

Primary side of ignition circuit is energized when breaker points are closed

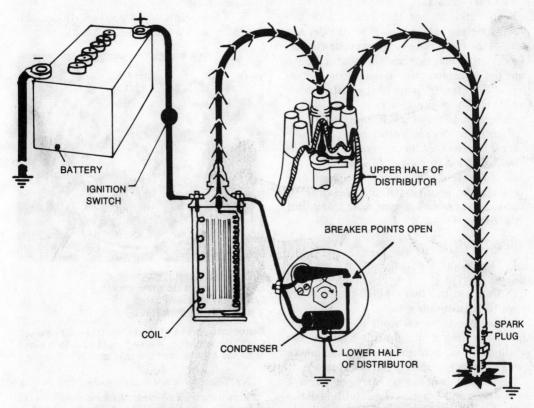

Secondary side of ignition circuit is energized when breaker points are open

electrical charge was not transferred elsewhere, the material on the contacts of the points would melt and that all-important gap between the contacts would start to change. If this gap is not maintained, the points will not break the primary circuit. If the primary circuit is not broken, the secondary circuit will not have enough voltage to fire the spark plugs. Enter the condenser.

The function of the condenser is to absorb the excessive voltage from the points when they open and thus prevent the points from becoming pitted or burned.

There are two ways to check breaker point gap: with a feeler gauge or with a dwell meter. Either way you set the points, you are adjusting the amount of time (in degrees of distributor rotation) that the points will remain open. If you adjust the points with a feeler gauge, you are setting the maximum amount the points will open when the rubbing block on the points is on a high point of the distributor cam. When you adjust the points with a dwell meter, you are measuring the number of degrees (of distributor cam rotation) that the points will remain closed before they start to open as a high point of the distributor cam approaches the rubbing block of the points.

If you still do not understand how the points function, take a friend, go outside, and remove the distributor cap from your engine. Have your friend operate the starter (make sure the transmission is not in gear) as you look at the exposed parts of the distributor.

NOTE: *There are two rules that should always be followed when adjusting or replacing points. The points and condenser are a matched set; never replace one without replacing the other. If you change the point gap or dwell of the engine, you also change the ignition timing. Therefore, if you adjust the points, you must also adjust the timing.*

INSPECTION

1. Disconnect the high-tension wire from the coil.

2. Unfasten the two retaining clips to remove the distributor cap.

3. Remove the rotor from the distributor shaft by pulling it straight up. Examine the condition of the rotor; if it is cracked or the metallic tip is excessively burned, replace it.

4. Pry the breaker points open with a screwdriver and examine the condition of the contact points. If the points are excessively

Pull the rotor straight up to remove it

worn, burned, or pitted they should be replaced.

NOTE: *Contact points which have been used for several thousand miles will have a gray, rough surface, but this is not necessarily an indication that they are malfunctioning. The roughness between the points matches so that a large contact area is maintained.*

5. If the points are in good condition, polish them with a point file.

1. Point gap adjusting screw
2. Breaker point retaining screws
3. Primary lead wire connection
4. Ground wire connection

Distributor breaker plate details—all except CVCC Hondamatic. Notice that the rubbing block is on the high spot of the cam lobe

NOTE: *Do not use emery cloth or sandpaper as they may leave particles on the points which could cause them to arc.*

After polishing the points, refer to the section following the breaker point replacement procedures for proper adjustment. If the points need replacing, refer to the following procedure.

Primary wire removal

REMOVAL AND INSTALLATION

1. Remove the small nut from the terminal screw located in the side of the distributor housing and remove the nut, screw, condenser wire, and primary wire from the terminal. Remove the terminal from the slot in the distributor housing.

2. Remove the screw(s) which attaches the condenser to the outside of the distributor housing (most models), or to the breaker plate inside the distributor (CVCC Hondamatic models), and remove the condenser.

3. Unscrew the Phillips head screw which holds the ground wire to the breaker point assembly and lift the end of the ground wire out of the way.

4. Remove the two Phillips head screws which attach the point assembly to the breaker plate and remove the point assembly.

NOTE: *You should use a magnetic or locking screwdriver. Trying to locate one of these tiny screws after you've dropped it can be an excruciating affair.*

5. Wipe all dirt and grease from the distributor plate and cam with a lint-free cloth. Apply a small amount of heat-resistant lubricant to the distributor cam. Although the lube is supplied with most breaker point kits,

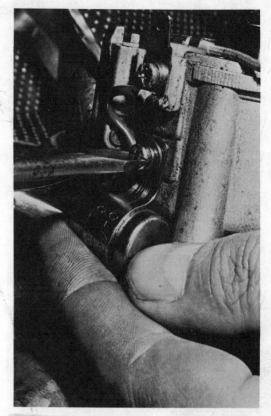

Condenser removal

Removing point set retaining screws

you can buy it at any auto parts store if necessary.

6. Properly position the new points on the breaker plate of the distributor and secure

with the two point screws. Attach the ground wire, with its screw, to the breaker plate assembly. Screw the condenser to its proper position on the distributor housing, or breaker plate.

7. Fit the terminal back into its notch in the distributor housing and attach the condenser and primary wires to the terminal screw and fasten with the nut.

ADJUSTMENT

With a Feeler Gauge

1. Rotate the crankshaft pulley until the point gap is at its greatest (where the rubbing block is on the high point of the cam lobe).

Crankshaft pulley bolt access window—CVCC models

Rotating crankshaft pulley by hand

Closeup of the points showing the rubbing block exactly on one of a high spot of the cam

This can be accomplished by using either a remote starter switch or by rotating the crankshaft pulley by hand.

2. At this position, insert the proper sized feeler gauge between the points. A slight drag should be felt. Point gap should be 0.018–0.022 in.

3. If no drag is felt, or if the feeler gauge cannot be inserted, loosen, but do not remove the two breaker point set screws.

4. Adjust the points as follows:

Insert a screwdriver through the hole in the breaker point assembly and into the notch provided on the breaker plate. Twist the screwdriver to open or close the points. When the correct gap has been obtained, retighten the point set screws.

Adjusting point gap with feeler gauge

5. Recheck the point gap to be sure that it did not change when the breaker point attaching screws were tightened.

6. Align the rotor with the distributor shaft and push the rotor onto the shaft until it is fully seated.

7. Reinstall the distributor cap and the coil high-tension wire.

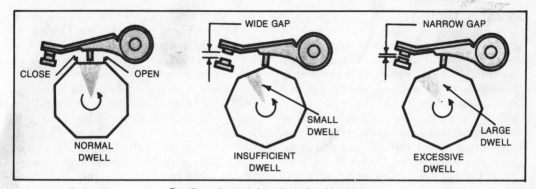

Dwell angle as a function of point gap

Dwell Angle

Dwell or cam angle refers to the amount of time the points remain closed, and is measured in degrees of distributor rotation. Dwell will vary according to the point gap, since dwell is a function of point gap. If the point gap is too wide, they open gradually, and dwell angle (the time they remain closed) is small. This wide gap causes excessive arcing at the points, leading to point burning. The insufficient dwell doesn't give the coil sufficient time to build up maximum energy, so coil output decreases. If the point gap is too small, dwell is increased and the idle becomes rough and starting is difficult. When setting points, remember: the wider the point opening, the smaller the dwell, and the smaller the point opening, the larger the dwell. When connecting a dwell meter, connect one lead (usually the black or negative lead) to a good ground on the engine, and the red or positive lead to the negative or distributor side of the coil. This terminal is easy to find; simply look for the terminal which has the small wire that leads to the distributor.

SETTING THE DWELL ANGLE

1. Connect a dwell-tach according to the manufacturer's instructions. See the preceding section for instructions on connecting the dwell meter.

2. With the engine warmed up and running at the specified idle speed, take a dwell reading.

3. If the point dwell is not within specifications, shut the engine off and adjust the point gap, as outlined earlier. Remember, increasing the point gap decreases the dwell angle and vice versa.

4. Check the dwell reading again and adjust it as required.

Ignition coil primary terminals

Taking a dwell reading. Notice the ground wire location

Ignition Timing

Ignition timing is the measurement, in degrees of crankshaft rotation, of the instant the spark plugs in the cylinders fire, in relation to the location of the piston, while the piston is on its compression stroke.

Ideally, the air/fuel mixture in the cylinder will be ignited (by the spark plug) and just beginning its rapid expansion as the piston passes top dead center (TDC) of the compression stroke. If this happens, the piston will be beginning the power stroke just as the compressed (by the movement of the piston) and ignited (by the spark plug) air/fuel mixture starts to expand. The expansion of the air/fuel mixture will then force the piston down on the power stroke and turn the crankshaft.

It takes a fraction of a second for the spark from the plug to completely ignite the mixture in the cylinder. Because of this, the spark plug must fire before the piston reaches TDC, if the mixture is to be completely ignited as the piston passes TDC. This measurement is given in degrees (of crankshaft rotation) *before* the piston reaches *top dead center* (BTDC). If the ignition timing setting for your engine is six degrees (6°) BTDC, this means that the spark plug must fire at a time when the piston for that cylinder is 6° before top dead center of its compression stroke. However, this only holds true while your engine is at idle speed.

As you accelerate from idle, the speed of your engine (rpm) increases. The increase in rpm means that the pistons are now traveling up and down much faster. Because of this, the spark plugs will have to fire even sooner if the mixture is to be completely ignited as the piston passes TDC. To accomplish this, the distributor incorporates means to advance the timing of the spark as engine speed increases.

The distributor has two means of advancing the ignition timing. One is called centrifugal advance and is actuated by weights in the distributor. The other is called vacuum advance and is controlled in that large circular housing on the side of the distributor.

In addition, some Honda distributors have a vacuum-retard mechanism which is contained in the same housing on the side of the distributor as the vacuum advance. Models having two hoses going to the distributor vacuum housing have both vacuum advance *and* retard. The function of this mechanism is to regulate the timing of the ignition spark under certain engine conditions. This causes more complete burning of the air/fuel mixture in the cylinder and consequently lowers exhaust emissions.

If ignition timing is set too far advanced (BTDC), the ignition and expansion of the air/fuel mixture in the cylinder will try to force the piston down the cylinder while it is still traveling upward. This causes engine "ping." If the ignition timing is too far retarded (after, or ATDC), the piston will have already started down on the power stroke when the air/fuel mixture ignites and expands. This will cause the piston to be forced down only a portion of its travel. This will result in poor engine performance and lack of power.

IGNITION TIMING CHECKING AND ADJUSTING

Honda recommends that the ignition timing be checked at 12,000 mile intervals (1973–74 models), or 15,000 mile intervals (1975 and later models). Also, the timing should always be adjusted after installing new points or adjusting the dwell angle. On all non-CVCC engines, the timing marks are located on the crankshaft pulley, with a pointer on the timing belt cover; all visible from the driver's side of the engine compartment. On all CVCC engines, the timing marks are located on the flywheel (manual transmission) or torque converter drive plate (automatic transmission), with a pointer on the rear of the cylinder block; all visible from the front right-side of the engine compartment after removing a special rubber access plug in the timing mark window. In all cases, the timing is checked with the engine warmed to operating temperature (176°F), idling in Neutral (manual trans.) or 2nd gear (Hondamatic), and with all vacuum hoses *connected*.

CVCC timing mark window location

Timing marks on the non-CVCC engines. The white mark is TDC

to the engine. The positive and negative leads connect to their corresponding battery terminals and the spark plug lead to No. 1 spark plug. The No. 1 spark plug is the one at the driver's side of the engine compartment.

3. Make sure that all wires are clear of the cooling fan and hot exhaust manifolds. Start the engine. Check that the idle speed is set to specifications with the transmission in Neutral (manual transmission) or 2nd gear (Hondamatic). If not, adjust as outlined in this chapter. At any engine speed other than the specified idle speed, the distributor advance or retard mechanisms will actuate, leading to an erroneous timing adjustment.

> CAUTION: *Make sure that the parking brake is firmly applied and the front wheels blocked to prevent the car from rolling forward when the automatic transmission is engaged.*

4. Point the timing light at the timing marks. On Non-CVCC cars, align the pointer with the "F" or red notch on the crankshaft pulley. On CVCC cars, align the pointer with the red notch on the flywheel or torque converter drive plate (except on cars where the timng specification is TDC in which case the "T" or white notch is used).

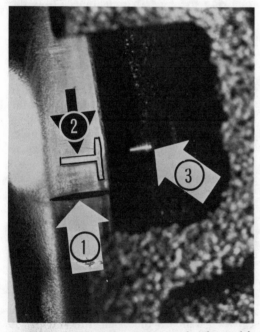

Details of CVCC engine timing marks. Arrow 1 is the red notch, which is the ignition timing mark. Arrow 2 is the TDC mark. The T has been outlined for clarity in this picture. Arrow 3 is the ignition timing pointer

1. Stop the engine, and hook up a tachometer. The positive lead connects to the distributor side terminal of the ignition coil, and the negative lead to a good ground, such as an engine bolt.

> NOTE: *On some models you will have to pull back the rubber ignition coil cover to reveal the terminals.*

2. Hook up a DC stroboscopic timing light

Checking the timing on a CVCC engine

NOTE: *The timing light flashes every time the spark plug for the No. 1 cylinder fires. Since the timing light flash makes the crankshaft pulley or flywheel seem stationary, you will be able to read the exact position of No. 1 piston on the timing scale.*

5. If necessary, adjust the timing by loosening the larger distributor hold-down (clamp) bolt and slowly rotate the distributor in the required direction while observing the timing marks.

CAUTION: *Do not grasp the top of the distributor cap while the engine is running as you might get a nasty shock. Instead, grab the distributor housing to rotate.*

After making the necessary adjustment,

Loosen this distributor hold-down (clamp) bolt to rotate the distributor for ignition timing adjustments

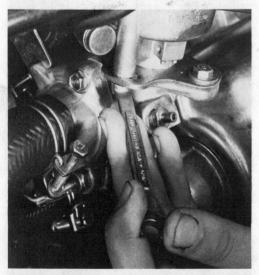

If the timing cannot be adjusted within the range of the upper (larger) clamp bolt, this smaller one can be loosened to provide extra adjustment

tighten the hold-down bolt, taking care not to disturb the adjustment.

NOTE: *There are actually two bolts which may be loosened to adjust ignition timing. There is a smaller bolt on the underside of the distributor swivel mounting plate. This smaller bolt should not be loosened unless you cannot obtain a satisfactory adjustment using the upper bolt. Its purpose is to provide an extra range of adjustment, such as in cases where the distributor was removed and then installed one tooth off.*

VALVE ADJUSTMENT

Valve adjustment is one factor which determines how far the intake and exhaust valves will open into the cylinder.

If the valve clearance is too large, part of the lift of the camshaft will be used up in removing the excessive clearance, thus the valves will not be opened far enough. This condition has two effects, the valve train components will emit a tapping noise as they take up the excessive clearance, and the engine will perform poorly, since the less the intake valves open, the smaller the amount of air/fuel mixture that will be admitted to the cylinders. The less the exhaust valves open, the greater the backpressure in the cylinder which prevents the proper air/fuel mixture from entering the cylinder.

If the valve clearance is too small, the intake and exhaust valves will not fully seat on the cylinder head when they close. When a valve seats on the cylinder head it does two things, it seals the combustion chamber so none of the gases in the cylinder can escape and it cools itself by transferring some of the heat it absorbed from the combustion process through the cylinder head and into the engine cooling system. Therefore, if the valve clearance is too small, the engine will run poorly (due to gases escaping from the combustion chamber), and the valves will overheat and warp (since they cannot transfer heat unless they are touching the seat in the cylinder head).

Honda recommends that the valve clearance be checked at 12,000 mile intervals (1973–74 models), or 15,000 mile intervals (1975 and later models).

NOTE: *While all valve adjustments must be as accurate as possible, it is better to have the valve adjustment slightly loose than slightly tight, as burned valves may result from overly tight adjustments.*

Distributor rotor at no. 1 piston Top Dead Center (TDC) position

All Non-CVCC Models

1. Adjust valves when the engine is cold (100°F or less).

2. Remove the valve cover and align the TDC (Top Dead Center) mark on the crankshaft pulley with the index mark on the timing belt cover. The TDC notch is the one immediately following the red 5° BTDC notch used for setting ignition timing.

3. When No. 1 cylinder is at TDC on the compression stroke, check and adjust the following valves (numbered from the crankshaft pulley end of the engine):

Intake—Nos. 1 and 2 cylinders
Exhaust—Nos. 1 and 3 cylinders
Adjust the valves as follows

   a. Check valve clearance with a feeler gauge between the tip of the rocker arm and the top of the valve. There should be a slight drag on the feeler gauge;

   b. If there is no drag or if the gauge cannot be inserted, loosen the valve adjusting screw locknut;

   c. Turn the adjusting screw with a screwdriver to obtain the proper clearance;

   d. Hold the adjusting screw and tighten the locknut;

   e. Recheck the clearance before reinstalling the valve cover.

4. Then rotate the crankshaft 360° and adjust:

Intake—Nos. 3 and 4 cylinders
Exhaust—Nos. 2 and 4 cylinders

CVCC Models

1. Make sure that the engine is cold (cylinder head temperature below 100°F).

2. Remove the valve cover. From the front of the engine, take a look at the forward face of the camshaft timing belt gear. When No. 1 cylinder as at Top Dead Center (TDC), the keyway for the woodruff key retaining the timing gear to the camshaft will be facing up. On 1976 and later models, the word "UP" will be at the top of the gear. You can double-check this by distributor rotor position. Take some chalk or crayon and make where the No. 1 spark plug wire goes into the distributor cap on the distributor body. Then, remove the cap and check that the rotor points toward that mark.

3. With the No. 1 cylinder at TDC, you can adjust the following valves (numbered from the crankshaft pulley end of the engine):

Intake—Nos. 1 and 2 cylinders

Valve adjustment—CVCC and non-CVCC models

Adjusting auxiliary valve clearance—CVCC models

Auxiliary Intake—Nos. 1 and 2 cylinders
Exhaust—Nos. 1 and 3 cylinders
Adjust the valves as follows:

a. Check valve clearance with a feeler gauge between the tip of the rocker arm and the top of the valve. There should be a slight drag on the feeler gauge;

b. If there is no drag or if the gauge cannot be inserted, loosen the valve adjusting screw locknut;

c. Turn the adjusting screw with a screwdriver to obtain the proper clearance;

d. Hold the adjusting screw and tighten the locknut;

e. Recheck the clearance before reinstalling the valve cover.

4. To adjust the remaining valves, rotate the crankshaft to the No. 4 cylinder TDC position. To get the No. 4 cylinder to the TDC position, rotate the crankshaft 360 de-

grees. This will correspond to an 180 degree movement of the distributor rotor and camshaft timing gear. The rotor will now be pointing opposite the mark you made for the No. 1 cylinder. The camshaft timing gear keyway or "UP" mark will now be at the bottom (6 o'clock position). At this position, you may adjust the remaining valves:

Intake—Nos. 3 and 4 cylinders
Auxiliary Intake—Nos. 3 and 4 cylinders
Exhaust—Nos. 2 and 4 cylinders

Carburetor Adjustments

This section contains only carburetor adjustments which apply to engine tune-up—namely, idle speed and mixture adjustments. Descriptions of the carburetors used and complete adjustment procedures can be found in the "Emission Controls" and "Fuel Systems" sections of Chapter 4.

Carburetor idle speed and mixture adjustment is the last step in any tune-up. Prior to making the final carburetor adjustments, make sure that the spark plugs, points and condenser, dwell angle, ignition timing, and valve clearance have all been checked, serviced, and, if necessary, adjusted. If any of these tune-up items have been overlooked, it may be difficult to obtain a proper carburetor adjustment.

NOTE: *All carburetor adjustments must be made with the engine fully warmed up to operating temperature (176°F).*

IDLE SPEED AND MIXTURE ADJUSTMENT

1973 Civic 1170 CC with Hitachi 2-bbl

1. Adjust the idle speed with the headlights on and the cooling fan off. The cooling fan can be disconnected by removing the leads from either the fan motor or the thermoswitch screwed into the base of the radiator, on the engine side.

Manual transmission models should be set in Neutral. Cars equipped with Hondamatic transmissions should be set in gear "1". Set the parking brake and block the front wheels.

2. Remove the limiter cap and turn the idle mixture screw counterclockwise, until engine speed drops. Now turn the idle speed screw in the reverse direction (clockwise) until the engine reaches its highest rpm. (If the idle speed reaches now above specification, repeat Steps 1 & 2.)

Idle speed and mixture screw locations on the Keihin 3-bbl carburetor used on the CVCC engines. Arrow 1 is the idle speed screw, and arrow 2 is the mixture screw. The 2-bbl carburetor used on the non-CVCC engines is similar

3. Continue to turn the idle mixture screw clockwise to obtain the specified rpm drop:

4-speed—40 rpm
Hondamatic—20 rpm

4. Replace the limiter cap and reconnect the cooling fan lines.

1974 and later non-CVCC Civic with Hitachi 2-bbl

1. The idle speed is adjusted with the headlights on and the radiator cooling fan off. To make sure that the cooling fan stays off while you are making your adjustments, disconnect the fan leads.

NOTE: *Do not leave the cooling fan leads disconnected for any longer than necessary, as the engine may overheat.*

Manual transmission cars are adjusted with the transmission in Neutral. On Hondamatic cars, the idle adjustments are made with the car in gear "1." As a safety precaution, firmly apply the parking brake and block the front wheels.

2. Remove the plastic limiter cap from the idle mixture screw. Hook up a tachometer to the engine with the positive lead connected to the distributor side (terminal) of the coil and the negative lead to a good ground. On 1976 models, disconnect the breather hose from the valve cover.

3. Start the engine and adjust first the

mixture screw (turn counterclockwise to richen), and then the idle speed screw for the best quality idle at 870 rpm (manual transmission), or 770 rpm (Hondamatic in gear).

4. Then, lean out the idle mixture (turn mixture screw clockwise), until the idle speed drops to 800 rpm (manual transmission), or 750 rpm (Hondamatic in gear).

5. Replace the limiter cap, connect the cooling fan, and disconnect the tachometer.

Civic and Accord CVCC with Keihin 3-bbl

1. The idle speed is adjusted with the headlights on and the radiator cooling fan on. With the engine warmed to operating temperature and idling, the cooling fan should come on. But, if it doesn't, you can load the engine's electrical system (for purposes of adjusting the idle speed), by turning the high-speed heater blower on instead. Do not have both the cooling fan and heater blower operating simultaneously, as this will load the engine too much and lower the idle speed abnormally. Manual transmission cars are adjusted with the transmission in Neutral. On Hondamatic cars, the idle adjustments are made with the car in gear "2" (that's right, Hi gear). As a safety precaution, apply the parking brake and block the front wheels.

2. Remove the plastic cap from the idle mixture screw. Hook up a tachometer to the engine with the positive lead connected to the distributor side (terminal) of the coil and the negative lead to a good ground.

3. Start the engine and rotate the idle mixture screw counterclockwise (rich), until the highest rpm is achieved. Then, adjust the idle speed screw to 910 rpm (manual transmission), or 801 rpm (Hondamatic in Second gear).

4. Finally, lean out the idle mixture (turn mixture screw in clockwise), until the idle speed drops to 850 rpm (manual transmission), or 750 rpm Hondamatic in Second gear).

5. Replace the limiter cap and disconnect the tachometer.

Troubleshooting

The following section is designed to aid in the rapid diagnosis of engine problems. The systematic format is used to diagnose problems ranging from engine starting difficulties to the need for engine overhaul. It is assumed that the user is equipped with basic hand tools and test equipment (tachdwell meter, timing light, voltmeter, and ohmmeter).

Troubleshooting is divided into two sections. The first, *General Diagnosis*, is used to locate the problem area. In the second, *Specific Diagnosis*, the problem is systematically evaluated.

General Diagnosis

Problem: Symptom	*Begin at Specific Diagnosis, Number* _____
Engine Won't Start:	
Starter doesn't turn	1.1, 2.1
Starter turns, engine doesn't	2.1
Starter turns engine very slowly	1.1, 2.4
Starter turns engine normally	3.1, 4.1
Starter turns engine very quickly	6.1
Engine fires intermittently	4.1
Engine fires consistently	5.1, 6.1
Engine Runs Poorly:	
Hard starting	3.1, 4.1, 5.1, 8.1
Rough idle	4.1, 5.1, 8.1
Stalling	3.1, 4.1, 5.1, 8.1
Engine dies at high speeds	4.1, 5.1
Hesitation (on acceleration from standing stop)	5.1, 8.1
Poor pickup	4.1, 5.1, 8.1
Lack of power	3.1, 4.1, 5.1, 8.1
Backfire through the carburetor	4.1, 8.1, 9.1
Backfire through the exhaust	4.1, 8.1, 9.1
Blue exhaust gases	6.1, 7.1
Black exhaust gases	5.1
Running on (after the ignition is shut off)	3.1, 8.1
Susceptible to moisture	4.1
Engine misfires under load	4.1, 7.1, 8.4, 9.1
Engine misfires at speed	4.1, 8.4
Engine misfires at idle	3.1, 4.1, 5.1, 7.1, 8.4

Engine Noise Diagnosis

Problem: Symptom	Probable Cause

Engine Noises:①

Problem: Symptom	Probable Cause
Metallic grind while starting	Starter drive not engaging completely
Constant grind or rumble	* Starter drive not releasing, worn main bearings
Constant knock	Worn connecting rod bearings
Knock under load	Fuel octane too low, worn connecting rod bearings
Double knock	Loose piston pin
Metallic tap	* Collapsed or sticky valve lifter, excessive valve clearance, excessive end play in a rotating shaft
Scrape	* Fan belt contacting a stationary surface
Tick while starting	S.U. electric fuel pump (normal), starter brushes
Constant tick	* Generator brushes, shreaded fan belt
Squeal	* Improperly tensioned fan belt
Hiss or roar	* Steam escaping through a leak in the cooling system or the radiator overflow vent
Whistle	* Vacuum leak
Wheeze	Loose or cracked spark plug

①—It is extremely difficult to evaluate vehicle noises. While the above are general definitions of engine noises, those starred (*) should be considered as possibly originating elsewhere in the car. To aid diagnosis, the following list considers other potential sources of these sounds.

Metallic grind:
Throwout bearing; transmission gears, bearings, or synchronizers; differential bearings, gears; something metallic in contact with brake drum or disc.

Metallic tap:
U-joints; fan-to-radiator (or shroud) contact.

Scrape:
Brake shoe or pad dragging; tire to body contact; suspension contacting undercarriage or exhaust; something non-metallic contacting brake shoe or drum.

Tick:
Transmission gears; differential gears; lack of radio suppression; resonant vibration of body panels; windshield wiper motor or transmission; heater motor and blower.

Squeal:
Brake shoe or pad not fully releasing; tires (excessive wear, uneven wear, improper inflation); front or rear wheel alignment (most commonly due to improper toe-in).

Hiss or whistle:
Wind leaks (body or window); heater motor and blower fan.

Roar:
Wheel bearings; wind leaks (body and window).

Index

  * The engine need not be running
** The engine must be running

Sample Section

Test and Procedure	Results and Indications	Proceed to
4.1—Check for spark: Hold each spark plug wire approximately ¼″ from ground with gloves or a heavy, dry rag. Crank the engine and observe the spark.	→ If no spark is evident:	→ **4.2**
	→ If spark is good in some cases:	→ **4.3**
	→ If spark is good in all cases:	→ **4.6**

Specific Diagnosis

This section is arranged so that following each test, instructions are given to proceed to another, until a problem is diagnosed.

1.1—Inspect the battery visually for case condition (corrosion, cracks) and water level.	If case is cracked, replace battery:	**1.4**
	If the case is intact, remove corrosion with a solution of baking soda and water (**CAUTION:** *do not get the solution into the battery*), and fill with water:	**1.2**
1.2—Check the battery cable connections: Insert a screwdriver between the battery post and the cable clamp. Turn the headlights on high beam, and observe them as the screwdriver is gently twisted to ensure good metal to metal contact.	If the lights brighten, remove and clean the clamp and post; coat the post with petroleum jelly, install and tighten the clamp:	**1.4**
	If no improvement is noted:	**1.3**

Testing battery cable connections using a screwdriver

1.3—Test the state of charge of the battery using an individual cell tester or hydrometer.	If indicated, charge the battery. **NOTE:** *If no obvious reason exists for the low state of charge (i.e., battery age, prolonged storage), the charging system should be tested:*	**1.4**

Spec. Grav. Reading	Charged Condition
1.260–1.280	Fully Charged
1.230–1.250	Three Quarter Charged
1.200–1.220	One Half Charged
1.170–1.190	One Quarter Charged
1.140–1.160	Just About Flat
1.110–1.130	All The Way Down

State of battery charge

The effect of temperature on the specific gravity of battery electrolyte

1.4—Visually inspect battery cables for cracking, bad connection to ground, or bad connection to starter.	If necessary, tighten connections or replace the cables:	**2.1**

Tests in Group 2 are performed with coil high tension lead disconnected to prevent accidental starting.

2.1—Test the starter motor and solenoid: Connect a jumper from the battery post of the solenoid (or relay) to the starter post of the solenoid (or relay).	If starter turns the engine normally:	**2.2**
	If the starter buzzes, or turns the engine very slowly:	**2.4**
	If no response, replace the solenoid (or relay).	**3.1**
	If the starter turns, but the engine doesn't, ensure that the flywheel ring gear is intact. If the gear is undamaged, replace the starter drive.	**3.1**

Test and Procedure	Results and Indications	Proceed to
2.2—Determine whether ignition override switches are functioning properly (clutch start switch, neutral safety switch), by connecting a jumper across the switch(es), and turning the ignition switch to "start".	If starter operates, adjust or replace switch: If the starter doesn't operate:	3.1 2.3
2.3—Check the ignition switch "start" position: Connect a 12V test lamp between the starter post of the solenoid (or relay) and ground. Turn the ignition switch to the "start" position, and jiggle the key.	If the lamp doesn't light when the switch is turned, check the ignition switch for loose connections, cracked insulation, or broken wires. Repair or replace as necessary: If the lamp flickers when the key is jiggled, replace the ignition switch.	3.1 3.3

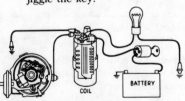

Checking the ignition switch "start" position

Test and Procedure	Results and Indications	Proceed to
2.4—Remove and bench test the starter, according to specifications in the car section.	If the starter does not meet specifications, repair or replace as needed: If the starter is operating properly:	3.1 2.5
2.5—Determine whether the engine can turn freely: Remove the spark plugs, and check for water in the cylinders. Check for water on the dipstick, or oil in the radiator. Attempt to turn the engine using an 18″ flex drive and socket on the crankshaft pulley nut or bolt.	If the engine will turn freely only with the spark plugs out, and hydrostatic lock (water in the cylinders) is ruled out, check valve timing: If engine will not turn freely, and it is known that the clutch and transmission are free, the engine must be disassembled for further evaluation:	9.2 **Next Chapter**
3.1—Check the ignition switch "on" position: Connect a jumper wire between the distributor side of the coil and ground, and a 12V test lamp between the switch side of the coil and ground. Remove the high tension lead from the coil. Turn the ignition switch on and jiggle the key.	If the lamp lights: If the lamp flickers when the key is jiggled, replace the ignition switch: If the lamp doesn't light, check for loose or open connections. If none are found, remove the ignition switch and check for continuity. If the switch is faulty, replace it:	3.2 3.3 3.3

Checking the ignition switch "on" position

Test and Procedure	Results and Indications	Proceed to
3.2—Check the ballast resistor or resistance wire for an open circuit, using an ohmmeter.	Replace the resistor or resistance wire if the resistance is zero.	**3.3**
3.3—Visually inspect the breaker points for burning, pitting or excessive wear. Gray coloring of the point contact surfaces is normal. Rotate the crankshaft until the contact heel rests on a high point of the distributor cam and adjust the point gap to specifications.	If the breaker points are intact, clean the contact surfaces with fine emery cloth, and adjust the point gap to specifications. If the points are worn, replace them.	**3.4**
3.4—Connect a dwell-meter between the distributor primary lead and ground. Crank the engine and observe the point dwell angle.	Adjust the dwell angle if necessary. **NOTE:** *Increasing the point gap decreases the dwell angle and vice-versa.* If the dwell meter shows little or no reading;	**3.6** **3.5**
3.5—Check the condenser for short: connect an ohmmeter across the condenser body and the pigtail lead. Checking the condenser for short OHMMETER	If any reading other than infinite is noted, replace the condenser:	**3.6**
3.6—Test the coil primary resistance: Connect an ohmmeter across the coil primary terminals, and read the resistance on the low scale. Note whether an external ballast resistor or resistance wire is utilized.	Coils utilizing ballast resistors or resistance wires should have approximately 1.0 ohms resistance. Coils with internal resistors should have approximately 4.0 ohms resistance. If values far from the above are noted, replace the coil.	**4.1**
4.1—Check for spark: Hold each spark plug wire approximately ¼″ from ground with gloves or a heavy, dry rag. Crank the engine, and observe the spark.	If no spark is evident: If spark is good in some cylinders: If spark is good in all cylinders:	**4.2** **4.3** **4.6**
4.2—Check for spark at the coil high tension lead: Remove the coil high tension lead from the distributor and position it approximately ¼″ from ground. Crank the engine and observe spark. **CAUTION:** *This test should not be performed on cars equipped with transistorized ignition.*	If the spark is good and consistent: If the spark is good but intermittent, test the primary electrical system starting at 3.3: If the spark is weak or non-existent, replace the coil high tension lead, clean and tighten all connections and retest. If no improvement is noted:	**4.3** **3.3** **4.4**
4.3—Visually inspect the distributor cap and rotor for burned or corroded contacts, cracks, carbon tracks, or moisture. Also check the fit of the rotor on the distributor shaft (where applicable).	If moisture is present, dry thoroughly, and retest per 4.1: If burned or excessively corroded contacts, cracks, or carbon tracks are noted, replace the defective part(s) and retest per 4.1: If the rotor and cap appear intact, or are only slightly corroded, clean the contacts thoroughly	**4.1** **4.1**

Test and Procedure	Results and Indications	Proceed to
	(including the cap towers and spark plug wire ends) and retest per 4.1:	
	If the spark is good in all cases:	**4.6**
	If the spark is poor in all cases:	**4.5**
4.4—Check the coil secondary resistance: Connect an ohmmeter across the distributor side of the coil and the coil tower. Read the resistance on the high scale of the ohmmeter. 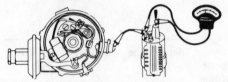 **Testing the coil secondary resistance**	The resistance of a satisfactory coil should be between 4,000 and 10,000 ohms. If resistance is considerably higher (i.e. 40,000 ohms) replace the coil and retest per 4.1. **NOTE:** *this does not apply to high performance coils.*	
4.5—Visually inspect the spark plug wires for cracking or brittleness. Ensure that no two wires are positioned so as to cause induction firing (adjacent and parallel). Remove each wire, one by one, and check resistance with an ohmmeter.	Replace any cracked or brittle wires. If any of the wires are defective, replace the entire set. Replace any wires with excessive resistance (over 8000Ω per foot for suppression wire), and separate any wires that might cause induction firing.	**4.6**
4.6—Remove the spark plugs, noting the cylinders from which they were removed, and evaluate according to the chart below.	See following.	**See following.**

	Condition	Cause	Remedy	Proceed to
	Electrodes eroded, light brown deposits.	Normal wear. Normal wear is indicated by approximately .001″ wear per 1000 miles.	Clean and regap the spark plug if wear is not excessive: Replace the spark plug if excessively worn:	**4.7**
	Carbon fouling (black, dry, fluffy deposits).	If present on one or two plugs:		
		Faulty high tension lead(s).	Test the high tension leads:	**4.5**
		Burnt or sticking valve(s).	Check the valve train: (Clean and regap the plugs in either case.)	**9.1**
		If present on most or all plugs: Overly rich fuel mixture, due to restricted air filter, improper carburetor adjustment, improper choke or heat riser adjustment or operation.	Check the fuel system:	**5.1**

	Condition	Cause	Remedy	Proceed to
	Oil fouling (wet black deposits)	Worn engine components. **NOTE:** *Oil fouling may occur in new or recently rebuilt engines until broken in.*	Check engine vacuum and compression: Replace with new spark plug	**6.1**
	Lead fouling (gray, black, tan, or yellow deposits, which appear glazed or cinder-like).	Combustion by-products.	Clean and regap the plugs: (Use plugs of a different heat range if the problem recurs.)	**4.7**
	Gap bridging (deposits lodged between the electrodes).	Incomplete combustion, or transfer of deposits from the combustion chamber.	Replace the spark plugs:	**4.7**
	Overheating (burnt electrodes, and extremely white insulator with small black spots).	Ignition timing advanced too far.	Adjust timing to specifications:	**8.2**
		Overly lean fuel mixture.	Check the fuel system:	**5.1**
		Spark plugs not seated properly.	Clean spark plug seat and install a new gasket washer: (Replace the spark plugs in all cases.)	**4.7**
	Fused spot deposits on the insulator.	Combustion chamber blow-by.	Clean and regap the spark plugs:	**4.7**
	Pre-ignition (melted or severely burned electrodes, blistered or cracked insulators, or metallic deposits on the insulator).	Incorrect spark plug heat range.	Replace with plugs of the proper heat range:	**4.7**
		Ignition timing advanced too far.	Adjust timing to specifications:	**8.2**
		Spark plugs not being cooled efficiently.	Clean the spark plug seat, and check the cooling system:	**11.1**
		Fuel mixture too lean.	Check the fuel system:	**5.1**
		Poor compression.	Check compression:	**6.1**
		Fuel grade too low.	Use higher octane fuel:	**4.7**

Test and Procedure	Results and Indications	Proceed to
4.7—Determine the static ignition timing. Using the crankshaft pulley timing marks as a guide, locate top dead center on the compression stroke of the number one cylinder.	The rotor should be pointing toward the no. 1 tower in the distributor cap, and the armature spoke for that cylinder should be lined up with the stator.	**4.8**

Test and Procedure	Results and Indications	Proceed to
4.8—Check coil polarity: Connect a voltmeter negative lead to the coil high tension lead, and the positive lead to ground (**NOTE: *reverse the hook-up for positive ground cars***). Crank the engine momentarily.	If the voltmeter reads up-scale, the polarity is correct:	**5.1**
	If the voltmeter reads down-scale, reverse the coil polarity (switch the primary leads):	**5.1**
5.1—Determine that the air filter is functioning efficiently: Hold paper elements up to a strong light, and attempt to see light through the filter.	Clean permanent air filters in gasoline (or manufacturer's recommendation), and allow to dry. Replace paper elements through which light cannot be seen:	**5.2**
5.2—Determine whether a flooding condition exists: Flooding is identified by a strong gasoline odor, and excessive gasoline present in the throttle bore(s) of the carburetor.	If flooding is not evident:	**5.3**
	If flooding is evident, permit the gasoline to dry for a few moments and restart. If flooding doesn't recur:	**5.6**
	If flooding is persistent:	**5.5**
5.3—Check that fuel is reaching the carburetor: Detach the fuel line at the carburetor inlet. Hold the end of the line in a cup (not styrofoam), and crank the engine.	If fuel flows smoothly:	**5.6**
	If fuel doesn't flow (**NOTE: *Make sure that there is fuel in the tank***), or flows erratically:	**5.4**
5.4—Test the fuel pump: Disconnect all fuel lines from the fuel pump. Hold a finger over the input fitting, crank the engine (with electric pump, turn the ignition or pump on); and feel for suction.	If suction is evident, blow out the fuel line to the tank with low pressure compressed air until bubbling is heard from the fuel filler neck. Also blow out the carburetor fuel line (both ends disconnected):	**5.6**
	If no suction is evident, replace or repair the fuel pump:	**5.6**
	NOTE: *Repeated oil fouling of the spark plugs, or a no-start condition, could be the result of a ruptured vacuum booster pump diaphragm, through which oil or gasoline is being drawn into the intake manifold (where applicable).*	
5.5—Check the needle and seat: Tap the carburetor in the area of the needle and seat.	If flooding stops, a gasoline additive (e.g., Gumout) will often cure the problem:	**5.6**
	If flooding continues, check the fuel pump for excessive pressure at the carburetor (according to specifications). If the pressure is normal, the needle and seat must be removed and checked, and/or the float level adjusted:	**5.6**
5.6—Test the accelerator pump by looking into the throttle bores while operating the throttle.	If the accelerator pump appears to be operating normally:	**5.7**
	If the accelerator pump is not operating, the pump must be reconditioned. Where possible, service the pump with the carburetor(s) installed on the engine. If necessary, remove the carburetor. Prior to removal:	**5.7**
5.7—Determine whether the carburetor main fuel system is functioning:	If the engine starts, runs for a few seconds, and dies:	**5.8**

Checking coil polarity

Test and Procedure	Results and Indications	Proceed to
Spray a commercial starting fluid into the carburetor while attempting to start the engine.	If the engine doesn't start:	**6.1**
5.8—Uncommon fuel system malfunctions: See below:	If the problem is solved: If the problem remains, remove and recondition the carburetor.	**6.1**

Condition	Indication	Test	Usual Weather Conditions	Remedy
Vapor lock	Car will not re-start shortly after running.	Cool the components of the fuel system until the engine starts.	Hot to very hot	Ensure that the exhaust manifold heat control valve is operating. Check with the vehicle manufacturer for the recommended solution to vapor lock on the model in question.
Carburetor icing	Car will not idle, stalls at low speeds.	Visually inspect the throttle plate area of the throttle bores for frost.	High humidity, 32–40°F.	Ensure that the exhaust manifold heat control valve is operating, and that the intake manifold heat riser is not blocked.
Water in the fuel	Engine sputters and stalls; may not start.	Pump a small amount of fuel into a glass jar. Allow to stand, and inspect for droplets or a layer of water.	High humidity, extreme temperature changes.	For droplets, use one or two cans of commercial gas dryer (Dry Gas) For a layer of water, the tank must be drained, and the fuel lines blown out with compressed air.

Test and Procedure	Results and Indications	Proceed to
6.1—Test engine compression: Remove all spark plugs. Insert a compression gauge into a spark plug port, crank the engine to obtain the maximum reading, and record.	If compression is within limits on all cylinders:	**7.1**
	If gauge reading is extremely low on all cylinders:	**6.2**
	If gauge reading is low on one or two cylinders: (If gauge readings are identical and low on two or more adjacent cylinders, the head gasket must be replaced.)	**6.2**

Testing compression
(© Chevrolet Div. G.M. Corp.)

Compression pressure limits
(© Buick Div. G.M. Corp.)

Maxi. Press. Lbs. Sq. In.	Min. Press. Lbs. Sq. In.	Maxi. Press. Lbs. Sq. In.	Min. Press. Lbs. Sq. In.	Max. Press. Lbs. Sq. In.	Min. Press. Lbs. Sq. In.	Max. Press. Lbs. Sq. In.	Min. Press. Lbs. Sq. In.
134	101	162	121	188	141	214	160
136	102	164	123	190	142	216	162
138	104	166	124	192	144	218	163
140	105	168	126	194	145	220	165
142	107	170	127	196	147	222	166
146	110	172	129	198	148	224	168
148	111	174	131	200	150	226	169
150	113	176	132	202	151	228	171
152	114	178	133	204	153	230	172
154	115	180	135	206	154	232	174
156	117	182	136	208	156	234	175
158	118	184	138	210	157	236	177
160	120	186	140	212	158	238	178

Condition	Indication	Test	Usual Weather Conditions	Remedy
6.2—Test engine compression (wet): Squirt approximately 30 cc. of engine oil into each cylinder, and retest per 6.1.			If the readings improve, worn or cracked rings or broken pistons are indicated:	**Next Chapter**
			If the readings do not improve, burned or excessively carboned valves or a jumped timing chain are indicated: **NOTE:** *A jumped timing chain is often indicated by difficult cranking.*	**7.1**
7.1—Perform a vacuum check of the engine: Attach a vacuum gauge to the intake manifold beyond the throttle plate. Start the engine, and observe the action of the needle over the range of engine speeds.			See below.	**See below**

	Reading	Indications	Proceed to
	Steady, from 17–22 in. Hg.	Normal:	**8.1**
	Low and steady.	Late ignition or valve timing, or low compression:	**6.1**
	Very low.	Vacuum leak:	**7.2**
	Needle fluctuates as engine speed increases.	Ignition miss, blown cylinder head gasket, leaking valve or weak valve spring:	**6.1, 8.3**
	Gradual drop in reading at idle.	Excessive back pressure in the exhaust system:	**10.1**
	Intermittent fluctuation at idle.	Ignition miss, sticking valve:	**8.3, 9.1**
	Drifting needle.	Improper idle mixture adjustment, carburetors not synchronized (where applicable), or minor intake leak. Synchronize the carburetors, adjust the idle, and retest. If the condition persists:	**7.2**
	High and steady.	Early ignition timing:	**8.2**

Test and Procedure	Results and Indications	Proceed to
7.2—Attach a vacuum gauge per 7.1, and test for an intake manifold leak. Squirt a small amount of oil around the intake manifold gaskets, carburetor gaskets, plugs and fittings. Observe the action of the vacuum gauge.	If the reading improves, replace the indicated gasket, or seal the indicated fitting or plug: If the reading remains low:	**8.1** **7.3**
7.3—Test all vacuum hoses and accessories for leaks as described in 7.2. Also check the carburetor body (dashpots, automatic choke mechanism, throttle shafts) for leaks in the same manner.	If the reading improves, service or replace the offending part(s): If the reading remains low:	**8.1** **6.1**
8.1—Check the point dwell angle: Connect a dwell meter between the distributor primary wire and ground. Start the engine, and observe the dwell angle from idle to 3000 rpm.	If necessary, adjust the dwell angle. **NOTE:** *Increasing the point gap reduces the dwell angle and vice-versa.* If the dwell angle moves outside specifications as engine speed increases, the distributor should be removed and checked for cam accuracy, shaft endplay and concentricity, bushing wear, and adequate point arm tension (**NOTE:** *Most of these items may be checked with the distributor installed in the engine, using an oscilloscope*):	**8.2**
8.2—Connect a timing light (per manufacturer's recommendation) and check the dynamic ignition timing. Disconnect and plug the vacuum hose(s) to the distributor if specified, start the engine, and observe the timing marks at the specified engine speed.	If the timing is not correct, adjust to specifications by rotating the distributor in the engine: (Advance timing by rotating distributor opposite normal direction of rotor rotation, retard timing by rotating distributor in same direction as rotor rotation.)	**8.3**
8.3—Check the operation of the distributor advance mechanism(s): To test the mechanical advance, disconnect all but the mechanical advance, and observe the timing marks with a timing light as the engine speed is increased from idle. If the mark moves smoothly, without hesitation, it may be assumed that the mechanical advance is functioning properly. To test vacuum advance and/or retard systems, alternately crimp and release the vacuum line, and observe the timing mark for movement. If movement is noted, the system is operating.	If the systems are functioning: If the systems are not functioning, remove the distributor, and test on a distributor tester:	**8.4** **8.4**
8.4—Locate an ignition miss: With the engine running, remove each spark plug wire, one by one, until one is found that doesn't cause the engine to roughen and slow down.	When the missing cylinder is identified:	**4.1**

Test and Procedure	Results and Indications	Proceed to
9.1—Evaluate the valve train: Remove the valve cover, and ensure that the valves are adjusted to specifications. A mechanic's stethoscope may be used to aid in the diagnosis of the valve train. By pushing the probe on or near push rods or rockers, valve noise often can be isolated. A timing light also may be used to diagnose valve problems. Connect the light according to manufacturer's recommendations, and start the engine. Vary the firing moment of the light by increasing the engine speed (and therefore the ignition advance), and moving the trigger from cylinder to cylinder. Observe the movement of each valve.	See below.	**See below**

Observation	Probable Cause	Remedy	Proceed to
Metallic tap heard through the stethoscope.	Sticking hydraulic lifter or excessive valve clearance.	Adjust valve. If tap persists, remove and replace the lifter:	**10.1**
Metallic tap through the stethoscope, able to push the rocker arm (lifter side) down by hand.	Collapsed valve lifter.	Remove and replace the lifter:	**10.1**
Erratic, irregular motion of the valve stem.*	Sticking valve, burned valve.	Recondition the valve and/or valve guide:	**Next Chapter**
Eccentric motion of the pushrod at the rocker arm.*	Bent pushrod.	Replace the pushrod:	**10.1**
Valve retainer bounces as the valve closes.*	Weak valve spring or damper.	Remove and test the spring and damper. Replace if necessary:	**10.1**

*—When observed with a timing light.

Test and Procedure	Results and Indications	Proceed to
9.2—Check the valve timing: Locate top dead center of the No. 1 piston, and install a degree wheel or tape on the crankshaft pulley or damper with zero corresponding to an index mark on the engine. Rotate the crankshaft in its direction of rotation, and observe the opening of the No. 1 cylinder intake valve. The opening should correspond with the correct mark on the degree wheel according to specifications.	If the timing is not correct, the timing cover must be removed for further investigation:	

Observation	Probable Cause	Remedy	Proceed to
10.1—Determine whether the exhaust manifold heat control valve is operating: Operate the valve by hand to determine whether it is free to move. If the valve is free, run the engine to operating temperature and observe the action of the valve, to ensure that it is opening.		If the valve sticks, spray it with a suitable solvent, open and close the valve to free it, and retest. If the valve functions properly:	**10.2**
		If the valve does not free, or does not operate, replace the valve:	**10.2**
10.2—Ensure that there are no exhaust restrictions: Visually inspect the exhaust system for kinks, dents, or crushing. Also note that gasses are flowing freely from the tailpipe at all engine speeds, indicating no restriction in the muffler or resonator.		Replace any damaged portion of the system:	**11.1**
11.1—Visually inspect the fan belt for glazing, cracks, and fraying, and replace if necessary. Tighten the belt so that the longest span has approximately ½″ play at its midpoint under thumb pressure.		Replace or tighten the fan belt as necessary:	**11.2**

Checking the fan belt tension

Observation	Probable Cause	Remedy	Proceed to
11.2—Check the fluid level of the cooling system.		If full or slightly low, fill as necessary:	**11.5**
		If extremely low:	**11.3**
11.3—Visually inspect the external portions of the cooling system (radiator, radiator hoses, thermostat elbow, water pump seals, heater hoses, etc.) for leaks. If none are found, pressurize the cooling system to 14–15 psi.		If cooling system holds the pressure:	**11.5**
		If cooling system loses pressure rapidly, reinspect external parts of the system for leaks under pressure. If none are found, check dipstick for coolant in crankcase. If no coolant is present, but pressure loss continues:	**11.4**
		If coolant is evident in crankcase, remove cylinder head(s), and check gasket(s). If gaskets are intact, block and cylinder head(s) should be checked for cracks or holes. If the gasket(s) is blown, replace, and purge the crankcase of coolant:	**12.6**
		NOTE: *Occasionally, due to atmospheric and driving conditions, condensation of water can occur in the crankcase. This causes the oil to appear milky white. To remedy, run the engine until hot, and change the oil and oil - filter.*	

Test and Procedure	Results and Indications	Proceed to
11.4— Check for combustion leaks into the cooling system: Pressurize the cooling system as above. Start the engine, and observe the pressure gauge. If the needle fluctuates, remove each spark plug wire, one by one, noting which cylinder(s) reduce or eliminate the fluctuation.  Radiator pressure tester	Cylinders which reduce or eliminate the fluctuation, when the spark plug wire is removed, are leaking into the cooling system. Replace the head gasket on the affected cylinder bank(s).	
11.5— Check the radiator pressure cap: Attach a radiator pressure tester to the radiator cap (wet the seal prior to installation). Quickly pump up the pressure, noting the point at which the cap releases.	If the cap releases within ± 1 psi of the specified rating, it is operating properly: If the cap releases at more than ± 1 psi of the specified rating, it should be replaced:	11.6 11.6

Testing the radiator pressure cap

Test and Procedure	Results and Indications	Proceed to
11.6— Test the thermostat: Start the engine cold, remove the radiator cap, and insert a thermometer into the radiator. Allow the engine to idle. After a short while, there will be a sudden, rapid increase in coolant temperature. The temperature at which this sharp rise stops is the thermostat opening temperature.	If the thermostat opens at or about the specified temperature: If the temperature doesn't increase: (If the temperature increases slowly and gradually, replace the thermostat.)	11.7 11.7
11.7— Check the water pump: Remove the thermostat elbow and the thermostat, disconnect the coil high tension lead (to prevent starting), and crank the engine momentarily.	If coolant flows, replace the thermostat and retest per 11.6: If coolant doesn't flow, reverse flush the cooling system to alleviate any blockage that might exist. If system is not blocked, and coolant will not flow, recondition the water pump.	11.6 —
12.1— Check the oil pressure gauge or warning light: If the gauge shows low pressure, or the light is on, for no obvious reason, remove the oil pressure sender. Install an accurate oil pressure gauge and run the engine momentarily.	If oil pressure builds normally, run engine for a few moments to determine that it is functioning normally, and replace the sender. If the pressure remains low: If the pressure surges: If the oil pressure is zero:	— 12.2 12.3 12.3
12.2— Visually inspect the oil: If the oil is watery or very thin, milky, or foamy, replace the oil and oil filter.	If the oil is normal: If after replacing oil the pressure remains low: If after replacing oil the pressure becomes normal:	12.3 12.3 —

Test and Procedure	Results and Indications	Proceed to
12.3—Inspect the oil pressure relief valve and spring, to ensure that it is not sticking or stuck. Remove and thoroughly clean the valve, spring, and the valve body.	If the oil pressure improves:	—
	If no improvement is noted:	**12.4**

Oil pressure relief valve
(© British Leyland Motors)

Test and Procedure	Results and Indications	Proceed to
12.4—Check to ensure that the oil pump is not cavitating (sucking air instead of oil): See that the crankcase is neither over nor underfull, and that the pickup in the sump is in the proper position and free from sludge.	Fill or drain the crankcase to the proper capacity, and clean the pickup screen in solvent if necessary. If no improvement is noted:	**12.5**
12.5—Inspect the oil pump drive and the oil pump:	If the pump drive or the oil pump appear to be defective, service as necessary and retest per 12.1:	**12.1**
	If the pump drive and pump appear to be operating normally, the engine should be disassembled to determine where blockage exists:	**Next Chapter**
12.6—Purge the engine of ethylene glycol coolant: Completely drain the crankcase and the oil filter. Obtain a commercial butyl cellosolve base solvent, designated for this purpose, and follow the instructions precisely. Following this, install a new oil filter and refill the crankcase with the proper weight oil. The next oil and filter change should follow shortly thereafter (1000 miles).		

Engine and Engine Rebuilding

ENGINE ELECTRICAL

Distributor

The distributor is bevel gear-driven by the camshaft. On non-CVCC engines, it is located at the crankshaft pulley end of the engine. On CVCC engines, the distributor is located in a special extension housing at the flywheel end of the engine.

All distributors utilize centrifugal advance mechanisms to increase ignition timing as engine speed increases. Centrifugal advance is controlled by a pair of weights located under the breaker point mounting plate. As the distributor shaft spins faster, the weights are affected by centrifugal force and move away from the shaft, advancing the timing.

In addition, all distributors use some kind of vacuum ignition control, although this varies from model to model.

Vacuum advance works as follows: When the engine is operating under low-load conditions (light acceleration), the vacuum diaphragm moves the breaker point mounting plate in the opposite direction of distributor rotation, thereby advancing the timing.

Vacuum retard, on the other hand, is actuated when the engine is operating under high-vacuum conditions (deceleration or idle), and moves the breaker point mounting

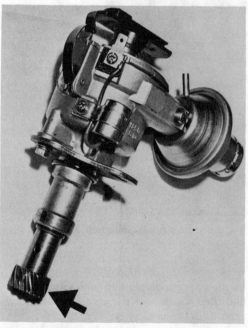

Honda distributor. Note the helical teeth on the drive gear (arrow)

plate in the same direction of rotation as the distributor, thereby retarding the spark. On models, equipped with both vacuum advance and retard, both these ignition characteristics are true. You can always tell a dual diaphragm distributor by its *two* hoses.

REMOVAL AND INSTALLATION

1. Disconnect the high tension and primary lead wires that run from the distributor to the coil.

2. Unsnap the two distributor cap retaining clamps and remove the distributor cap. Position it out of the way.

3. Using chalk or paint, carefully mark the position of the distributor rotor in relation to the distributor housing, and mark the relation of the distributor housing to the engine block. When this is done, you should have a line on the distributor housing directly in line with the tip of the rotor, and another line on the engine block directly in line with the mark on the distributor housing.

NOTE: *This aligning procedure is very important because the distributor must be reinstalled in the exact location from which it was removed, if correct ignition timing is to be maintained.*

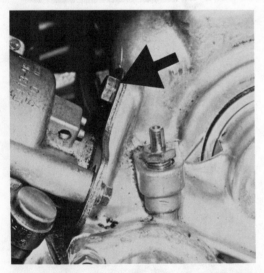

CVCC distributor hold-down bolt; non-CVCC similar

4. Note the position of the vacuum line(s) on the vacuum diaphragm with masking tape and then disconnect the lines from the vacuum unit.

5. Remove the bolt which attaches the distributor to the engine block or distributor extension housing (CVCC), and remove the distributor from the engine.

CAUTION: *Do not disturb the engine while the distributor is removed. If you attempt to start the engine with the distributor removed, you will have to retime the engine.*

6. To install, place the rotor on the distributor shaft and align the tip of the rotor with the line that you made on the distributor housing.

7. With the rotor and housing aligned, insert the distributor into the engine while aligning the mark on the housing with the mark on the block, or extension housing (CVCC).

NOTE: *Since the distributor pinion gear has helical teeth, the rotor will turn slightly as the gear on the distributor meshes with the gear on the camshaft. Allow for this when installing the distributor by aligning the mark on the distributor with the mark on the block, but poisitioning the tip of the rotor slightly to the side of the mark on the distributor.*

The rotor will move approximately 30 degrees during removal and installation

8. When the distributor is fully seated in the engine, install and tighten the distributor retaining bolt.

9. Align and install the distributor cap and snap the retaining clamps into place.

10. Install the high-tension and primary wires onto the coil.

11. Check the ignition timing as outlined in Chapter 2.

Installation When Engine Has Been Disturbed

If the engine was cranked with the distributor removed, it will be necessary to retime the engine. If you have installed the distributor incorrectly and the engine will not start, remove the distributor from the engine and start from scratch.

1. Install the distributor with No. 1 cylinder at the top dead center position on the compression stroke (the "TDC" mark on the

crankshaft pulley (or flywheel) aligned with the index mark on the timing belt cover or crankcase).

2. Line up the metal end of the rotor head with the protrusion on the distributor housing.

3. Carefully insert the distributor into the cylinder head opening with the attaching plate bolt slot aligned with the distributor mounting hole in the cylinder head. Then secure the plate at the center of the adjusting slot. The rotor head must face No. 1 cylinder.

NOTE: *Since the distributor pinion gear has helical teeth, the rotor will turn slightly as the gear on the distributor meshes with the gear on the camshaft. Allow for this when installing the distributor by positioning the tip of the rotor to the side of the protrusion.*

4. Inspect and adjust the point gap and ignition timing.

Alternator

The alternator converts the mechanical energy which is supplied by the drive belt into electrical energy by electromagnetic induction. When the ignition switch is turned on, current flows from the battery, through the charging system light or ammeter, to the voltage regulator, and finally to the alternator. When the engine is started, the drive belt turns the rotating field (rotor) in the stationary windings (stator), inducing alternating current. This alternating current is converted into usable direct current by the diode rectifier. Most of this current is used to charge the battery and power the electrical components of the vehicle. A small part is returned to the field windings of the alternator enabling it to increase its output. When the current in the field windings reaches a predetermined control voltage, the voltage regulator grounds the circuit, preventing any further increase. The cycle is continued so that the voltage remains constant.

On non-CVCC models, the alternator is located beneath the distributor toward the rear of the engine compartment. On CVCC models, the alternator is located near the No. 1 spark plug at the front of the engine compartment. On CVCC models equipped with air conditioning, the alternator is mounted on a special vibration-absorbing bracket at the driver's side of the engine compartment.

Alternator mounting—CVCC models with air conditioning

PRECAUTIONS

1. Observe the proper polarity of the battery connections by making sure that the positive (+) and negative (−) terminal connections are not reversed. Misconnection will allow current to flow in the reverse direction, resulting in damaged diodes and an overheated wire harness.

2. Never ground or short out any alternator or alternator regulator terminals.

CVCC alternator mounting

3. Never operate the alternator with any of its or the battery's leads disconnected.

4. Always remove the battery or disconnect its output lead while charging it.

5. Always disconnect the ground cable when replacing any electrical components.

6. Never subject the alternator to excessive heat or dampness.

7. Never use arc-welding equipment with the alternator connected.

REMOVAL AND INSTALLATION
All Models

1. Disconnect the negative (−) battery terminal.

Alternator wiring connections—CVCC shown

2. Unplug the wires from the plugs on the rear of the alternator.

3. Loosen and remove the two alternator mounting bolts and remove the V-belt and alternator assembly.

4. To install, reverse the removal procedure. Adjust the alternator belt tension according to the "Belt Tension Adjustment" section below.

BELT TENSION ADJUSTMENT

The initial inspection and adjustment to the alternator drive belt should be performed after the first 3,000 miles or if the alternator has been moved for any reason. Afterwards, you should inspect the belt tension every 12,000 miles. Before adjusting, inspect the belt to see that it is not cracked or worn. Be sure that its surfaces are free of grease and oil.

1. Push down on the belt halfway between pulleys with a force of about 24 lbs. The belt should deflect 0.47–0.67 in. (12–117 mm).

2. If the belt tension requires adjustment, loosen the adjusting link bolt and move the

alternator with a pry bar positioned against the front of the alternator housing.

CAUTION: *Do not apply pressure to any other part of the alternator.*

3. After obtaining the proper tension, tighten the adjusting link bolt.

CAUTION: *Do not overtighten the belt; damage to the alternator bearings could result.*

Firing Order

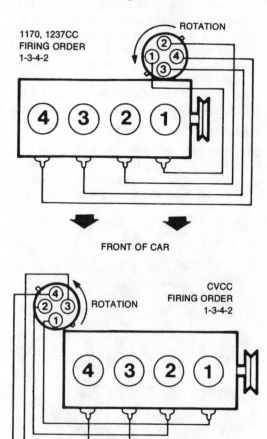

1170, 1237CC
FIRING ORDER
1-3-4-2

ROTATION

FRONT OF CAR

CVCC
FIRING ORDER
1-3-4-2

ROTATION

FRONT OF CAR

Regulator

The regulator is a device which controls the output of the alternator. If the regulator did not limit the voltage output of the alternator, the excessive output could burn out components of the electrical system, as well as the alternator itself.

Alternator and Regulator Specifications

		ALTERNATOR			REGULATOR						
						Field Relay			Regulator		
Year	Engine Displacement (cc)	Part No. or Manufacturer	Field Current @ 12 V (amps)	Output (amps) @ 5,000 rpm	Part No. or Manufacturer	Yoke Gap (in.)	Point Gap (in.)	Volts to Close	Yoke Gap (in.)	Point Gap (in.)	Volts @ 5,000 rpm
1973–78	1170, 1237	Hitachi	2.5	40① 35②	Hitachi	0.008– 0.018	0.0016– 0.0472	4.5– 5.8	0.008– 0.024	0.010– 0.018	13.5– 14.5
1975–78	1487, 1600 CVCC	Nippon Denso	2.5	35③ 45④	Nippon Denso	—	—	—	—	0.016– 0.020	13.5– 14.5

① From No. 1011759
② Up to No. 1011158
③ Without A/C
④ With A/C

REMOVAL AND INSTALLATION

All Models

The regulator is inside the engine compartment, attached to the right fenderwall just above the battery.

1. Disconnect the negative (−) terminal from the battery.

2. Remove the regulator terminal lead wires.

NOTE: *You should label these wires to avoid confusion during installation.*

3. Unscrew the two regulator retaining bolts and remove the regulator from the car.

4. To install, reverse the removal procedure.

Starter

The starter is located on the firewall side of the engine block, adjacent to the flywheel or torque converter housing. 1170 cc and 1237 cc models use a direct drive-type starter, while the CVCC uses a gear reduction starter. Otherwise, the two units are similar in operation and service. Both starters are four-pole, series-wound, DC units to which an outboard solenoid is mounted. When the ignition is turned to the "start" position, the solenoid armature is drawn in, engaging the starter pinion with the flywheel. When the starter pinion and flywheel are fully engaged, the solenoid armature closes the main contacts for the starter, causing the starter to crank the engine. When the engine starts, the increased speed of the flywheel causes the gear to overrun the starter clutch and rotor. The gear continues in full mesh until the ignition is switched from the "start" to the "on" position, interrupting the starter current. The shift lever spring then returns the gear to its neutral position.

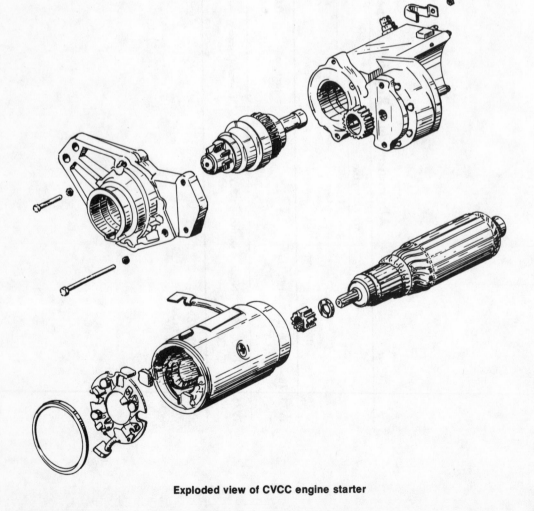

Exploded view of CVCC engine starter

CVCC starter showing rear bolt (arrow)

Non-CVCC engine starter showing mounting bolts (arrows)

REMOVAL AND INSTALLATION

1. Disconnect the ground cable at the battery negative (−) terminal, and the starter motor cable at the positive terminal.

2. Disconnect the starter motor cable at the motor.

3. Remove the starter motor by loosening the two attaching bolts. On CVCC models,
the bolts attach from opposing ends of the starter.

4. Reverse the removal procedure to install the motor. Be sure to tighten the attaching bolts to 29–36 ft lbs and make sure that all wires are securely connected.

STARTER DRIVE REPLACEMENT

1170, 1237 cc Models

1. Remove the solenoid by loosening and removing the attaching bolts.

2. Remove the two brush holder plate retaining screws from the rear cover. Also pry off the rear dust cover along with the clip and thrust washer(s).

3. Remove the two through bolts from the rear cover and lightly tap the rear cover with a mallet to remove it.

4. Remove the four carbon brushes from the brush holder and remove the brush holder.

5. Separate the yoke from the case. The yoke is provided with a hole for positioning, into which the gear case lock pin is inserted.

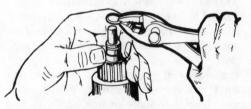

Removing pinion gear from armature

6. Pull the yoke assembly from the gear case, being sure to carefully detach the shift lever from the pinion.

7. Remove the armature unit from the yoke casing and the field coil.

8. To remove the pinion gear from the armature, first set the armature on end with the pinion end facing upward and pull the clutch stop collar downward toward the pinion. Then remove the pinion stop clip and

Battery and Starter Specifications

Year	Engine Displacement (cc)	Battery			Starter							Brush Spring Tension (oz)
		Ampere Hour Capacity	Volts	Terminal Grounded	Lock Test			No-Load Test				
					Amps	Volts	Torque (ft lbs)	Amps	Volts	RPM		
1973–78	1170, 1237	45	12	Negative	380 or less	4.9	5.42	Less than 70	12	7000+		56.448

Battery and Starter Specifications (cont.)

Year	Engine Displacement (cc)	Battery			Starter				Min Brush Length (in.)
		Ampere Hour Capacity	Volts	Terminal Grounded	Load		No-Load		
					Amps	Volts	Amps	Volts	
1975–78	1487, 1600 CVCC	45	12	Negative	160 @ 68° F	9.6	Less than 80	11.5	0.39

pull the pinion stop and gears from the armature shaft as a unit.

9. To assemble and install the starter motor, reverse the disassembly and removal procedures. Be sure to install new clips, and be careful of the installation direction of the shift lever.

ENGINE MECHANICAL

Understanding the Engine

NOTE: *The following discussion is intended to be a general one. Characteristics specific to the engines described in this book will be discussed in the following section.*

The basic piston engine is a metal block containing a series of chambers. The upper engine block is usually an iron or aluminum alloy casting, consisting of outer walls, which form hollow jackets around the cylinder walls. The lower block provides a number of rigid mounting points for the bearings which hold the crankshaft in place, and is known as the crankcase. The hollow jackets of the upper block add to the rigidity of the engine and contain the liquid coolant which carries the heat away from the cylinders and other engine parts. The block of an air cooled engine consists of a crankcase which provides for the rigid mounting of the crankshaft and for studs which hold the cylinders in place. The cylinders are individual, single-wall castings, finned for cooling, and are usually bolted to the crankcase, rather than cast integrally with the block. In a water-cooled engine, only the cylinder head is bolted to the top of the block. The water pump is mounted directly to the block.

The crankshaft is a long iron or steel shaft mounted rigidly in the bottom of the crankcase, at a number of points (usually 4–7). The crankshaft is free to turn and contains a number of counterweighted crank-pins (one for each cylinder; that are offset several inches from the center of the crankshaft and turn in a circle as the crankshaft turns. The crank-pins are centered under each cylinder. Pistons with circular rings to seal the small space between the pistons and wall of the cylinders are connected to the crankpins by steel connecting rods. The rods connect the pistons at their upper ends with the crank-pins at their lower ends.

When the crankshaft spins, the pistons move up and down in the cylinders, varying the volume of each cylinder, depending on the position of the piston. Two openings in each cylinder head (above the cylinders) allow the intake of the air/fuel mixture and the exhaust of burned gasses. The volume of the combustion chamber must be variable for the engine to compress the fuel charge before combustion, to make use of the expansion of the burning gasses and to exhaust the burned gasses and take in a fresh fuel mixture. As the pistons are forced downward by the expansion of burning fuel, the connecting rods convert the reciprocating (up and down) motion of the pistons into rotary (turning) motion of the crankshaft. A round flywheel at the rear of the crankshaft provides a large, stable mass to smooth out the rotation.

The cylinder heads form tight covers for the tops of the cylinders and contain machined chambers into which the fuel mixture is forced as it is compressed by the pistons reaching the upper limit of their travel. Each combustion chamber contains one intake valve, one exhaust valve and one spark plug per cylinder. The spark plugs are screwed into holes in the cylinder head so that the tips protrude into the combustion chambers. The valve in each opening in the cylinder head is opened and closed by the action of the camshaft. The camshaft is driven by the crankshaft through a chain or belt at ½ crankshaft speed (the camshaft gear is twice the size of the crankshaft gear). The valves are operated either through rocker arms and pushrods (overhead valve engine) or directly by the camshaft (overhead cam engine).

Lubricating oil is stored in a pan at the bottom of the engine and is force fed to all parts of the engine by a gear type pump, driven from the crankshaft. The oil lubricates the entire engine and also seals the piston rings, giving good compression.

Honda Engine Design

The engines used in the Honda Civic and Accord are water-cooled, overhead cam, transversely mounted, inline four cylinder powerplants. They can be divided into two different engine families; CVCC and non-CVCC.

The non-CVCC engines have been offered in two different displacements; 1170 cc (1973 only), and 1237 cc (1974 and later). These engines are somewhat unusual in that both the engine and the cylinder head are aluminum. The cylinder head is a crossflow design. The block uses sleeved cylinder liners and a main bearing girdle to add rigidity to the block. The engine uses five main bearings.

The CVCC (Compound Vortex Controlled Combustion) engine is unique in that its cyl-

Frontal view of CVCC engine

inder head is equipped with three valves per cylinder, instead of the usual two. Besides the intake and exhaust valve, each cylinder has an auxiliary intake valve which is much smaller than the regular intake valve. This auxiliary intake valve has its own separate precombustion chamber (adjacent to the main chamber with a crossover passage), its own intake manifold passages, and its own carburetor circuit.

Briefly, what happens is this; at the beginning of the intake stroke, a small but very rich mixture is introduced into the precombustion chamber, while next door in the main combustion chamber, a large but very lean mixture makes its debut. At the end of the compression stroke, ignition occurs. The spark plug, located in the precombustion chamber, easily ignites the rich auxiliary mixture and this ignition spreads out into the main combustion chamber, where the large lean mixture is ignited. This two-stage combustion process allows the engine to operate efficiently with a much leaner overall air/fuel ratio. So, whereas the 1975 and later non-CVCC engines require a belt-driven air injection system to control pollutants, the CVCC accomplishes this internally and gets better gas mileage.

The CVCC engine has its cylinder block constructed of cast iron and the CVCC cylinder head is aluminum. Like the non-CVCC engine, it utilizes five main bearings.

Engine Removal and Installation

CAUTION: *If any repair operation requires the removal of a component of the air conditioning system (on vehicles so equipped), do not disconnect the refrigerant lines. If it is impossible to move the component out of the way with the lines attached, have the air conditioning system evaluated by a trained serviceman. The air conditioning system contains freon under pressure. This gas can be very dangerous. Therefore, under no circumstances should an untrained person attempt to disconnect the air-conditioner refrigerant lines.*

1170, 1237 cc Models

1. Raise the front of the car and support it with safety stands.
2. Remove the front wheels.
3. Drain the engine, transmission, and radiator.

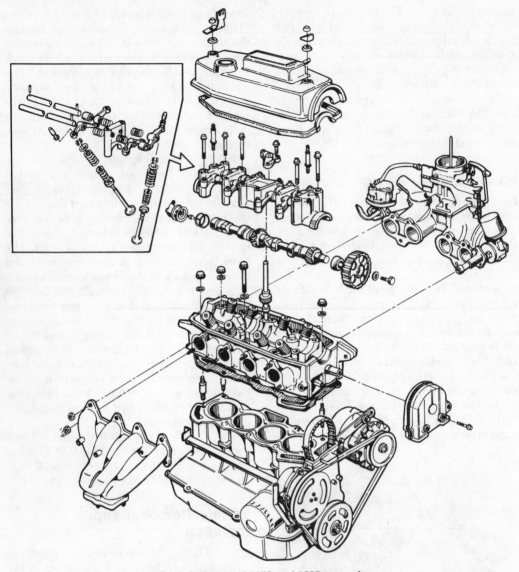

Exploded view of 1170 and 1237 cc engine

4. Remove the front turn signal lights and grille.

5. Remove the hood support bolts and the hood. Remove the fan shroud, if so equipped.

6. Remove the air cleaner case, and air intake pipe at the air cleaner.

7. Disconnect the battery and engine ground cables at the battery and the valve cover.

8. Disconnect the hose from the fuel vapor storage canister at the carburetor.

9. Disconnect the fuel line at the fuel pump.

NOTE: *Plug the line so that gas does not siphon from the tank.*

10. Disconnect the lower coolant hose at the water pump connecting tube and the upper hose at the thermostat cover.

11. Disconnect the following control cables and wires from the engine:

a. Throttle and choke cables at the carburetor;

b. Clutch cable at the release arm;

c. Ignition coil wires at the distributor;

d. Starter motor positive battery cable connection and solenoid wire;

e. Back-up light switch and T.C.S. (Transmission Controlled Spark) switch wires from the transmission casing;

f. Speedometer and tachometer cables;

CAUTION: *When removing the speedome-*

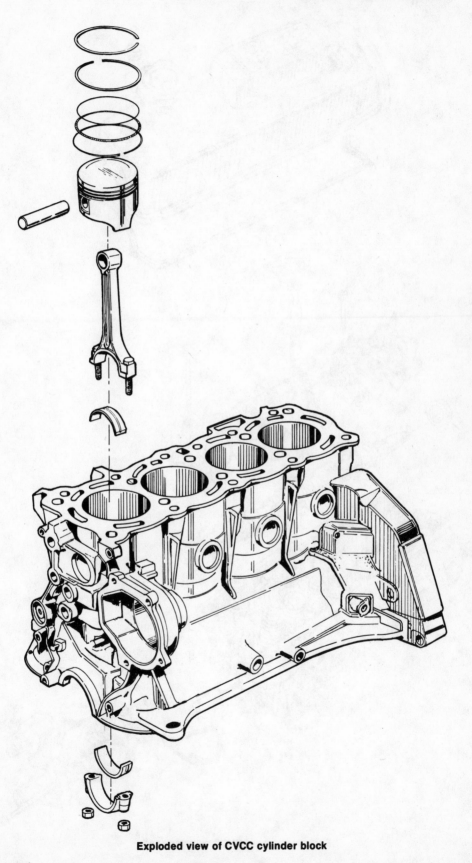

Exploded view of CVCC cylinder block

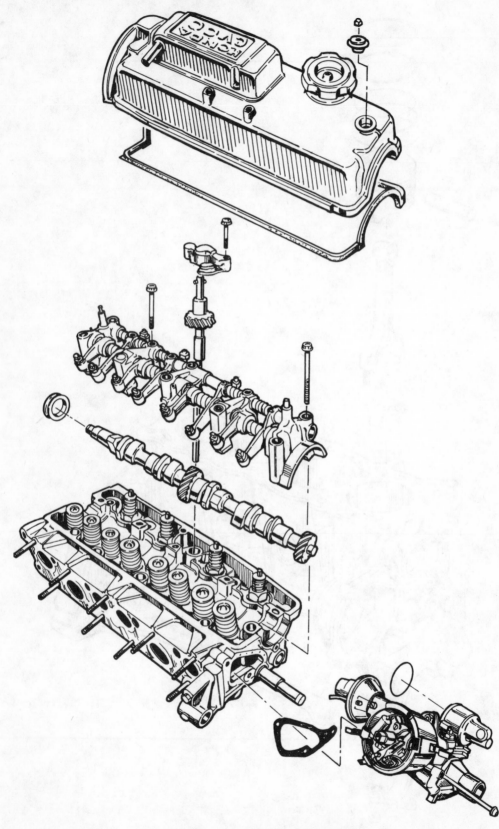

Exploded view of CVCC cylinder head

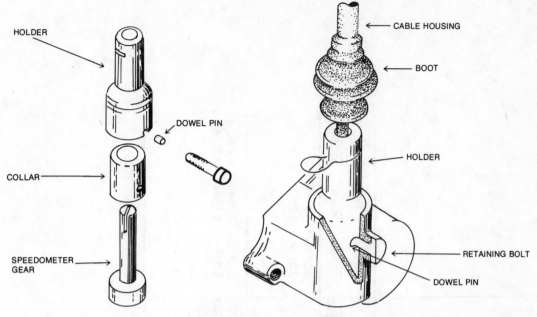

HOLDER

DOWEL PIN

COLLAR

SPEEDOMETER GEAR

CABLE HOUSING

BOOT

HOLDER

RETAINING BOLT

DOWEL PIN

Speedometer cable removal

ter cable from the transmission, it is not necessary to remove the entire cable holder. Remove the end boot (gear holder seal) and the cable retaining clip and then pull the cable out of the holder. In no way should you disturb the holder unless it is absolutely necessary.

The holder consists of three pieces: the holder, collar, and a dowel pin. The dowel pin indexes the holder and collar and is held in place by the bolt that retains the holder. If the bolt is removed and the holder rotated, the dowel pin can fall into the transmission case, necessitating transmis-

General Engine Specifications

Model	Year	Engine Displacement (cc)	Carburetor Type	Horsepower @ rpm	Bore x Stroke (in.)	Compression Ratio	Torque @ rpm (ft lbs)
Civic	1973	1170	Hitachi 2 bbl	50 @ 5000	2.76 x 2.99	8.3 : 1	59 @ 3000
Civic	1974	1237	Hitachi 2 bbl	Not Published	2.83 x 2.99	8.1 : 1	Not Published
Civic AIR	1975–78	1237	Hitachi 2 bbl	Not Published	2.83 x 2.99	8.1 : 1	Not Published
Civic CVCC	1975	1487	Keihin 3 bbl	53 @ 5000	2.91 x 3.41	8.1 : 1	68 @ 3000
Civic CVCC	1976–78	1487	Keihin 3 bbl	53 @ 5000	2.91 x 3.41	7.9 : 1	68 @ 3000
Accord CVCC	1976–78	1600	Keihin 3 bbl	Not Published	2.91 x 3.66	8.2 : 1	Not Published

Valve Specifications

Year	Engine Displacement (cc)	Seat Angle (deg)	Face Angle (deg)	Spring Installed Height (in.)	Stem to Guide Clearance (in.)			Stem Diameter (in.)		
					Intake	Exhaust	Auxiliary	Intake	Exhaust	Auxiliary
1973–78	1170, 1237	45	45	Inner— 1.6535 Outer— 1.5728	0.005– 0.007	0.005– 0.007	—	0.2591– 0.2594	0.2579– 0.2583	—
1975–78	1487, 1600	45	45	Inner— 1.358 Outer— 1.437 Auxiliary— 0.906	0.0004– 0.0016	0.0020– 0.0031	0.0008– 0.0020	0.2592– 0.2596	0.2580– 0.2584	0.2162– 0.2166

Crankshaft and Connecting Rod Specifications
All measurements given in in.

Year	Engine Displacement (cu in.)	Crankshaft				Connecting Rod		
		Main Brg Journal Dia	Main Brg Oil Clearance	Shaft End Play	Thrust on No.	Journal Dia	Clearance Oil	Side Clearance
1973–78	1170, 1237	1.9685– 1.9673	0.0009– 0.0017	0.0039– 0.0138	3	1.5736– 1.548	0.0008– 0.0015	0.0079– 0.0177①
1975–78	1600, 1487 CVCC	1.9687– 1.9697	0.0010– 0.0021	0.0039– 0.0138	3	1.6525– 1.6535	0.0008– 0.0015	0.0059– 0.0118

① 1974–76 1237 cc engines—0.0059–0.0118 in.

Piston and Ring Specifications
All measurements are given in inches

Year	Engine Displacement (cc)	Piston Clearance	Ring Gap			Ring Side Clearance		
			Top Compression	Bottom Compression	Oil Control	Top Compression	Bottom Compression	Oil Control
1973	1170	0.0012– 0.0039	0.008– 0.016	0.008– 0.016	0.008– 0.035	0.0008– 0.0018	0.0008– 0.0018	0.0008– 0.0018
1974–78	1237	0.0012– 0.0039	0.0098– 0.0157	0.0098– 0.0577	0.0118– 0.0394	0.0008– 0.0018	0.0008– 0.0018	Snug
1975–78	1600, 1487 CVCC	0.0012– 0.0039	0.0079– 0.0157	0.0079– 0.0157	0.0079– 0.0354	0.0008– 0.0018	0.0008– 0.0018	Snug

Torque Specifications
All readings are given in ft lbs

Year	Engine Displacement (cc)	Cylinder Head Bolts	Main Bearing Bolts	Rod Bearing Bolts	Crankshaft Pulley Bolts	Flywheel to Crankshaft Bolts	Manifold		Spark Plugs	Oil Pan Drain Bolt
							In	Ex		
1973–78	1170, 1237	30–35① 37–42②	27–31	18–21	34–38	34–38	13– 17	13– 17③	11–18	29–36
1975–78	1600, 1487 CVCC	40–47	30–35	18–21	34–38	34–38	15– 17	15– 17	11–18	29–36

① To engine number EB 1-1019949
② From engine number EB 1-1019950
③ 1975–76 models w/AIR—22–33 ft lbs

sion disassembly to remove the pin. To insure that this does not happen when the holder must be removed, do not rotate the holder more than 30° in either direction when removing it. Once removed, make sure that the pin is still in place. Use the same precaution when installing the holder.

g. Alternator wire and wire harness connector;

h. The wires from both water temperature thermal switches on the intake manifold;

i. Cooling fan connector and radiator thermoswitch wires;

j. Oil pressure sensor;

k. On 1975–76 models, vacuum hose to throttle opener at opener, and vacuum hose from carburetor insulator to throttle opener;

1. On 1976–76 models, by-pass valve assemble and bracket.

NOTE: *It would be a good idea to tag all of these wires to avoid confusion during installation.*

12. Disconnect the heater hose by removing the "H" connector from the two hoses in the firewall.

13. Remove the engine torque rod from the engine and firewall.

14. Remove the starter motor.

15. Remove the radiator from the engine compartment.

16. Remove the exhaust pipe-to-manifold clamp.

17. Remove the exhaust pipe flange nuts and lower the exhaust pipe.

18. Disconnect the left and right lower control arm ball joints at the knuckle, using a ball joint remover (or special tool 07941-6340000).

19. Hold the brake disc and pull the right and left drive shafts out of the differential case.

20a. Manual transmission only: Drive out the gearshift rod pin (8 mm) with a drift and disconnect the rod at the transmission case.

NOTE: *Do not disconnect the shift lever end of the gearshift rod and extension.*

20b. Hondamatic only: Disconnect shift cable at console and cooler line at transmission.

21. Disconnect the gearshift extension at the engine (man. trans. only).

22. Screw in two engine hanger bolts in the torque rod bolt hole and the bolt hole just to the left of the distributor. Then, engage

Driving gearshift rod pin out using pin driver

the lifting chain hooks to the hanger bolts and lift the engine just enough to take the load off the engine mounts.

23. After being sure that the engine is properly supported, remove the two center mount bracket nuts.

Center mount nut locations (arrows)

24. Remove the center beam (1973–74 only).

25. Remove the left engine mount.

26. Lift the engine out slowly, taking care not to allow the engine to damage other parts of the car.

27. To install, reverse the removal procedure. Pay special attention to the following points:

a. Lower the engine into position and install the left mount. On 1973–74 models, install the center beam with the front end between the stabilizer bar and frame. Do not attach mounting bolts at this time.

NOTE: *On 1973–74 models, be sure that the lower mount has the mount stop installed between the center beam and the rubber mount.*

b. Align the center mount studs with the beam and tighten the nuts and washer serveral turns (just enough to support the beam). On 1973–74 models, attach the rear end of the center beam to the subframe;

c. On 1973–74 models, attach the front end of the center beam. Torque the center beam bolts but do not tighten the lower mount nuts. Lower the engine so it rests on the lower mount. Torque the lower mount nuts.

d. Use a new shift rod pin;

e. After installing the driveshafts, attempt to move the inner joint housing in and out of the differential housing. If it moves easily, the driveshaft end clips should be replaced;

f. Make sure that the control cables and wires are connected properly;

g. When connecting the heater hoses, the upper hose goes to the water pump connecting pipe and the lower hose to the intake manifold;

h. Refill the engine, transmission, and radiator with their respective fluids to the proper levels;

i. On Hondamatic cars, check shift cable adjustment.

1487 cc CVCC Models

1. Raise the front of the car and support it with jackstands. Remove both front wheels.

2. Remove the headlight rim attaching screws and the rims.

3. Open the hood. Disconnect both parking light connectors. Remove the parking light retaining bolts and backing plate and remove the parking lights.

4. Remove the lower grille molding and remove the six grille retaining bolts and the grille.

5. Disconnect the windshield washer hose and remove it from the underside of the hood.

Thermosensors and coolant temperature sending unit locations. Arrow 1 is the temperature sending unit, arrow 2 is thermosensor "A", and arrow 3 is the thermosensor "B"

6. Disconnect the negative battery cable and the tranmission bracket-to-body ground cable.

7. Remove the upper torque (engine locating) arm.

8. Disconnect the vacuum hose at the power brake booster, thermosensors "A" and "B" at their wiring connectors, and the coolant temperature gauge sending unit wire.

9. Drain the radiator. After all coolant has drained, install the drain bolt finger-tight.

10. Disconnect all four coolant hoses. Disconnect cooling fan motor connector and the temperature sensor. Remove the radiator hose to the overflow tank.

11. On Hondamatic cars only, remove both ATF cooler line bolts.

NOTE: *Save the washers from the cooler line banjo connectors and replace if damaged.*

12. Remove the radiator.

13. Label and disconnect the starter motor wires. Remove the two starter mount-

Emission control black box—1976 type shown

ing bolts (one from each end of the starter), and remove the starter.

14. Label and disconnect the spark plug wires at the plugs. Remove the distributor cap and scribe the position of the rotor on the side of the distributor housing. Remove the top distributor swivel bolt and remove the distributor (the rotor will rotate 30° as the drive gear is beveled).

15. On manual transmission cars, remove the C-clip retaining the clutch cable at the firewall. Then, remove the end of the clutch cable from the clutch release arm and bracket. First, pull up on the cable, and then push it out to release it from the bracket. Remove the end form the release arm.

16. Disconnect the back-up light switch wires. Disconnect the control valve vacuum hose, the air intake hose, and the preheat air intake hose. Disconnect the air bleed valve hose from the air cleaner. Label and disconnect all remaining vacuum hoses from the underside of the air cleaner. Remove the air cleaner.

17. Label and disconnect all remaining emission control vacuum hoses from the engine. Disconnect the emission box wiring connector and remove the black emission box from the firewall.

18. Remove the engine mount heat shield.

19. Disconnect the engine-to-body ground strap at the valve cover.

20. Disconnect the alternator wiring connector and oil pressure sensor leads.

21. Disconnect the vacuum hose from the start control and electrical leads to both cut-off solenoid valves.

22. Disconnect the vacuum hose from the charcoal canister and both fuel lines to the carburetor. Mark the adjustment and disconnect the choke and throttle cables at the carburetor.

23. On Hondamatic cars only, remove the center console and disconnect the gear selector control cable at the console. This may be accomplished after removing the retaining clip and pin.

24. Drain the transmission oil.

25. Remove the fender well shield under the right fender, exposing the speedometer drive cable. Remove the set screw securing the speedometer drive holder. Then, slowly pull the cable assembly out of the transmission, taking care not to drop the pin or drive gear. Finally, remove the pin, collar, and drive gear from the cable assembly.

26. Disconnect the front suspension stabilizer bar from its mounts on both sides. Also, remove the bolt retaining the lower control arm to the sub-frame on both sides.

27. Remove the forward mounting nut on the radius rod on both sides. Then, pry the constant velocity joint out about ½ in. and pull the stub axle out of the transmission case. Repeat for other side.

28. Remove the six retaining bolts and remove the center beam.

29. On manual transmission cars only, drive out the pin retaining the shift linkage.

30. Disconnect the lower torque arm from the transmission.

31. On Hondamatic cars only, remove the bolt retaining the control cable stay at the transmission. Loosen the two U-bolt nuts and pull the cable out of its housing.

32. Disconnect the exhaust pipe at the manifold. Disconnect the retaining clamp also.

33. Remove the rear engine mount nut.

34. Attach a chain pulley hoist to the engine. Honda recommends using the threaded bolt holes at the extreme right and left ends of the cylinder head (with special hardened bolts) as lifting points, as opposed to wrapping a chain around the entire block and risk damaging some components such as the carburetor, etc.

35. Raise the engine enough to place a slight tension on the chain, remove the nut retaining the front engine mount. Then, remove the three bolts retaining the front mount. While lifting the engine, remove the mount.

36. Remove the three retaining bolts and push the left engine support into its shock mount bracket to the limit of its travel.

37. Slowly raise the engine out of the vehicle.

38. Installation is the reverse of removal.

Accord CVCC Models

1. Disconnect the negative battery terminal.

2. Drain the radiator of coolant, and drain the engine and transmission oil.

3. Jack up the front of the car and remove the front wheels. Be sure to support the car with safety stands.

4. Remove the air cleaner.

5. Remove the following wires and hoses:
   a. The coil wire and the ignition primary wire from the distributor.
   b. The engine subharness and the

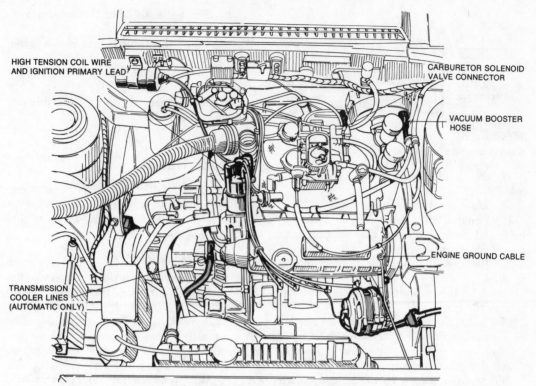

Accord component removal points

HIGH TENSION COIL WIRE AND IGNITION PRIMARY LEAD

CARBURETOR SOLENOID VALVE CONNECTOR

VACUUM BOOSTER HOSE

ENGINE GROUND CABLE

TRANSMISSION COOLER LINES (AUTOMATIC ONLY)

starter wires. (Mark the wires before removal to ease installation.)

c. The vacuum tube from the brake booster.

d. On Hondamatic models, remove the ATF cooler hose from the transmission.

e. The engine ground cable.

f. Alternator wiring harness.

g. Carburetor solenoid valve connector

h. Carburetor fuel line.

6. Remove the choke and throttle cables.

7. Remove the radiator and heater hoses.

8. Remove the emission control "black box".

9. Remove the clutch slave cylinder with the hydraulic line attached.

10. Remove the speedometer cable. Pull the wire clip from the housing, and remove the cable from the housing. Do not, under any circumstances, remove the housing from the transmission.

11. Attach an engine hoist to the engine block, and raise the engine just enough to remove the slack from the chain.

12. Disconnect the right and left lower ball joints, and the tie rod ends. You will need a ball joint remover tool for this operation. An alternative method is to leave the ball joints connected, and remove the lower

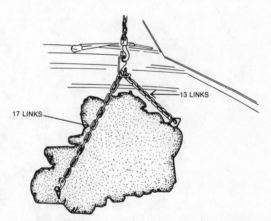

13 LINKS

17 LINKS

Accord engine removal. Note the chain positioning

control arm inner bolts, and the radius rods from the lower control arms.

13. Remove the driveshafts from the transmission by prying the snap ring off the groove in the end of the shaft. The pull the shaft out by holding the knuckle.

14. Remove the center engine mount.

15. Remove the shift rod positioner from the transmission case.

16. Drive out the pin from the shift rod using a small pin driver.

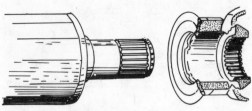

Accord driveshaft removal

17. On Hondamatics, remove the control cable.

18. Disconnect the exhaust pipe.

19. Remove the three engine support bolts and push the left engine support into the shock mount bracket.

20. Remove the front and rear engine mounts.

21. Raise the engine carefully and remove it from the car.

22. Install the engine in the reverse order of removal, making the following checks:

a. Make sure that the clip at the end of the driveshaft seats in the groove in the differential. **Failure to do so may lead to the wheels falling off.**

b. Bleed the air from the cooling system.

c. Adjust the throttle and choke cable tension.

d. Check the clutch for the correct free play.

e. Make sure that the transmission shifts properly.

Cylinder Head

REMOVAL AND INSTALLATION

NOTE: *You will need a 12 point socket to remove and install the head bolts on the CVCC engine.*

Removal Precautions

a. To prevent warping, the cylinder head should be removed when the engine is cold.

b. Remove oil, scale or carbon deposits accumulated from each part. When decarbonizing take care not to score or scratch the mating surfaces.

c. After washing the oil holes or orifices in each part, make sure they are not

Disassembled CVCC cylinder head showing major components

restricted by blowing out with compressed air.

d. If parts will not be reinstalled immediately after washing, spray parts with a rust preventive to protect from corrosion.

NOTE: *If the engine has already been removed from the car, begin with Step 12 in the following procedure.*

1. Remove the turn signals, grille, and hood. Disconnect the negative battery cable.

2. Drain the radiator.

3. Disconnect the upper radiator hose at the thermostat cover.

3a. On CVCC models, remove distributor cap, ignition wires and primary wire. Also, loosen the alternator bracket and remove the upper mounting bolt from the cylinder head.

4. Remove the air cleaner case.

5. Disconnect the tube running between the canister and carburetor at the canister.

6. Disconnect the throttle and choke control cables. Label and disconnect all vacuum hoses.

7. Disconnect the heater hose at the intake manifold.

8. Disconnect the wires from both thermoswitches.

9. Disconnect the fuel line.

9a. On CVCC models, disconnect the temperature gauge sending unit wire, idle cut-off solenoid valve, and primary/main cut-off solenoid valve.

10. Disconnect the engine torque rod.

11. Disconnect the exhaust pipe at the exhaust manifold.

12. Remove the valve cover bolts and the valve cover.

13. Remove the two timing belt upper cover bolts and the cover.

14. Bring No. 1 piston to top dead center. Do this by aligning the notch next to the red notch you use for setting ignition timing, with the index mark on the timing belt cover (1170, 1237 cc) or rear of engine block (CVCC).

15. Loosen, but do not remove, the timing belt adjusting bolt and pivot bolt.

16. On 1170 and 1237 cc models only, remove the camshaft pulley bolt. Do not let the woodruff key fall inside the timing cover. Remove the pulley with a pulley remover (or special tool 07935-6110000).

CAUTION: *Use care when handling the timing belt. Do not use sharp instruments to remove the belt. Do not get oil or grease*

Timing belt pivot and adjustment bolts

Closeup of non-CVCC engine crankshaft showing gear removed, with woodruff key remaining

on the belt. Do not bend or twist the belt more than 90°.

17. On 1170 and 1237 cc models only, remove the fuel pump and distributor.

18. On 1170 and 1237 cc models only, remove the oil pump gear holder and remove the pump gear and shaft.

19. Loosen and remove the cylinder head bolts in the *reverse* order given in the head bolt tightening sequence diagram. The number one cylinder head bolt is hidden underneath the oil pump.

20. Remove the cylinder head with the carburetor and manifolds attached.

21. Remove the intake and exhaust manifolds from the cylinder head.

Cylinder head bolt removal. The rocker arms have been removed for clarity

Hidden bolt next to oil pump gear (arrow)

NOTE: *After removing the cylinder head, cover the engine with a clean cloth to prevent materials from getting into the cylinders.*

22. To install, reverse the removal procedure, being sure to pay attention to the following points:

a. Be sure that No. 1 cylinder is at top dead center before positioning the cylinder head in place;

b. Use a new head gasket and make sure the head, engine block, and gasket are clean;

c. The cylinder head aligning dowel pins should be in their proper place in the block before installing the cylinder head;

d. Tighten the head bolts according to the diagram;

e. After the head bolts have been tightened, install the woodruff key and camshaft pulley (if removed), and tighten the pulley bolt according to specification. On the non-CVCC engine, align the marks on the camshaft pulley so they are parallel with the top of the head and the woodruff key is facing up; On the CVCC engine, the word "up" should be facing upward and the mark on the cam gear should be aligned with the arrow on the cylinder head. See the illustration in the timing belt removal and installation procedure.

f. After installing the pulley (if removed), install the timing belt. Be careful not to disturb the timing position already set when installing the belt.

OVERHAUL (SEE "ENGINE REBUILDING" SECTION)

Valve Guide

REMOVAL AND INSTALLATION

All Models

1. Using a valve spring compressor, remove the valve keepers, retainers, springs, and seats. Then remove the valves.

2. Remove the valve guides with a hammer and a valve guide driver. Drive the guides out from the combustion chamber side.

NOTE: *On aluminum alloy heads, as used with 1170 and 1237 cc engines, an application of heat (approx. 200° F) may be necessary before the valve guides will be "loose" enough to drive out.*

3. Use the guide driver and a hammer to press the valve back into the head.

4. After installing a valve guide, use a valve guide reamer to obtain a proper valve stem fit. Use the reamer with an in-out motion while rotating. For the finished dimension of the valve guide, check the "Valve Specifications" chart.

NOTE: *Do not forget to install valve guide seals.*

Cylinder Head Bolt Torque Sequence—All Models

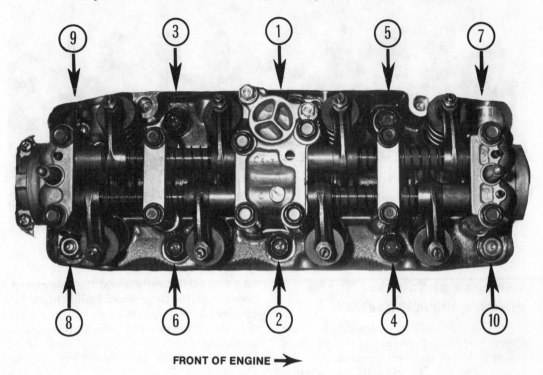

FRONT OF ENGINE ➔

Rocker arm assembly showing bolts partially removed

Rocker arm assembly—CVCC engine

Camshaft and Rocker Shafts
REMOVAL AND INSTALLATION

NOTE: *To facilitate installation, make sure that No. 1 piston is at Top Dead Center before removal of camshaft.*

1. Follow the "Cylinder Head" removal procedure before attempting to remove the camshaft.
2. Loosen the camshaft and rocker arm shaft holder bolts in a criss-cross pattern, beginning on the outside holder.
3. Remove the rocker arms, shafts, and holders as an assembly.
4. Lift out the camshaft and right head seal (or tachometer body if equipped).
5. To install, reverse the removal procedure, being sure to install the holder bolts in the reverse order of removal.

NOTE: *Back off valve adjusting screws before installing rockers. Then adjust valves as outlined in Chapter 2.*

Intake Manifold
REMOVAL AND INSTALLATION
1170, 1237 cc Models

1. Drain the radiator.
2. Remove the air cleaner and case.
3. Remove the carburetor from the intake manifold (see "Carburetor—Removal and Installation" in Chapter 4).
4. Remove the emission control hoses from the manifold T-joint. One hose leads to the condensation chamber and the other leads to the charcoal canister.
5. Remove the hose connected to the in-

take manifold directly above the T-joint and underneath the carburetor, leading to the air cleaner check valve (refer to Chapter 4 for diagrams of the various emission control hose connections).
6. Remove the thermo-switch wires from the switches.
7. Remove the solenoid valve located next to the thermo-switch.
8. Remove the six (6) intake manifold attaching nuts in a crisscross pattern, beginning from the center and moving out to both ends. Then remove the manifold.
9. Clean all old gasket material from the manifold and the cylinder head.
10. If the intake manifold is to be replaced, transfer all necessary components to the new manifold.
11. To install, reverse the removal procedure, being sure to observe the following points:

   a. Apply a water-resistant sealer to the new intake manifold gasket before positioning it in place;

   b. Be sure all hoses are properly connected;

   c. Tighten the manifold attaching nuts in the reverse order of removal.

Exhaust Manifold
REMOVAL AND INSTALLATION
1170, 1237 cc Models

CAUTION: *Do not perform this operation on a warm or hot engine.*

1. Remove the front grille.
2. Remove the three (3) exhaust pipe-to-

manifold nuts and disconnect the exhaust pipe at the manifold.

2a. On 1975 and later models, disconnect the air injection tubes from the exhaust manifold and remove the air injection manifold.

3. Remove the hot air cover, held by two bolts, from the exhaust manifold.

4. Remove the eight (8) manifold attaching nuts in a crisscross pattern starting from the center, and remove the manifold.

5. To install, reverse the removal procedure. Be sure to use new gaskets and be sure to tighten the manifold bolts in the reverse order of removal, and to the proper tightening torque.

Intake and Exhaust Manifolds

REMOVAL AND INSTALLATION

CVCC Models

1. Drain the radiator. Disconnect manifold coolant hoses.

2. Remove the air cleaner assembly.

3. Label and disconnect all emission control vacuum hoses and electrical leads.

3. Label and disconnect all emission control vacuum hoses and electrical leads.

5. Remove the carburetor from the intake manifold.

6. Remove the upper heat shield. Loosen, but do not remove the four bolts retaining the intake manifold to the exhaust manifold.

When reinstalling the combination manifold on CVCC models, tighten these four bolts *after* the manifolds have been attached to the engine. You'll crack the manifold ears if you tighten them beforehand

7. Disconnect the exhaust pipe from the exhaust manifold.

8. Remove the nine nuts retaining the intake and exhaust manifolds to the cylinder

head. The two manifolds are removed as a unit.

9. Reverse the above procedure to install, using new gaskets. The thick washers used beneath the cylinder head-to-manifold retaining nuts must be installed with the dished (concave), side toward the engine. Readjust the choke and throttle linkage and bleed the cooling system.

Timing Gear Cover

REMOVAL AND INSTALLATION

1. Align the crankshaft pulley (1170 and 1237 cc), or flywheel pointer (CVCC), at Top Dead Center (TDC).

Engine showing timing belt upper cover removed

2. Remove the two bolts which hold the timing belt upper cover and remove the cover.

3. Loosen the alternator and air pump (if so equipped), and remove the pulley belt(s).

4. Remove the three water pump pulley bolts and the water pump pulley.

5. Remove the crankshaft pulley attaching bolt. Use a two-jawed puller to remove the crankshaft pulley.

NOTE: *The crankshaft bolt cannot be reused. It must be replaced every time it is removed.*

6. Remove the timing gear cover retaining bolts and the timing gear cover.

The small washers can be removed from behind the tensioner and adjusting bolt to allow removal of the cover. Be sure to reinstall the washers

7. To install, reverse the removal procedure. Make sure that the timing guide plates, pulleys and front oil seal are properly installed on the crankshaft end before replacing the cover.

CAUTION: *Be sure not to upset the timing position already set (TDC).*

Timing Belt and Tensioner
REMOVAL AND INSTALLATION

1. Turn the crankshaft pulley until it is at Top Dead Center.

2. Remove the pulley belt, water pump pulley, crankshaft pulley, and timing gear cover. Mark the direction of timing belt rotation.

3. Loosen, *but do not remove,* the tensioner adjusting bolt and pivot bolt.

4. Slide the timing belt off of the camshaft timing gear and the crankshaft pulley gear and remove it from the engine.

5. To remove the camshaft timing gear pulley, first remove the center bolt and then remove the pulley with a pulley remover or a brass hammer. This can be accomplished by simply removing the timing belt upper cover, loosening the tensioner bolts, and sliding the timing belt off of the gear to expose the gear for removal.

NOTE: *If you remove the timing gear with the timing belt cover in place, be sure not to let the woodruff key fall inside the tim-*

Inspecting the timing belt

ing cover when removing the gear from the camshaft.

Inspect the timing belt. Replace if over 10,000 miles old, if oil soaked (find source of oil leak also), or if worn on leading edges of belt teeth.

6. To install, reverse the removal procedure. Be sure to install the crankshaft pulley and the camshaft timing gear pulley in the top dead center position. (See "Cylinder Head Removal" for further details). On the non-CVCC engine, align the marks on the camshaft timing gear so they are parallel with the top of the cylinder head and the woodruff key is facing up. See the photograph for details on CVCC timing.

When installing the timing belt, do not allow oil to come in contact with the belt. Oil will cause the rubber to swell. Be careful not

Closeup of the adjustment and pivot bolts. The upper bolt is the pivot bolt, and the lower bolt is the adjustment bolt

On CVCC engines, when the camshaft pulley is in the correct position, the word "UP" will be facing up and the small mark on the camshaft pulley will be aligned with the arrow on the cylinder head. The marks are just slightly off in this photograph. On the opposite side of the cam gear, there is a small arrow pointing at a small line. This is used by Honda to indicate when the gear has been installed 180 degrees out of time. The marks are not really necessary since then the word "UP" would be pointing down

Frontal view of a non-CVCC engine showing the timing belt correctly installed. Note that the crankshaft key is pointing straight up and the marks on the cam gear are parallel with the top of the cylinder head

On non-CVCC engines, align the marks on the cam gear parallel with the top of the cylinder head

to bend or twist the belt unnecessarily, since it is made of fiberglass; nor should you use tools having sharp edges when installing or removing the belt. Be sure to install the belt with the arrow facing in the same direction it was facing during removal.

After installing the timing belt, adjust the belt tension by first rotating the crankshaft counterclockwise ¼ turn. Then, retighten the adjusting bolt and finally the tensioner pivot bolt.

CAUTION: *Do not remove the adjusting or pivot bolts, only loosen them. When adjusting, do not use any force other than the adjuster spring. If the belt is too tight, it will result in a shortened belt life.*

Pistons and Connecting Rods

REMOVAL AND INSTALLATION

For removal with the engine out of the car, begin with Step 8.

1. Remove the turn signals, grille, and engine hood.

2. Drain the radiator.

3. Drain the engine oil.

4. Raise the front of the car and support it with safety stands.

5. Attach a chain to the clutch cable bracket on the transmission case and raise just enough to take the load off of the center mount.

NOTE: *Do not remove the left engine mount.*

6. Remove the center beam and engine lower mount.

7. Remove the cylinder head (see "Cylinder Head Removal and Installation").

8. Loosen the oil pan bolts and remove

the oil pan and flywheel dust shield. Loosen the oil pan bolts in a criss-cross pattern beginning with the outside bolt. To remove the oil pan, lightly tap the corners of the oil pan with a mallet. It is not necessary to remove the gasket unless it is damaged.

CAUTION: *Do not pry the oil pan off with the tip of a screwdriver.*

Mark the pistons for installation if they aren't already marked from the factory

Oil pump removal. There is a bolt hidden under the screen. See the photograph under "Oil Pump Removal"

9. Remove the oil passage block and the oil pump assembly.

CAUTION: *As soon as the oil passage block bolts are loosened, the oil in the oil line may flow out.*

NOTE: *Before removing the pistons, check the top of the cylinder bore for carbon build-up or a ridge. Remove the carbon or use a ridge-reamer to remove the ridge before removing the pistons.*

10. Working from the underside of the car, remove the connecting rod bearing caps. Using the wooden handle of a hammer, push the pistons and connecting rods out of the cylinders.

NOTE: *Bearing caps, bearings, and pistons should be marked to indicate their location for reassembly.*

11. When removing the piston rings, be

sure not to apply excessive force as the rings are made of cast iron and can be easily broken.

NOTE: *A hydraulic press is necessary for removing the piston pin. This is a job best left to the professional, if you need to go this far.*

The piston pins must be removed with a press

Piston assembly

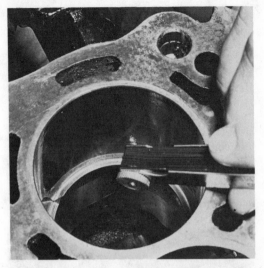

Check the ring end gap before installing the rings on the pistons

Piston ring installation. Tools like this aren't really necessary, as rings can be easily installed by hand

12. Observe the following points when installing the piston rings:

a. When installing the three-piece oil ring, first place the spacer and then the rails in position. The spacer and rail gaps must be staggered 0.787–1.181 in. (2–3 cm);

b. Install the second and top rings on the piston with their markings facing upward;

c. After installing all rings on the piston, rotate them to be sure they move smoothly without signs of binding;

d. The ring gaps must be staggered 120° and must NOT be in the direction of the piston pin boss or at right angles to the pin. The gap of the three-piece oil ring refers to that of the middle spacer.

NOTE: *Pistons and rings are also available in four oversizes, 0.010 in. (0.25 mm), 0.020 in. (0.50 mm), 0.030 in. (0.75 mm), and 0.040 in. (1.00 mm).*

13. Using a ring compressor, install the piston into the cylinder with the skirt protruding about ⅓ of the piston height below the ring compressor. Prior to installation, apply a thin coat of oil to the rings and to the cylinder wall.

NOTE: *When installing the piston, the connecting rod oil jet hole or the mark on the piston crown faces the intake manifold.*

14. Using the wooden handle of a hammer, slowly press the piston into the cylinder. Guide the connecting rod so it does not damage the crankshaft journals.

15. Reassemble the remaining components in the reverse order of removal. Install the connecting rod bearing caps so that the recess in the cap and the recess in the rod are on the same side. After tightening the cap bolts, move the rod back and forth on the journal to check for binding.

Make sure the recess in the cap and recess on the rod are on the same side (Arrows)

Torquing the connecting rod cap

ENGINE LUBRICATION

Oil Pan
REMOVAL AND INSTALLATION

1. Drain the engine oil.
2. Raise the front of the car and support it with safety stands.

3. Attach a chain to the clutch cable bracket on the transmission case and raise just enough to take the load off the center mount.

NOTE: *Do not remove the left engine mount.*

4. Remove the center beam and engine lower mount.

5. Loosen the oil pan bolts and remove the oil pan flywheel dust shield.

NOTE: *Loosen the bolts in a criss-cross pattern beginning with the outside bolt. To remove the oil pan, lightly tap the corners of the oil pan with a mallet. It is not necessary to remove the gasket unless it is damaged.*

6. To install, reverse the removal procedure. Apply a coat of sealant to the entire mating surface of the cylinder block, except the crankshaft oil seal, before fitting the oil pan.

Rear Main Oil Seal
REPLACEMENT

The rear oil seal on the Honda is installed in the rear main bearing cap. Replacement of the seal requires the removal of the transmission, flywheel and clutch housing, as well as the oil pan. Refer to the appropriate sections for the removal and installation of the above components. Both the front and rear main seal are installed after the crankshaft has been torqued, in the event it was removed. Special drivers are used.

Driving in the rear main seal using the Honda special tool

Removing the oil pump screen

Torquing the oil pump retaining bolts

Installing the oil pump screen

Oil Pump
REMOVAL AND INSTALLATION

To remove the oil pump, follow the procedure given for oil pan removal and installation. After the oil pan has been dropped, simply unbolt the oil passage block and oil pump assembly from the engine. Remove the oil pump screen to find the last bolt. When installing the pump, torque the bolts to no more than 8 ft lbs.

ENGINE COOLING

The Honda employs water-cooling for engine heat dissipation. Air is forced through the radiator by an electric fan which is, in turn, activated by a water temperature sensor screwed into the base of the radiator.

Radiator
REMOVAL AND INSTALLATION

NOTE: *When removing the radiator, take care not to damage the core and fins.*

1. Drain the radiator.
2. Disconnect the thermo-switch wire and the fan motor wire. Remove the fan shroud, if so equipped.
3. Disconnect the upper coolant hose at the upper radiator tank and the lower hose at the water pump connecting pipe.

Hidden oil pump retaining bolt (arrow)

4. Remove the turn signals and front grille.

5. Detach the radiator mounting bolts and remove the radiator with the fan attached. The fan can be easily unbolted from the back of the radiator.

6. To install, reverse the removal procedure. Bleed the cooling system.

Water Pump

REMOVAL AND INSTALLATION

1. Drain the radiator.

2. On 1170 and 1237 cc cars only, loosen the alternator bolts. Move the alternator toward the cylinder block and remove the drive belt.

3. Loosen the pump mounting bolts and remove the pump together with the pulley and the seal rubber.

4. To install, reverse the removal procedure using a new gasket. Bleed the cooling system.

Thermostat

REMOVAL AND INSTALLATION

1. On 1170 and 1237 cc cars, the thermostat is located on the intake manifold, under the air cleaner nozzle, so you will first have to remove the air cleaner housing. On CVCC

Thermostat housing and bleed bolt location—non-CVCC models

cars, it is located at the rear of the distributor housing.

2. Unbolt and remove the thermostat cover and pull the thermostat from the housing.

3. To install, reverse the removal procedure. Always install the spring end of the thermostat toward the engine. Tighten the two cover bolts to 7 ft lbs. Always use a new gasket. Bleed the cooling system.

Thermostat housing and bleed bolt location—CVCC models

Thermostat installation

Engine Rebuilding

This section describes, in detail, the procedures involved in rebuilding a Honda engine.

The section is divided into two sections. The first, Cylinder Head Reconditioning, assumes that the cylinder head is removed from the engine, all manifolds are removed, and the cylinder head is on a workbench. The camshaft should be removed. The second section, Cylinder Block Reconditioning, covers the block, pistons, connecting rods and crankshaft. It is assumed that the engine is mounted on a work stand, and the cylinder head and all accessories are removed.

Procedures are identified as follows:

Unmarked—Basic procedures that must be performed in order to successfully complete the rebuilding process.

Torque (ft. lbs.)*

U.S./Bolt Grade (SAE)

Bolt Diameter (inches)	1 and 2	5	6	8	Wrench Size (inches) Bolt	Nut
1/4	5	7	10	10.5	3/8	7/16
5/16	9	14	19	22	1/2	9/16
3/8	15	25	34	37	9/16	5/8
7/16	24	40	55	60	5/8	3/4
1/2	37	60	85	92	3/4	13/16
9/16	53	88	120	132	7/8	7/8
5/8	74	120	167	180	15/16	1
3/4	120	200	280	296	1 1/8	1 1/8
7/8	190	302	440	473	1 5/16	1 5/16
1	282	466	660	714	1 1/2	1 1/2

Metric/Bolt Grade

Bolt Diameter (mm)	5D	8G	10K	12K	Wrench Size (mm) Bolt and Nut
6	5	6	8	10	10
8	10	16	22	27	14
10	19	31	40	49	17
12	34	54	70	86	19
14	55	89	117	137	22
16	83	132	175	208	24
18	111	182	236	283	27
22	182	284	394	464	32
24	261	419	570	689	36

*—Torque values are for lightly oiled bolts. CAUTION: Bolts threaded into aluminum require much less torque.

Starred (*)—Procedures that should be performed to ensure maximum performance and engine life.

In many cases, a choice of methods is also provided. Methods are identified in the same manner as procedures. The choice of method for a procedure is at the discretion of the user.

The tools required for the basic rebuilding procedure should, with minor exceptions, be those included in a mechanic's tool kit. An accurate torque wrench, and a dial indicator (reading in thousandths) mounted on a universal base should be available. Bolts and nuts with no torque specification should be tightened according to size (see chart). Special tools, where required, all are readily available from the major tool suppliers (i.e., Craftsman, Snap-On, K-D). The services of a competent automotive machine shop must also be readily available.

When assembling the engine, any parts that will be in frictional contact must be pre-lubricated, to provide protection on initial start-up. Vortex Pre-Lube, STP, or any product specifically formulated for this purpose may be used. NOTE: *Do not use engine oil.* Where semi-permanent (locked but removable) installation of bolts or nuts is desired, threads should be cleaned and coated with Loctite. Studs may be permanently installed using Loctite Stud and Bearing Mount.

Aluminum has become increasingly popular for use in engines, due to its low weight and excellent heat transfer characteristics. The following precautions must be observed when handling aluminum engine parts:

—Never hot-tank aluminum parts.

—Remove all aluminum parts (identification tags, etc.) from engine parts before hot-tanking (otherwise they will be removed during the process).

—Always coat threads lightly with engine oil or anti-seize compounds before installation, to prevent seizure.

—Never over-torque bolts or spark plugs in aluminum threads. Should stripping occur, threads can be restored according to the following procedure, using Heli-Coil thread inserts:

Tap drill the hole with the stripped threads to the specified size (see chart). Using the specified tap (NOTE: *Heli-Coil tap sizes refer to the size thread being replaced, rather than the actual tap size*), tap the hole for the Heli-Coil. place the insert on the proper installation tool (see chart). Apply pressure on the insert while winding it clockwise into the hole, until the top of the insert is one turn below the surface. Remove the installation tool, and break the installation tang from the bottom of the insert by moving it up and down. If the Heli-Coil must be removed, tap the removal tool firmly into the hole, so that it engages the top thread, and turn the tool counter-clockwise to extract that insert.

Snapped bolts or studs may be removed,

STANDARD SCREW FITS IN

Heli-Coil installation
(© Chrysler Corp.)

HELI-COIL INSERT IN   HELI-COIL
TAPPED HOLE

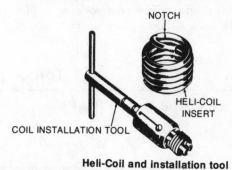

NOTCH

HELI-COIL INSERT

COIL INSTALLATION TOOL

Heli-Coil and installation tool

Heli-Coil Specifications

	Heli-Coil Insert			Drill	Tap	Insert. Tool	Extracting Tool
	Thread Size	Part No.	Insert Length (In.)	Size	Part No.	Part No.	Part No.
	1/2 -20	1185-4	3/8	17/64(.266)	4 CPB	528-4N	1227-6
	5/16-18	1185-5	15/32	Q(.332)	5 CPB	528-5N	1227-6
	3/8 -16	1185-6	9/16	X(.397)	6 CPB	528-6N	1227-6
	7/16-14	1185-7	21/32	29/64(.453)	7 CPB	528-7N	1227-16
	1/2 -13	1185-8	3/4	33/64(.516)	8 CPB	528-8N	1227-16

using a stud extractor (unthreaded) or Vise-Grip pliers (threaded). Penetrating oil (e.g., Liquid Wrench) will often aid in breaking frozen threads. In cases where the stud or bolt is flush with, or below the surface, proceed as follows:

Drill a hole in the broken stud or bolt, approximately ½ its diameter. Select a screw extractor (e.g., Easy-Out) of the proper size, and tap it into the stud or bolt. Turn the extractor counter-clockwise to remove the stud or bolt.

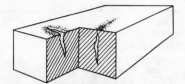

Magnaflux indication of cracks

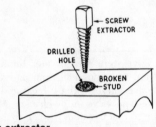

Screw extractor

Magnaflux and Zyglo are inspection techniques used to locate material flaws, such as stress cracks. Magnafluxing coats the part with fine magnetic particles, and subjects the part to a magnetic field. Cracks cause breaks in the magnetic field, which are outlined by the particles. Since Magnaflux is a magnetic process, it is applicable only to ferrous materials. The Zyglo process coats the material with a fluorescent dye penetrant, and then subjects it to blacklight inspection, under which cracks glow brightly. Parts made of any material may be tested using Zyglo. While Magnaflux and Zyglo are excellent for general inspection, and locating hidden defects, specific checks of suspected cracks may be made at lower cost and more readily using spot check dye. The dye is sprayed onto the suspected area, wiped off, and the area is then sprayed with a developer. Cracks then will show up brightly. Spot check dyes will only indicate surface cracks; therefore, structural cracks below the surface may escape detection. When questionable, the part should be tested using Magnaflux or Zyglo.

Cylinder Head Reconditioning

NOTE: *This engine rebuilding section is a guide to accepted engine rebuilding procedures. Every effort is made to illustrate the engine(s) used by this manufacturer; but, occasionally, typical examples of standard engine rebuilding practice are illustrated.*

Procedure	Method
Remove the rocker arms:	Remove the rocker arms with shaft(s). Wire the sets of rockers, balls and nuts together, and identify according to the corresponding valve.

CVCC cylinder head showing rocker arm retaining bolts

Procedure	Method

Remove the valves and springs:

Honda cylinder head showing major components

Using an appropriate valve spring compressor (depending on the configuration of the cylinder head), compress the valve springs. Lift out the keepers with needlenose pliers, release the compressor, and remove the valve, spring, and spring retainer. Be sure to keep the valves in order as you remove them. The best way to do this is to drill a series of holes in a piece of wood and then number the holes. Place each valve in the appropriate hole and there will be no chance of a mixup.

Check the valve stem-to-guide clearance:

Checking the valve stem-to-guide clearance

Clean the valve stem with lacquer thinner or a similar solvent to remove all gum and varnish. Clean the valve guides using solvent and an expanding wire-type valve guide cleaner. Mount a dial indicator so that the stem is at 90° to the valve stem, as close to the valve guide as possible. Move the valve off its seat, and measure the valve guide-to-stem clearance by moving the stem back and forth to actuate the dial indicator. Measure the valve stems using a micrometer, and compare to specifications, to determine whether stem or guide wear is responsible for excessive clearance.

De-carbon the cylinder head and valves:

Cylinder head showing cleaned combustion chambers vs dirty ones

Chip carbon away from the valve heads, combustion chambers, and ports, using a chisel made of hardwood. Remove the remaining deposits with a stiff wire brush. **NOTE:** *Ensure that the deposits are actually removed, rather than burnished.*

Hot-tank the cylinder head:

Closeup of Honda cylinder head. Note that no bearings are used. The cam rides directly in the journals

Clean the cylinder head with a safe solvent to remove grease, corrosion, and scale from the water passages. Make sure that the hot tank solution cleans aluminum instead of dissolving it.

Procedure	Method
Degrease the remaining cylinder head parts:	Using solvent (i.e., Gunk), clean the rocker shaft(s), nuts, springs, spring retainers, and keepers. Do not remove the protective coating from the springs.

Check the cylinder head for warpage:

1 & 3 CHECK DIAGONALLY
2 CHECK ACROSS CENTER

1

2

3

Checking the cylinder head for warpage

Place a straight-edge across the gasket surface of the cylinder head. Using feeler gauges, determine the clearance at the center of the straight-edge. Measure across both diagonals, along the longitudinal centerline, and across the cylinder head at several points. If warpage exceeds .003″ in a 6″ span, or .006″ over the total length, the cylinder head must be resurfaced. **NOTE:** *If warpage exceeds the manufacturers maximum tolerance for material removal, the cylinder head must be replaced.*

Replacing the valve guides: NOTE: *Valve guides should only be replaced if damaged or if an oversize valve stem is not available.*

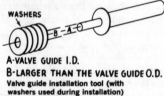

A-VALVE GUIDE I.D.
B-SLIGHTLY SMALLER THAN VALVE GUIDE O.D.

Valve guide removal tool

WASHERS

A-VALVE GUIDE I.D.
B-LARGER THAN THE VALVE GUIDE O.D.
Valve guide installation tool (with washers used during installation)

Press or tap the valve guides out of the head using a stepped drift (see illustration). Determine the height above the boss that the guide must extend, and obtain a stack of washers, their I.D. similar to the guide's O.D., of that height. Place the stack of washers on the guide, and insert the guide into the boss. **NOTE:** *Valve guides ar often tapered or beveled for installation.* Using the stepped installation tool (see illustration), press or tap the guides into position. Ream the guides according to the size of the valve stem.

Replacing valve seat inserts:

Replacement of valve seat inserts which are worn beyond resurfacing or broken, if feasible, must be done by a machine shop.

Resurfacing (grinding) the valve face:

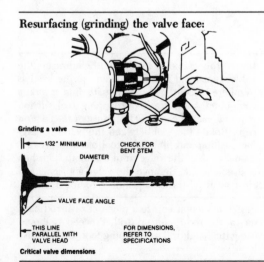

Grinding a valve

1/32″ MINIMUM
DIAMETER
CHECK FOR BENT STEM

VALVE FACE ANGLE

THIS LINE PARALLEL WITH VALVE HEAD
FOR DIMENSIONS, REFER TO SPECIFICATIONS

Critical valve dimensions

Using a valve grinder, resurface the valves according to specifications. **CAUTION:** *Valve face angle is not always identical to valve seat angle.* A minimum margin of $^1/_{32}$″ should remain after grinding the valve. The valve stem tip should also be squared and resurfaced, by placing the stem in the V-block of the grinder, and turning it while pressing lightly against the grinding wheel.

Procedure	Method

Resurfacing the valve seats using reamers:

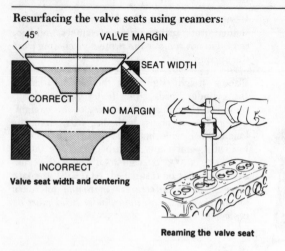

Valve seat width and centering

Reaming the valve seat

Select a reamer of the correct seat angle, slightly larger than the diameter of the valve seat, and assemble it with a pilot of the correct size. Install the pilot into the valve guide, and using steady pressure, turn the reamer clockwise. **CAUTION:** *Do not turn the reamer counter-clockwise.* Remove only as much material as necessary to clean the seat. Check the concentricity of the seat (see below). If the dye method is not used, coat the valve face with Prussian blue dye, install and rotate it on the valve seat. Using the dye marked area as a centering guide, center and narrow the valve seat to specifications with correction cutters. **NOTE:** *When no specifications are available, minimum seat width for exhaust valves should be* $5/64''$, *intake valves* $1/16''$. After making correction cuts, check the position of the valve seat on the valve face using Prussian blue dye.

* **Resurfacing the valve seats using a grinder:**

Select a pilot of the correct size, and a coarse stone of the correct seat angle. Lubricate the pilot if necessary, and install the tool in the valve guide. Move the stone on and off the seat at approximately two cycles per second, until all flaws are removed from the seat. Install a fine stone, and finish the seat. Center and narrow the seat using correction stones, as described above.

Checking the valve seat concentricity:

Checking the valve seat concentricity using a dial gauge

Coat the valve face with Prussian blue dye, install the valve, and rotate it on the valve seat. If the entire seat becomes coated, and the valve is known to be concentric, the seat is concentric.

* Install the dial gauge pilot into the guide, and rest the arm on the valve seat. Zero the gauge, and rotate the arm around the seat. Run-out should not exceed .002″.

* Invert the cylinder head, lightly lubricate the valve stems, and install the valves in the head as numbered. Coat valve seats with fine grinding compound, and attach the lapping tool suction cup to a valve head (**NOTE:** *Moisten the suction cup*). Rotate the tool between the palms, changing position and lifting the tool often to prevent grooving. Lap the valve until a smooth, polished seat is evident. Remove the valve and tool, and rinse away all traces of grinding compound.

** Fasten a suction cup to a piece of drill rod, and mount the rod in a hand drill. Proceed as above, using the hand drill as a lapping tool. **CAUTION:**

Procedure	**Method**

* Lapping the valves: NOTE: *Valve lapping is done to ensure efficient sealing of resurfaced valves and seats. Valve lapping alone is not recommended for use as a resurfacing procedure.*

Due to the higher speeds involved when using the hand drill, care must be exercised to avoid grooving the seat. Lift the tool and change direction of rotation often.

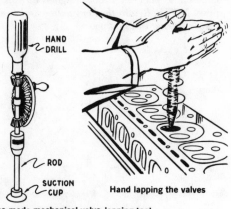

HAND DRILL

ROD

SUCTION CUP

Hand lapping the valves

Home made mechanical valve lapping tool

Check the valve springs:

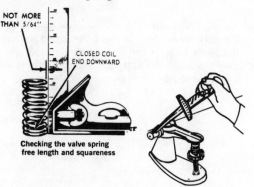

NOT MORE THAN 5/64"

CLOSED COIL END DOWNWARD

Checking the valve spring free length and squareness

Checking the valve spring tension

Place the spring on a flat surface next to a square. Measure the height of the spring, and rotate it against the edge of the square to measure distortion. If spring height varies (by comparison) by more than $1/16''$ or if distortion exceeds $1/16''$, replace the spring.

** In addition to evaluating the spring as above, test the spring pressure at the installed and compressed (installed height minus valve lift) height using a valve spring tester. Springs used on small displacement engines (up to 3 liters) should be ± 1 lb of all other springs in either position. A tolerance of ± 5 lbs is permissible on larger engines.

---

* Install valve stem seals:

RETAINER

SPRING

INTAKE VALVE

SEAL

Valve stem seal installation

* Due to the pressure differential that exists at the ends of the intake valve guides (atmospheric pressure above, manifold vacuum below), oil is drawn through the valve guides into the intake port. This has been alleviated somewhat since the addition of positive crankcase ventilation, which lowers the pressure above the guides. Several types of valve stem seals are available to reduce blow-by. Certain seals simply slip over the stem and guide boss, while others require that the boss be machined. Recently, Teflon guide seals have become popular. Consult a parts supplier or machinist concerning availability and suggested usages. **NOTE:** *When installing seals, ensure that a small amount of oil is able to pass the seal to lubricate the valve guides; otherwise, excessive wear may result.*

Procedure	Method

Install the valves:

Auxiliary intake valves used in the CVCC cylinder head. Note that there have been three different sizes used over the years. Also note the different face sizes

Lubricate the valve stems, and install the valves in the cylinder head as numbered. Lubricate and position the seals (if used, see above) and the valve springs. Install the spring retainers, compress the springs, and insert the keys using needlenose pliers or a tool designed for this purpose. **NOTE:** *Retain the keys with wheel bearing grease during installation.*

Checking valve spring installed height:

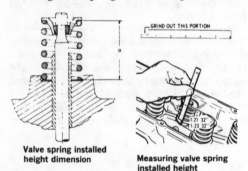

Valve spring installed height dimension

Measuring valve spring installed height

Measure the distance between the spring pad and the lower edge of the spring retainer, and compare to specifications. If the installed height is incorrect, use new springs.

Inspect the rocker shaft(s) and rocker arms

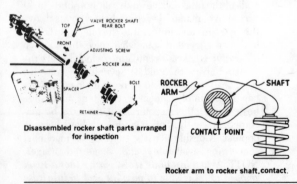

Disassembled rocker shaft parts arranged for inspection

Rocker arm to rocker shaft contact

Remove rocker arms, springs and washers from rocker shaft. **NOTE:** *Lay out parts in the order they are removed.* Inspect rocker arms for pitting or wear on the valve contact point, or excessive bushing wear. Bushings need only be replaced if wear is excessive, because the rocker arm normally contacts the shaft at one point only. Grind the valve contact point of rocker arm smooth if necessary, removing as little material as possible. If excessive material must be removed to smooth and square the arm, it should be replaced. Clean out all oil holes and passages in rocker shaft. If shaft is grooved or worn, replace it. Lubricate and assemble the rocker shaft.

Inspect the camshaft bushings and the camshaft (overhead cam engines):

See next section.

Cylinder Block Reconditioning

Procedure	Method

Checking the main bearing clearance:

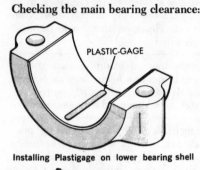

PLASTIC-GAGE

Installing Plastigage on lower bearing shell

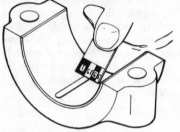

Measuring Plastigage to determine bearing clearance

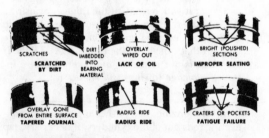

SCRATCHES	DIRT IMBEDDED INTO BEARING MATERIAL	OVERLAY WIPED OUT	BRIGHT (POLISHED) SECTIONS
SCRATCHED BY DIRT		LACK OF OIL	IMPROPER SEATING
OVERLAY GONE FROM ENTIRE SURFACE	RADIUS RIDE	CRATERS OR POCKETS
TAPERED JOURNAL	RADIUS RIDE	FATIGUE FAILURE

Causes of bearing failure

On the CVCC engine, one main bearing bolt is hidden by the oil pump (arrow)

Invert engine, and remove cap from the bearing to be checked. Using a clean, dry rag, thoroughly clean all oil from crankshaft journal and bearing insert. **NOTE:** *Plastigage is soluble in oil; therefore, oil on the journal or bearing could result in erroneous readings.* Place a piece of Plastigage along the full length of journal, reinstall cap, and torque to specifications. Remove bearing cap, and determine bearing clearance by comparing width of Plastigage to the scale on Plastigage envelope. Journal taper is determined by comparing width of the Plastigage strip near its ends. Rotate crankshaft 90° and retest, to determine journal eccentricity. **NOTE:** *Do not rotate crankshaft with Plastigage installed.* If bearing insert and journal appear intact, and are within tolerances, no further main bearing service is required. If bearing or journal appear defective, cause of failure should be determined before replacement.

* Remove crankshaft from block (see below). Measure the main bearing journals at each end twice (90° apart) using a micrometer, to determine diameter, journal taper and eccentricity. If journals are within tolerances, reinstall bearing caps at their specified torque. Using a telescope gauge and micrometer, measure bearing I.D. parallel to piston axis and at 30° on each side of piston axis. Subtract journal O.D. from bearing I.D. to determine oil clearance. If crankshaft journals appear defective, or do not meet tolerances, there is no need to measure bearings; for the crankshaft will require grinding and/or undersize bearings will be required. If bearing appears defective, cause for failure should be determined prior to replacement.

Procedure	Method
Checking the connecting rod bearing clearance:	Connecting rod bearing clearance is checked in the same manner as main bearing clearance, using Plastigage. Before removing the crankshaft, connecting rod side clearance also should be measured and recorded.
	* Checking connecting rod bearing clearance, using a micrometer, is identical to checking main bearing clearance. If no other service is required, the piston and rod assemblies need not be removed.
Removing the crankshaft:	Using a punch, mark the corresponding main bearing caps and saddles according to position (i.e., one punch on the front main cap and saddle, two on the second, three on the third, etc.). Using number stamps, identify the corresponding connecting rods and caps, according to cylinder (if no numbers are present). Remove the main and connecting rod caps, and place sleeves of plastic tubing over the connecting rod bolts, to protect the journals as the crankshaft is removed. Lift the crankshaft out of the block.
Remove the ridge from the top of the cylinder: 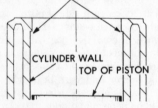 Cylinder bore ridge	In order to facilitate removal of the piston and connecting rod, the ridge at the top of the cylinder (unknown area; see illustration) must be removed. Place the piston at the bottom of the bore, and cover it with a rag. Cut the ridge away using a ridge reamer, exercising extreme care to avoid cutting too deeply. Remove the rag, and remove cuttings that remain on the piston. **CAUTION:** *If the ridge is not removed, and new rings are installed, damage to rings will result.*
Removing the piston and connecting rod:  Removing the piston	Invert the engine, and push the pistons and connecting rods out of the cylinders. If necessary, tap the connecting rod boss with a wooden hammer handle, to force the piston out. **CAUTION:** *Do not attempt to force the piston past the cylinder ridge* (see above).
Service the crankshaft:	Ensure that all oil holes and passages in the crankshaft are open and free of sludge. If necessary, have the crankshaft ground to the largest possible undersize.
Removing freeze plugs:	Drill a small hole in the center of the freeze plugs. Thread a large sheet metal screw into the hole and remove the plug with a slide hammer.

Procedure	Method
Remove the oil gallery plugs:	Threaded plugs should be removed using an appropriate (usually square) wrench. To remove soft, pressed in plugs, drill a hole in the plug, and thread in a sheet metal screw. Pull the plug out by the screw using a slide hammer.
Hot-tank the block:	Clean the block with a safe solvent to remove grease, corrosion, and scale from the water jackets. **NOTE:** *Consult the operator to determine whether the camshaft bearings will be damaged during the hot-tank process.*

Check the block for cracks:	Visually inspect the block for cracks or chips. The most common locations are as follows:
	    Adjacent to freeze plugs.
	    Between the cylinders and water jackets.
	    Adjacent to the main bearing saddles.
	    At the extreme bottom of the cylinders.
	Check only suspected cracks using spot check dye (see introduction). If a crack is located, consult a machinist concerning possible repairs.

Install the oil gallery plugs and freeze plugs:	Coat freeze plugs with sealer and tap into position using a piece of pipe, slightly smaller than the plug, as a driver. To ensure retention, stake the edges of the plugs. Coat threaded oil gallery plugs with sealer and install. Drive replacement soft plugs into block using a large drift as a driver.
	* Rather than reinstalling lead plugs, drill and tap the holes, and install threaded plugs.

Check the bore diameter and surface:

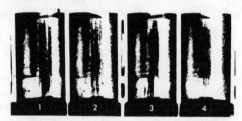

1, 2, 3 Piston skirt seizure resulted in this pattern. Engine must be rebored

4. Piston skirt and oil ring seizure caused this damag Engine must be rebored

5, 6 Score marks caused by a split piston skirt. Damage is not serious enough to warrant reboring

7. Ring seized longitudinally, causing a score mark 1 3/16" wide, on the land side of the piston groove. The honing pattern is destroyed and the cylinder must be rebored

Visually inspect the cylinder bores for roughness, scoring, or scuffing. If evident, the cylinder bore must be bored or honed oversize to eliminate imperfections, and the smallest possible oversize piston used. The new pistons should be given to the machinist with the block, so that the cylinders can be bored or honed exactly to the piston size (plus clearance). If no flaws are evident, measure the bore diameter using a telescope gauge and micrometer, or dial gauge, parallel and perpendicular to the engine centerline, at the top (below the ridge) and bottom of the bore. Subtract the bottom measurements from the top to determine taper, and the parallel to the centerline measurements from the perpendicular measurements to determine eccentricity. If the measurements are not within specifications, the cylinder must be bored or honed, and an oversize piston installed. If the measurements are within specifications the cylinder may be used as is, with only finish honing (see below). **NOTE:** *Prior to submitting the block for boring, perform the following operation(s).*

Procedure	Method

8. Result of oil ring seizure. Engine must be rebored

9. Oil ring seizure here was not serious enough to warrant reboring. The honing marks are still visible

Cylinder wall damage
(© Daimler-Benz A.G.)

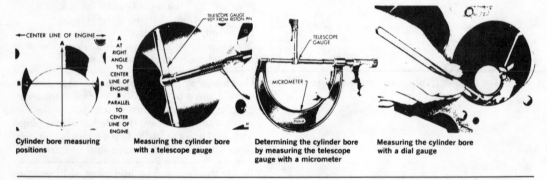

Cylinder bore measuring positions

Measuring the cylinder bore with a telescope gauge

Determining the cylinder bore by measuring the telescope gauge with a micrometer

Measuring the cylinder bore with a dial gauge

Check the block deck for warpage:

Using a straightedge and feeler gauges, check the block deck for warpage in the same manner that the cylinder head is checked (see Cylinder Head Reconditioning). If warpage exceeds specifications, have the deck resurfaced. **NOTE:** *In certain cases a specification for total material removal (Cylinder head and block deck) is provided. This specification must not be exceeded.*

* Check the deck height:

The deck height is the distance from the crankshaft centerline to the block deck. To measure, invert the engine, and install the crankshaft, retaining it with the center main cap. Measure the distance from the crankshaft journal to the block deck, parallel to the cylinder centerline. Measure the diameter of the end (front and rear) main journals, parallel to the centerline of the cylinders, divide the diameter in half, and subtract it from the previous measurement. The results of the front and rear measurements should be identical. If the difference exceeds .005″, the deck height should be corrected. **NOTE:** *Block deck height and warpage should be corrected concurrently.*

Procedure	Method
Check the cylinder block bearing alignment:  Checking main bearing saddle alignment	Remove the upper bearing inserts. Place a straightedge in the bearing saddles along the centerline of the crankshaft. If clearance exists between the straightedge and the center saddle, the block must be align-bored.
Clean and inspect the pistons and connecting rods: 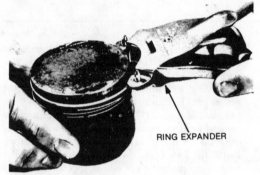 Removing the piston rings 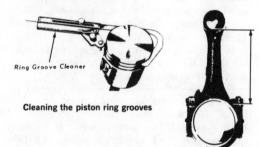 Cleaning the piston ring grooves Connecting rod length checking dimension	Using a ring expander, remove the rings from the piston. Remove the retaining rings (if so equipped) and remove piston pin. **NOTE:** *If the piston pin must be pressed out, determine the proper method and use the proper tools; otherwise the piston will distort.* Clean the ring grooves using an appropriate tool, exercising care to avoid cutting too deeply. Thoroughly clean all carbon and varnish from the piston with solvent. **CAUTION:** *Do not use a wire brush or caustic solvent on pistons.* Inspect the pistons for scuffing, scoring, cracks, pitting, or excessive ring groove wear. If wear is evident, the piston must be replaced. Check the connecting rod length by measuring the rod from the inside of the large end to the inside of the small end using calipers (see illustration). All connecting rods should be equal length. Replace any rod that differs from the others in the engine.
	* Have the connecting rod alignment checked in an alignment fixture by a machinist. Replace any twisted or bent rods.
	* Magnaflux the connecting rods to locate stress cracks. If cracks are found, replace the connecting rod.
Fit the pistons to the cylinders:  Checking the cylinder bore with a dial indicator	Using a telescope gauge and micrometer, or a dial gauge, measure the cylinder bore diameter perpendicular to the piston pin, 2½″ below the deck. Measure the piston perpendicular to its pin on the skirt. The difference between the two measurements is the piston clearance. If the clearance is within specifications or slightly below (after boring or honing), finish honing is all that is required. If the clearance is excessive, try to obtain a slightly larger piston to bring clearance within specifications. Where this is not possible, obtain the first oversize piston, and hone (or if necessary, bore) the cylinder to size.

RING EXPANDER

Ring Groove Cleaner

Procedure	*Method*

Measuring the piston with a micrometer

Assemble the pistons and connecting rods:

Pressing in a new piston pin

Inspect piston pin, connecting rod small end bushing, and piston bore for galling, scoring, or excessive wear. If evident, replace defective part(s). Measure the I.D. of the piston boss and connecting rod small end, and the O.D. of the piston pin. If within specifications, assemble piston pin and rod. **CAUTION:** *If piston pin must be pressed in, determine the proper method and use the proper tools; otherwise the piston will distort.* Install the lock rings; ensure that they seat properly. If the parts are not within specifications, determine the service method for the type of engine. In some cases, piston and pin are serviced as an assembly when either is defective. Others specify reaming the piston and connecting rods for an oversize pin. If the connecting rod bushing is worn, it may in many cases be replaced. Reaming the piston and replacing the rod bushing are machine shop operations.

Clean and inspect the camshaft:

Checking camshaft runout with a dial indicator

Degrease the camshaft, using solvent, and clean out all oil holes. Visually inspect cam lobes and bearing journals for excessive wear. If a lobe is questionable, check all lobes as indicated below. If a journal or lobe is worn, the camshaft must be reground or replaced. **NOTE:** *If a journal is worn, there is a good chance that the bushings are worn.* If lobes and journals appear intact, place the front and rear journals in V-blocks, and rest a dial indicator on the center journal. Rotate the camshaft to check straightness. If deviation exceeds .001″, replace the camshaft.

* Check the camshaft lobes with a micrometer, by measuring the lobes from the nose to base and again at 90° (see illustration). The lift is determined by subtracting the second measurement from the first. If all exhaust lobes and all intake lobes are not identical, the camshaft must be reground or replaced.

Camshaft lobe measurement

Procedure	Method

Finish hone the cylinders:

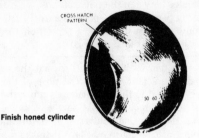

Finish honed cylinder

Chuck a flexible drive hone into a power drill, and insert it into the cylinder. Start the hone, and move it up and down in the cylinder at a rate which will produce approximately a 60° cross-hatch pattern (see illustration). **NOTE:** *Do not extend the hone below the cylinder bore.* After developing the pattern, remove the hone and recheck piston fit. Wash the cylinders with a detergent and water solution to remove abrasive dust, dry, and wipe several times with a rag soaked in engine oil.

Check piston ring end-gap:

Checking ring end-gap

Compress the piston rings to be used in a cylinder, one at a time, into that cylinder, and press them approximately 1″ below the deck with an inverted piston. Using feeler gauges, measure the ring end-gap, and compare to specifications. Pull the ring out of the cylinder and file the ends with a fine file to obtain proper clearance. **CAUTION:** *If inadequate ring end-gap is utilized, ring breakage will result.*

Install the piston rings:

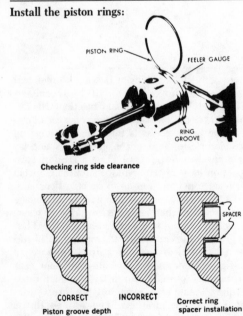

Checking ring side clearance

CORRECT INCORRECT

Piston groove depth

Correct ring spacer installation

Inspect the ring grooves in the piston for excessive wear or taper. If necessary, recut the groove(s) for use with an overwidth ring or a standard ring and spacer. If the groove is worn uniformly, overwidth rings, or standard rings and spacers may be installed without recutting. Roll the outside of the ring around the groove to check for burrs or deposits. If any are found, remove with a fine file. Hold the ring in the groove, and measure side clearance. If necessary, correct as indicated above. **NOTE:** *Always install any additional spacers above the piston ring.* The ring groove must be deep enough to allow the ring to seat below the lands (see illustration). In many cases, a "go-no-go" depth gauge will be provided with the piston rings. Shallow grooves may be corrected by recutting, while deep grooves require some type of filler or expander behind the piston. Consult the piston ring supplier concerning the suggested method. Install the rings on the piston, lowest ring first, using a ring expander. **NOTE:** *Position the ring markings as specified by the manufacturer.*

Install the camshaft:

Liberally lubricate the camshaft lobes and journals, and slide the camshaft into the head. Install and tighten the camshaft thrust plate retaining bolts.

Procedure	Method

Check camshaft end-play:

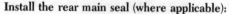

Checking camshaft
end-play with a
feeler gauge

DIAL INDICATOR

CAMSHAFT

Checking camshaft end-play with a
dial indicator

Using feeler gauges, determine whether the clearance between the camshaft boss (or gear) and backing plate is within specifications. Install shims behind the thrust plate, or reposition the camshaft gear and retest end-play.

* Mount a dial indicator stand so that the stem of the dial indicator rests on the nose of the camshaft, parallel to the camshaft axis. Push the camshaft as far in as possible and zero the gauge. Move the camshaft outward to determine the amount of camshaft end-play. If the end-play is not within tolerance, install shims behind the thrust plate, or reposition the camshaft gear and retest.

Install the rear main seal (where applicable):

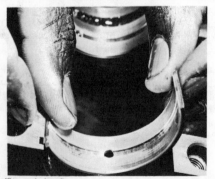

Installing the rear main seal. Note the special tool

Position the block with the bearing saddles facing upward. Lay the rear main seal in its groove and press it lightly into its seat. Use the Honda special tool. Make sure the crank is torqued first.

Install the crankshaft:

Installing the thrust bearing. Note that the grooved side faces outward. The thickness *cannot* be changed by shimming or grinding

Installing main bearing

Thoroughly clean the main bearing saddles and caps. Place the upper halves of the bearing inserts on the saddles and press into position. **NOTE:** *Ensure that the oil holes align.* Press the corresponding bearing inserts into the main bearing caps. Lubricate the upper main bearings, and lay the crankshaft in position. Place a strip of Plastigage on each of the crankshaft journals, install the main caps, and torque to specifications. Remove the main caps, and compare the Plastigage to the scale on the Plastigage envelope. If clearances are within tolerances, remove the Plastigage, turn the crankshaft 90°, wipe off all oil and retest. If all clearances are correct, remove all Plastigage, thoroughly lubricate the main caps and bearing journals, and install the main caps. Torque all main caps, excluding the thrust bearing cap, to specifications. Tighten the thrust bearing cap finger tight. To properly align the thrust bearing, pry the crankshaft the extent of its axial travel several times, the last movement held toward the front of the engine, and torque the thrust bearing cap to specifications. Determine the crankshaft end-play (see below).

Procedure	Method

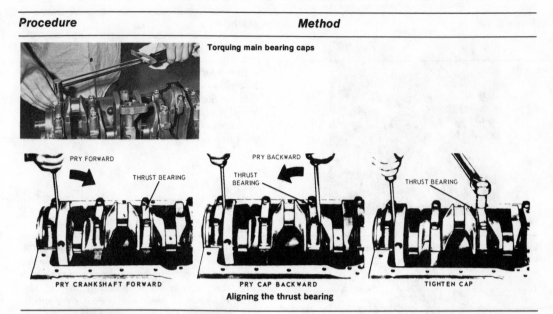

Torquing main bearing caps

PRY FORWARD THRUST BEARING

PRY CRANKSHAFT FORWARD

PRY BACKWARD THRUST BEARING

PRY CAP BACKWARD

THRUST BEARING

TIGHTEN CAP

Aligning the thrust bearing

Measure crankshaft end-play:

Checking crankshaft end-play with a dial indicator

Mount a dial indicator stand on the front of the block, with the dial indicator stem resting on the nose of the crankshaft, parallel to the crankshaft axis. Pry the crankshaft the extent of its travel rearward, and zero the indicator. Pry the crankshaft forward and record crankshaft end-play. **NOTE:** *Crankshaft end-play also may be measured at the thrust bearing, using feeler gauges (see illustration).*

Checking crankshaft end-play with a feeler gauge

Install the pistons:

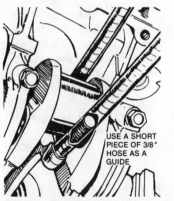

USE A SHORT PIECE OF 3/8" HOSE AS A GUIDE

Tubing used as guide when installing a piston

Press the upper connecting rod bearing halves into the connecting rods, and the lower halves into the connecting rod caps. Position the piston ring gaps according to specifications (see car section), and lubricate the pistons. Install a ring compresser on a piston, and press two long (8″) pieces of plastic tubing over the rod bolts. Using the plastic tubes as a guide, press the pistons into the bores and onto the crankshaft with a wooden hammer handle. After seating the rod on the crankshaft journal, remove the tubes and install the cap finger tight. Install the remaining pistons in the same manner. Invert the engine and check the bearing clearance at two points (90° apart) on each journal with Plastigage. **NOTE:** *Do not turn the crankshaft with Plastigage installed.* If clearance is within tolerances, remove *all* Plastigage,

Procedure	Method

Piston installation

thoroughly lubricate the journals, and torque the rod caps to specifications. If clearance is not within specifications, install different thickness bearing inserts and recheck. **CAUTION:** *Never shim or file the connecting rods or caps.* Always install plastic tube sleeves over the rod bolts when the caps are not installed, to protect the crankshaft journals.

Check connecting rod side clearance:

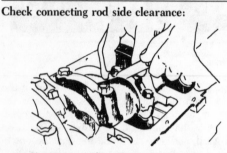

Checking connecting rod side clearance

Determine the clearance between the sides of the connecting rods and the crankshaft, using feeler gauges. If clearance is below the minimum tolerance, the rod may be machined to provide adequate clearance. If clearance is excessive, substitute an unworn rod, and recheck. If clearance is still outside specifications, the crankshaft must be welded and reground, or replaced.

Inspect the timing belt:

Visually inspect the timing belt for any signs of wear. If the belt has over 10,000 miles on it, replace it.

Completing the Rebuilding Process

Following the above procedures, complete the rebuilding process as follows:

Fill the oil pump with oil, to prevent cavitating (sucking air) on initial engine start up. Install the oil pump and the pickup tube on the engine. Coat the oil pan gasket as necessary, and install the gasket and the oil pan. Mount the flywheel and the crankshaft vibrational damper or pulley on the crankshaft. NOTE: *Always use new bolts when installing the flywheel.* Inspect the clutch shaft pilot bushing in the crankshaft. If the bushing is excessively worn, remove it with an expanding puller and a slide hammer, and tap a new bushing into place.

Position the engine, cylinder head side up. Lubricate the lifters, and install them into their bores. Install the cylinder head, and torque it as specified in the car section. Insert the pushrods (where applicable), and install the rocker shaft(s) (if so equipped) or position the rocker arms on the pushrods. If solid lift-ers are utilized, adjust the valves to the "cold" specifications.

Mount the intake and exhaust manifolds, the carburetor(s), the distributor and spark plugs. Adjust the point gap and the static ignition timing. Mount all accessories and install the engine in the car. Fill the radiator with coolant, and the crankcase with high quality engine oil.

Break-in Procedure

Start the engine, and allow it to run at low speed for a few minutes, while checking for leaks. Stop the engine, check the oil level, and fill as necessary. Restart the engine, and fill the cooling system to capacity. Check the point dwell angle and adjust the ignition timing and the valves. Run the engine at low to medium speed (800–2500 rpm) for approximately ½ hour, and retorque the cylinder head bolts. Road test the car, and check again for leaks.

Follow the manufacturer's recommended engine break-in procedure and maintenance schedule for new engines.

4

Emission Controls and Fuel System

EMISSION CONTROLS

Emission controls on the Honda fall into one of three basic systems: A. Crankcase Emission Control System, B. Exhaust Emission Control System, C. Evaporative Emission Control System.

A. Crankcase Emission Control System

The Honda's engine is equipped with a "Dual Return System" to prevent crankcase vapor emissions. Blow-by gas is returned to the combustion chamber through the intake manifold and carburetor air cleaner. When the throttle is partially opened, blow-by gas is returned to the intake manifold through breather tubes leading into the tee orifice located on the outside of the intake manifold. When the throttle is opened wide and vacuum in the air cleaner rises, blow-by gas is returned to the intake manifold through an additional passage in the air cleaner case.

B. Exhaust Emission Control System

1973–74 Models

Control of exhaust emissions, hydrocarbon (HC), carbon monoxide (CO), and Oxides of nitrogen (NO^x), is achieved by a combination of engine modifications and special control devices. Improvements to the combustion chamber, intake manifold, valve timing, carburetor, and distributor comprise the engine modifications. These modifications, in conjunction with the special control devices, enable the engine to produce low emission with leaner air-fuel mixtures while maintaining good driveability. The special control devices consist of the following:

a. Intake air temperature control;

b. Throttle opener;

c. Ignition timing retard unit (1973 models only);

d. Transmission and temperature controlled spark advance (TCS) for the 4-speed transmission;

e. Temperature controlled spark advance for Hondamatic automatic transmission (1973 models only).

Intake Air Temperature Control

Intake air temperature control is designed to provide the most uniform carburetion possible under various ambient air temperature conditions by maintaining the intake air temperature within a narrow range. When the temperature in the air cleaner is below 100° F (approx.), the air bleed valve, which con-

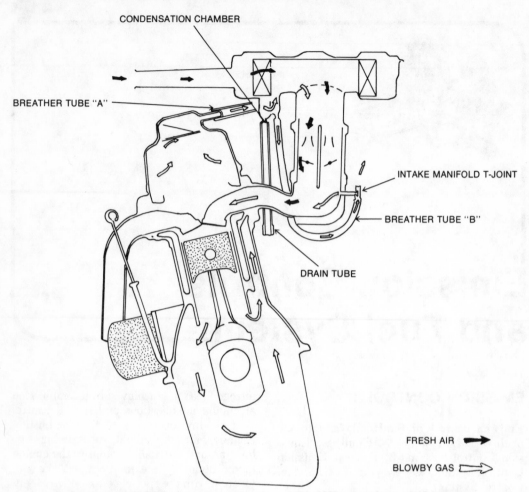

CONDENSATION CHAMBER

BREATHER TUBE "A"

INTAKE MANIFOLD T-JOINT

BREATHER TUBE "B"

DRAIN TUBE

FRESH AIR

BLOWBY GAS

Crankcase ventilation system operation—1170, 1237 cc engines—CVCC similar

sists of a bimetallic strip and a rubber seal, remains closed. Intake manifold vacuum is then led to a vacuum motor, located on the snorkel of the air cleaner case, which moves the air control valve door, allowing only pre-heated air to enter the air cleaner.

When the temperature in the air cleaner becomes higher than approx. 100° F, the air bleed valve opens and the air control valve door returns to the open position allowing only unheated air through the snorkel.

Throttle Opener

When the throttle is closed suddenly at high engine speed, hydrocarbon (HC) emissions increase due to engine misfire caused by an incombustible mixture. The throttle opener is designed to prevent misfiring during de-celeration by causing the throttle valve to re-main slightly open, allowing better mixture

control. The control valve is set to allow the passage of vacuum to the throttle opener dia-phragm when the engine vacuum is equal to or greater than the control valve preset vac-uum (21.6 ± 1.6 in. Hg) during acceleration.

Under running conditions, other than fully closed throttle deceleration, the intake mani-fold vacuum is less than the control valve set vacuum; therefore the control valve is not ac-tuated. The vacuum remaining in the throttle opener and control valve is returned to atmo-spheric pressure by the air passage at the valve center.

Ignition Timing Retard Unit

On 1973 models, when the engine is idling, the vacuum produced in the carburetor re-tarder port is communicated to the spark re-tard unit and the ignition timing, at idle, is retarded.

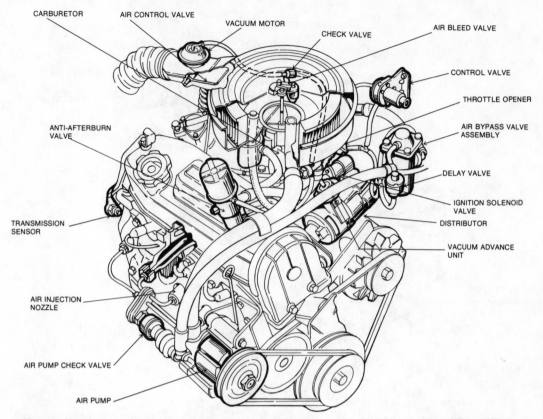

Location of emission control system components—1975 1237 cc AIR models with manual transmission; other years similar

TCS System

The transmission and temperature controlled spark advance for 4-speed transmissions is designed to reduce NO^x emissions during normal vehicle operation.

On 1973 models, when the coolant temperature is approximately 120° or higher, and the transmission is in First, Second, or Third gear, the solenoid valve cuts off the vacuum to the spark advance unit, resulting in lower NO^x levels.

On 1974 models, the vacuum is cut off to the spark advance unit regardless of temperature when First, Second, or Third gear is selected. Vacuum advance is restored when Fourth gear is selected.

Temperature Controlled Spark Advance

Temperature controlled spark advance on 1973 cars equipped with Hondamatic transmission is designed to reduce NO^x emissions by disconnecting the vacuum to the spark advance unit during normal vehicle operation.

When the coolant temperature is approximately 120° or higher, the solenoid valve is energized, cutting off vacuum to the advance unit.

1975–78 1237 CC AIR MODELS

Intake Air Temperature Control

Same as 1973–74 *models.*

Throttle Opener

Same as 1973–74 models.

Transmission Controlled Spark Advance

Same as 1974 models, with no coolant control override.

Ignition Timing Retard Unit

Same as 1973 models, but is used only on Hondamatic models and has no vacuum advance mechanism.

Air Injection System

Beginning with the 1975 model year, an air injection system is used to control hydrocar-

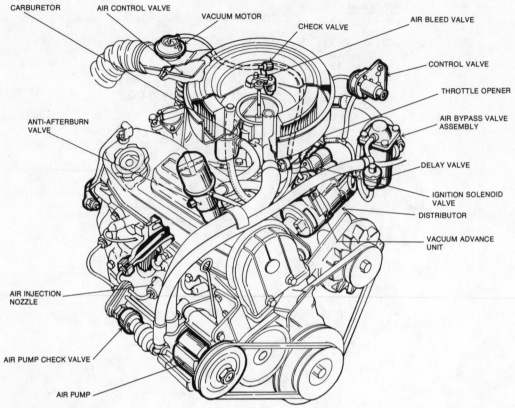

CARBURETOR

AIR CONTROL VALVE

VACUUM MOTOR

CHECK VALVE

AIR BLEED VALVE

CONTROL VALVE

THROTTLE OPENER

AIR BYPASS VALVE ASSEMBLY

ANTI-AFTERBURN VALVE

DELAY VALVE

IGNITION SOLENOID VALVE

DISTRIBUTOR

VACUUM ADVANCE UNIT

AIR INJECTION NOZZLE

AIR PUMP CHECK VALVE

AIR PUMP

Location of emission control system components—1975 1237 cc AIR models with Hondamatic—other years similar

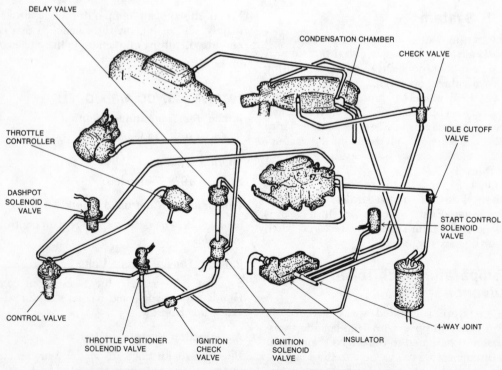

DELAY VALVE

CONDENSATION CHAMBER

CHECK VALVE

IDLE CUTOFF VALVE

THROTTLE CONTROLLER

DASHPOT SOLENOID VALVE

START CONTROL SOLENOID VALVE

CONTROL VALVE

4-WAY JOINT

THROTTLE POSITIONER SOLENOID VALVE

IGNITION CHECK VALVE

IGNITION SOLENOID VALVE

INSULATOR

Emission controls system schematic—Accord with manual transmission

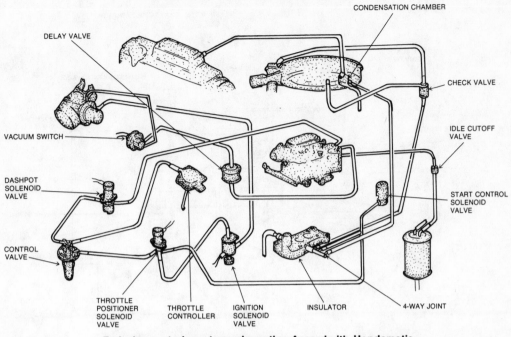

Emission controls system schematic—Accord with Hondamatic

bon and carbon monoxide emissions. With this system, a belt-driven air pump delivers filtered air under pressure to injection nozzles located at each exhaust port. Here, the additional oxygen supplied by the vane-type pump reacts with any uncombusted fuel mixture, promoting an afterburning effect in the hot exhaust manifold. To prevent a reverse

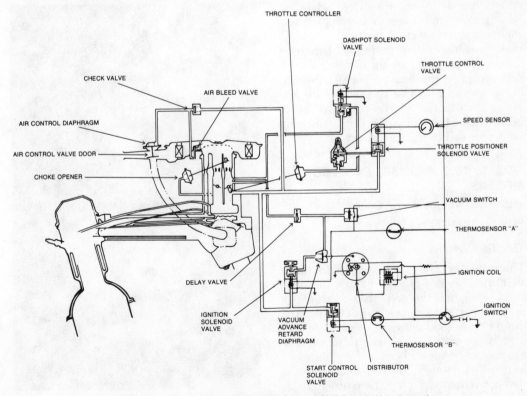

Emission control system schematic—Civic CVCC with Hondamatic

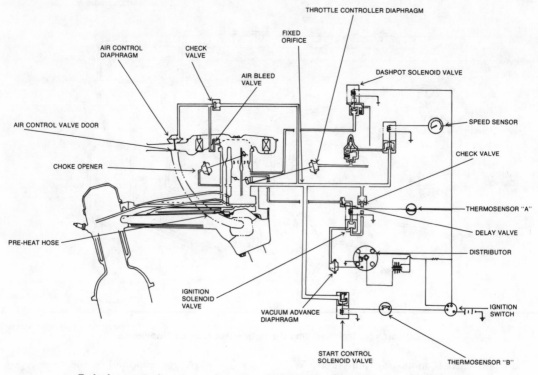

Emission control system schematic—Civic CVCC with manual transmission

flow in the air injection manifold when exhaust gas pressure exceeds air supply pressure, a nonreturn check valve is used. To prevent exhaust afterburning or backfiring during deceleration, an anti-afterburn valve delivers air to the intake manifold instead. When manifold vacuum rises above the preset vacuum of the air control valve and/or below that of the air by-pass valve, air pump air is returned to the air cleaner.

1975–78 1487 AND 1600 CC CVCC MODELS

Intake Air Temperature Control

Same as 1973–74 models.

Throttle Controls

This system controls the closing of the throttle during periods of gear shifting, deceleration, or anytime the gas pedal is released. In preventing the sudden closing of the throttle during these conditions, an overly rich mixture is prevented which controls excessive emissions of hydrocarbons and carbon monoxide. This system has two main parts; a dashpot system and a throttle positioner system. The dashpot diaphragm and solenoid

Vacuum delay valve mounted on air cleaner

valve act to dampen or slow down the throttle return time to 1–4 seconds. The throttle positioner part consists of a speed sensor, a solenoid valve, a control valve and an opener diaphragm which will keep the throttle open and predetermined minimum amount any time the gas pedal is released when the car is traveling 15 mph or faster, and closes it when the car slows to 10 mph.

Ignition Timing Controls

This system uses a coolant temperature sensor to switch distributor vacuum ignition timing controls on or off to reduce hydrocarbon and oxides of nitrogen emissions. The coolant switch is calibrated at 149° F.

Hot Start Control

This system is designed to prevent an over-rich mixture condition in the intake manifold due to vaporization of residual fuel when starting a hot engine. This reduces hydrocarbon and carbon monoxide emissions.

Thermosensors located on engine block. The upper thermosensor energizes a solenoid when the engine is cold, giving vacuum advance. The lower thermosensor is used when the engine is warm (1977 and earlier)

CVCC Engine Modifications

By far, the most important part of the CVCC engine emission control system is the Compound Vortex Controlled Combustion (CVCC) cylinder head itself. Each cylinder has three valves: a conventional intake and conventional exhaust valve, and a smaller auxiliary intake valve. There are actually *two* combustion chambers per cylinder: a pre-combustion or auxiliary chamber, and the main chamber. During the intake stroke, an extremely lean mixture is drawn into the main combustion chamber. Simultaneously, a very rich mixture is drawn into the smaller precombustion chamber via the auxiliary intake valve. The spark plug, located in the precombustion chamber, easily ignites the rich pre-mixture, and this combustion spreads out into the main combustion chamber where the lean mixture is ignited. Due to the fact that the volume of the auxiliary chamber is much smaller than the main chamber, the overall mixture is very lean (about 18 parts air to one part fuel). The result is low hydrocarbon emissions due to the slow, stable combustion of the lean mixture in the main chamber; low carbon monoxide emissions due to the excess oxygen available; and low oxides of nitrogen emissions due to the lowered peak combustion temperatures. An added benefit of burning the lean mixture is the excellent gas mileage.

C. Evaporative Emission Control System

This system prevents gasoline vapors from escaping into the atmosphere from the fuel tank and carburetor and consists of the components listed in the illustration.

Fuel vapor is stored in the expansion chamber, in the fuel tank, and in the vapor line up to the one-way valve. When the vapor pressure becomes higher than the set pressure of the one-way valve, the valve opens and allows vapor into the charcoal canister. While the engine is stopped or idling, the idle cut-off valve in the canister is closed and the vapor is absorbed by the charcoal.

At partially opened throttle, the idle cut-off valve is opened by manifold vacuum. The vapor that was stored in the charcoal canister and in the vapor line is purged into the intake manifold. Any excessive pressure or vacuum which might build up in the fuel tank is relieved by the two-way valve in the filler cap.

Maintenance and Service
COMPONENTS PERTAINING TO EMISSION CONTROLS

The proper control of exhaust emissions depends not only on the primary components of the emission controls mentioned above, but also on such related areas as ignition timing, spark plugs, valve clearance, engine oil, cooling system, etc. Before tackling the primary emission controls, you should determine if the related components are functioning properly, and correct any deficiencies.

A. CRANKCASE EMISSION CONTROL SYSTEM

1. Squeeze the lower end of the drain tube and drain any oil or water which may have collected.

2. Make sure that the intake manifold T-joint is clear by passing the shank end of a No. 65 (0.035 in. dia.) drill through both ends (orifices) of the joint.

3. Check for any loose, disconnected, or deteriorated tubes and replace if necessary.

B. EXHAUST EMISSION CONTROL SYSTEM

Intake Air Temperature Control System (Engine Cold)

1. Inspect for loose, disconnected, or deteriorated vacuum hoses and replace as necessary.

2. Remove the air cleaner cover and element.

3. With the transmission in Neutral and the blue distributor disconnected, engage the starter motor for approximately two (2) seconds. Manifold vacuum to the vacuum motor should completely raise the air control valve door. Once opened, the valve door should stay open unless there is a leak in the system.

4. If the valve door does not open, check the intake manifold port by passing a No. 78 (0.016 in. dia.) drill or compressed air through the orifice in the manifold.

5. If the valve door still does not open, proceed to the following steps:

a. Vacuum Motor Test—Disconnect the vacuum line from the vacuum motor inlet pipe. Fully open the air control valve door, block the vacuum motor inlet pipe, then release the door. If the door does not remain open, the vacuum motor is defective. Replace as necessary and repeat Steps 1–3;

b. Air Bleed Valve Test—Unblock the inlet pipe and make sure that the valve door fully closes without sticking or binding. Reconnect the vacuum line to the vacuum motor inlet pipe. Connect a vacuum source (e.g. hand vacuum pump) to the manifold vacuum line (disconnect at the intake manifold fixed orifice) and draw enough vacuum to fully open the valve door. If the valve door closes with the

manifold vacuum line plugged (by the vacuum pump), then vacuum is leaking through the air bleed valve. Replace as necessary and repeat Steps 1–3;

CAUTION: *Never force the air bleed valve (bi-metal strip) on or off its valve seat. The bi-metal strip and the valve seat may be damaged.*

c. Check Valve Test—Again draw a vacuum (at the manifold vacuum line) until the valve door opens. Unplug the line by disconnecting the pump from the manifold vacuum line. If the valve door closes, vacuum is leaking past the check valve. Replace as necessary and repeat Steps 1–3.

6. After completing the above steps, replace the air cleaner element and cover and fit a vacuum gauge into the line leading to the vacuum motor.

7. Start the engine and raise the idle to 1500–2000 rpm. As the engine warms, the vacuum gauge reading should drop to zero.

NOTE: *Allow sufficient time for the engine to reach normal operating temperature—when the cooling fan cycles on and off.*

If the reading does not drop to zero before the engine reaches normal operating temperature, the air bleed valve is defective and must be replaced. Repeat Step 3 as a final check.

Temperature and Transmission Controlled Spark Advance (Engine Cold)—All Models

1. Check for loose, disconnected, or deteriorated vacuum hoses and replace as necessary.

2. Check the coolant temperature sensor switch for proper operation with an ohmmeter or 12V light. The switch should normally be open (no continuity across the switch terminals) when the coolant temperature is below approximately 120° F (engine cold). If the switch is closed (continuity across the terminals), replace the switch and repeat the check.

3. On manual transmission models, check the transmission sensor switch. The switch should be open (no continuity across the connections) when Fourth gear is selected, and closed (continuity across the connections) in all other gear positions. Replace if necessary and repeat the check.

4. Remove the spark control vacuum tube, leading between the spark advance/retard unit and the solenoid valve, and connect

Start control solenoid valve

a vacuum gauge to the now-vacant hole in the solenoid valve, according to the diagram.

5. Start the engine and raise the idle to 2000 rpm. With a cold engine, the vacuum gauge should read approximately 3 in./Hg or more. As the coolant temperature reaches 120° F (and before the radiator fan starts), the vacuum reading should drop to zero. On manual transmission models, vacuum should return when Fourth gear is selected (and the transmission switch is opened). If this is not the case, proceed to the following steps:

NOTE: *If the engine is warm from the previous test, disconnect the coolant temperature switch wires when making the following tests.*

Emission control "black box" for electrical and vacuum hose connections

6. If vacuum is not initially available, disconnect the vacuum signal line from the charcoal canister and plug the open end, which will block a possible vacuum leak from the idle cut-off valve of the canister. With the line plugged, again check for vacuum at 2000 rpm. If vacuum is now available, reconnect the vacuum signal line and check the canister for vacuum leaks. (Refer to the "Evaporative Emission Control System" check.) If vacuum is still not available, stop the engine and disconnect the vacuum line from the solenoid valve (the line between the solenoid valve and the manifold T-joint) and insert a vacuum gauge in the line. If vacuum is not available, the vacuum port is blocked. Clear the port with compressed air and repeat the test sequence beginning with Step 3.

7. If vacuum is available in Step 5 after the engine is warm and in all ranges of the automatic transmission and in First, Second, and Third of the manual transmission, stop the engine and check for electrical continuity between the terminals of the coolant temperature sensor:

NOTE: *After completing the following steps, repeat the test procedure beginning with Step 4.*

a. If there is no continuity (and the engine is warm), replace the temperature sensor switch and recheck for continuity;

b. If there is continuity, check the battery voltage to the vacuum solenoid. If no voltage is available (with the ignition switch ON), check the wiring, fuses, and connections;

c. If there is battery voltage and the temperature sensor is operating correctly, check connections and/or replace the solenoid valve.

C. EVAPORATIVE EMISSION CONTROL SYSTEM (ENGINE AT NORMAL OPERATING TEMPERATURE)

Charcoal Canister

1. Check for loose, disconnected, or deteriorated vacuum hoses and replace where necessary.

2. Pull the free end of the purge air guide tube out of the body frame and plug it securely.

3. Disconnect the fuel vapor line from the charcoal canister and connect a vacuum gauge to the charcoal canister vapor inlet according to the diagram.

4. Start the engine and allow it to idle.

Since the vacuum port in the carburetor is closed off at idle, the vacuum gauge should register no vacuum. If vacuum is available, replace the charcoal canister and recheck for no vacuum. A vacuum reading indicates that the charcoal canister idle cut-off valve is broken or stuck.

5. Open the throttle to 2000 rpm and make sure that the charcoal canister idle cut-off valve is opening by watching the vacuum.

a. Disconnect the vacuum signal line and connect the vacuum gauge to the carburetor T-joint orifice formerly occupied by the signal line. The vacuum reading at 2000 rpm should be greater than 3 in./Hg. If vacuum is now available (with the throttle open), replace the charcoal canister and repeat Steps 4 & 5. If vacuum is still not available, or is below 3 in./Hg, proceed to the next step;

b. If vacuum is less than 3 in./Hg (with the throttle open), the carburetor vacuum port or T-joint might be plugged. Clear the passages with compressed air. If vacuum is now available, repeat Steps 4 & 5. If vacuum is not available, or below 3 in./Hg, the carburetor vacuum port is blocked. Repair or replace as necessary and repeat Steps 4 & 5. If vacuum is *still* not available, proceed to the next step;

c. Plug the solenoid valve vacuum line (the other line to the carburetor T-joint) and recheck for vacuum. If vacuum is now available, the leak is in the advance/retard solenoid valve. Repair or replace as necessary and repeat Steps 4 & 5.

FUEL SYSTEM

1170 and 1237 cc models use a two-barrel downdraft Hitachi carburetor. Fuel pressure is provided by a camshaft-driven mechanical fuel pump. A replaceable fuel filter is located in the engine compartment in-line between the fuel pump and carburetor.

On the 1487 and 1600 cc CVCC Civic, and Accord, a Keihin three-barrel carburetor is used. On this carburetor, the primary and secondary venturis deliver a lean air/fuel mixture to the main combustion chamber. Simultaneously, the third or auxiliary venturi which has a completely separate fuel metering circuit, delivers a small (in volume) but very rich air/fuel mixture to the precombustion chamber. Fuel pressure is provided by an electric fuel pump which is actuated when

the ignition switch is turned to the "on" position. The electric pump is located under the rear seat beneath a special access plate on sedan and hatchback models, and located under the rear of the car adjacent to the fuel tank on station wagon and Accord models. A replaceable in-line fuel filter located on the inlet side of the electric fuel pump is used on all CVCC models.

Mechanical Fuel Pump
REMOVAL AND INSTALLATION
All Except CVCC

The fuel pump in the Civic is located in back of the engine, underneath the air cleaner snorkel.

1. Remove the air cleaner and cover assembly.

2. Remove the inlet and outlet fuel lines at the pump.

3. Loosen the pump nuts and remove the pump.

NOTE: *Do not disassemble the pump. Disassembly may cause fuel or oil leakage. If the pump is defective, replace it as an assembly.*

4. To install the fuel pump, reverse the removal procedure.

INSPECTION

1. Check the following items:
   a. Looseness of the pump connector.

Mechanical fuel pump location. Arrow indicates air hole

Checking the fuel pump with a fuel pressure gauge

b. Looseness of the upper and lower body and cover screws.

c. Looseness of the rocker arm pin.

d. Contamination or clogging of the air hole.

e. Improper operation of the pump.

2. Check to see if there are signs of oil or fuel around the air hole. If so, the diaphragm is damaged and you must replace the pump.

3. To inspect the pump for operation, first disconnect the fuel line at the carburetor. Connect a fuel pressure gauge to the delivery side of the pump. Start the engine and measure the pump delivery pressure.

4. After measuring, stop the engine and check to see if the gauge drops suddenly. If the gauge drops suddenly and/or the delivery pressure is incorrect, check for a fuel or oil leak from the diaphragm or from the valves.

5. To test for volume, disconnect the fuel line from the carburetor and inset it into a one quart container. Crank the engine for 64 seconds at 600 rpm, or 40 seconds at 3,000 rpm. The bottle should be half full (1 pint).

Mechanical Fuel Pump Performance Specifications

Engine rpm	Delivery Pressure (lb/in.²)	Vacuum (in. Hg)	Displacement (in.³/minute)
600	2.56	17.72	27
3,000	2.56	7.87–11.81	43
6,000	2.56	7.87–11.81	46

Electrical Fuel Pump

REMOVAL AND INSTALLATION

CVCC Models

1. Remove the gas filler cap to relieve any excess pressure in the system.

2. Obtain a pair of clothes pins or other suitable clamps to pinch shut the fuel lines to the pump.

3. Disconnect the negative battery cable.

4. Locate the fuel pump. On sedan and hatchback models, you will first have to remove the rear seat by removing the bolt at the rear center of the bottom cushion and pivoting the seat forward from the rear. The pump and filter are located on the driver's side of the rear seat floor section beneath an access plate retained by four phillips head screws.

On station wagon and Accord models, you will probably have to raise the rear of the car, or park it with two wheels up on a curb to obtain access. In all cases, make sure, if you are crawling under the car, that the car is securely supported. *Do not venture beneath the car when it is supported only by the tire changing jack.*

5. Pinch the inlet and outlet fuel lines shut. Loosen the hose clamps. On station wagon models, remove the filter mounting clip on the left hand side of the bracket.

6. Disconnect the positive lead wire and ground wire from the pump at their quick disconnect.

7. Remove the two fuel pump retaining bolts, taking care not to lose the two spacers and bolt collars.

8. Remove the fuel lines and fuel pump.

9. Reverse the above procedure to install. The pump cannot be disassembled and must be replaced if defective. Operating fuel pump pressure is 2–3 psi.

Carburetors

The carburetor performs the following tasks: Opens and closes its intake port to maintain a predetermined amount of gasoline in its reservoir, channels air into the engine through the air cleaner, atomizes measured amounts of gasoline, and introduces the vapor into the incoming air stream, provides metered amounts of air/fuel mixture to the deceleration valve while it is operating, acts as a vacuum source for the distributor vacuum advance mechanism, and changes the air/fuel mixture it supplies to the engine for normal warm weather driving, acceleration, maximum power, cold engine operation, and idling. It looks complicated because it is. There are, however, many carburetor adjustments and repairs that can be performed by those who have a certain amount of mechanical aptitude.

Application

1170, 1237 cc—Hitachi 2-bbl; 1487 and 1600 cc—Keihin 3-bbl

CARBURETOR TROUBLESHOOTING

Carburetor problems are among the most difficult internal combustion engine malfunctions to diagnose. If you have a carburetor problem, read the description of carburetor systems in the beginning of the carburetor section of this chapter. Consider which system or combination of systems are in operation when the problem occurs. Some troubleshooting tips are given in the system operation descriptions. Additional troubleshooting information can be found in the "Troubleshooting" section in chapter two, subject five.

The most reliable way for a nonprofessional to diagnose a bad carburetor is to eliminate all other possible sources of the problem. If you suspect the carburetor is the problem, perform the adjustments given in this chapter. Check the ignition system to ensure that the spark plugs, contact points, and condenser are in good shape and adjusted properly. Check the emission control equipment following the instructions given in the first part of this chapter. Check the ignition timing adjustment. Check all vacuum hoses on the engine for loose connections or splits or breaks. Make sure the carburetor and intake manifold attaching bolts are tightened to the proper torque.

If you do determine that the carburetor is malfunctioning, and the adjustments in this chapter don't help, you have three alternatives: you can take it to a professional mechanic and let him fix it, you can buy a new or rebuilt carburetor to replace the one now on your car, or you can buy a carburetor rebuilding kit and overhaul your carburetor.

Overhaul

All Types

Efficient carburetion depends greatly on careful cleaning and inspection during over-

haul since dirt, gum, water, or varnish in or on the carburetor parts are often responsible for poor performance.

Overhaul your carburetor in a clean, dust-free area. Carefully disassemble the carburetor, referring often to the exploded views. Keep all similar and look-alike parts segregated during disassembly and cleaning to avoid accidental interchange during assembly. Make a note of all jet sizes.

When the carburetor is disassembled, wash all parts (except diaphragms, electric choke units, pump plunger, and any other plastic, leather, fiber, or rubber parts) in clean carburetor solvent. Do not leave parts in the solvent any longer than is necessary to sufficiently loosen the deposits. Excessive cleaning may remove the special finish from the float bowl and choke valve bodies, leaving these parts unfit for service. Rinse all parts in clean solvent and blow them dry with compressed air or allow them to air dry. Wipe clean all cork, plastic, leather, and fiber parts with a clean, lint-free cloth.

Blow out all passages and jets with compressed air and be sure that there are no restrictions or blockages. Never use wire or similar tools to clean jets, fuel passages, or air bleeds. Clean all jets and valves separately to avoid accidental interchange.

Check all parts for wear or damage. If wear or damage is found, replace the defective parts. Especially check the following:

1. Check the float needle and seat for wear. If wear is found, replace the complete assembly.

2. Check the float hinge pin for wear and the float(s) for dents or distortion. Replace the float if fuel has leaked into it.

3. Check the throttle and choke shaft bores for wear or an out-of-round condition. Damage or wear to the throttle arm, shaft, or shaft bore will often require replacement of the throttle body. These parts require a close tolerance of fit; wear may allow air leakage, which could affect starting and idling.

NOTE: *Throttle shafts and bushings are not included in overhaul kits. They can be purchased separately.*

4. Inspect the idle mixture adjusting needles for burrs or grooves. Any such condition requires replacement of the needle, since you will not be able to obtain a satisfactory idle.

5. Test the accelerator pump check valves. They should pass air one way but not the other. Test for proper seating by blowing and

Troubleshooting Basic Fuel System Problems

Many problems in the fuel system can be traced to dirt or moisture in the system, or to clogged fuel or air filters. Changing filters at regular intervals will eliminate most problems.

The Problem	Is Caused By	What to Do
Engine cranks, but won't start (or is hard to start) when cold	• Empty fuel tank • Incorrect starting procedure • Defective fuel pump • No fuel in carburetor • Clogged fuel filter • Engine flooded • Defective choke	• Check for fuel in tank • Follow correct procedure • Check pump output • Check for fuel in the carburetor • Replace fuel filter • Wait 15 minutes; try again • Check choke plate
Engine cranks, but is hard to start (or does not start) when hot—(presence of fuel is assumed)	• Defective choke • Vapor lock	• Check choke plate • Allow the engine to cool. If possible, cool the fuel line and fuel pump with wet rags or ice.
Rough idle or engine runs rough	• Dirt or moisture in fuel • Clogged air filter • Faulty fuel pump	• Replace fuel filter • Replace air filter • Check fuel pump output
Engine stalls or hesitates on acceleration	• Dirt or moisture in the fuel • Dirty Carburetor • Defective fuel pump • Incorrect float level, defective accelerator pump	• Replace fuel filter • Clean the carburetor • Check fuel pump output • Have carburetor checked
Poor gas mileage	• Clogged air filter • Dirty carburetor • Defective choke, faulty carburetor adjustment	• Replace air filter • Clean carburetor • Have carburetor checked
Engine is flooded (won't start accompanied by smell of raw fuel)	• Improperly adjusted choke or carburetor	• Wait 15 minutes and try again, without pumping gas pedal. • If it won't start, have carburetor checked

sucking on the valve. Replace the valve if necessary. If the valve is satisfactory, wash the valve again to remove breath moisture.

6. Check the bowl cover for warped surfaces with a straightedge.

7. Closely inspect the valves and seats for wear and damge, replacing as necessary.

8. After the carburetor is assembled, check the choke valve for freedom of operation.

Carburetor overhaul kits are recommended for each overhaul. These kits contain all gaskets and new parts to replace those that deteriorate most rapidly. Failure to replace all parts supplied with the kit (especially gaskets) can result in poor performance later.

Some carburetor manufacturers supply overhaul kits of three basic types: minor repair; major repair; and gasket kits. Basically, they contain the following:

Minor Repair Kits:
    All gaskets
    Float needle valve
    Volume control screw
    All diaphragms
    Spring for the pump diaphragm

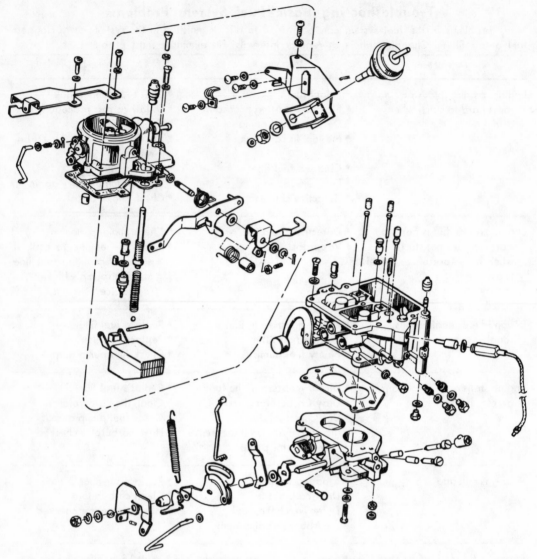

Exploded view of Hitachi 2-bbl used on non-CVCC engines

Major Repair Kits:
    All jets and gaskets
    All diaphragms
    Float needle valve
    Volume control screw
    Pump ball valve
    Main jet carrier
    Float
    Complete intermediate rod
    Intermediate pump lever
    Complete injector tube
    Some cover hold-down screws and
    washers
Gasket Kits:
    All gaskets

After cleaning and checking all components, reassemble the carburetor, using new parts and referring to the exploded view. When reassembling, make sure that all screws and jets are tight in their seats, but do not overtighten, as the tips will be distorted. Tighten all screws gradually, in rotation. Do not tighten needle vales into their seats; uneven jetting will result. Always use new gaskets. Be sure to adjust the float level when reassembling.

REMOVAL AND INSTALLATION

1. Disconnect the following:
    a. Hot air tube.

b. Vacuum hose between the one-way valve and the manifold—at the manifold.

c. Breather chamber (on air cleaner case) to intake manifold at the breather chamber.

d. Hose from the air cleaner case to the valve cover.

e. Hose from the carbon canister to the carburetor—at the carburetor.

f. Throttle opener hose—at the throttle opener.

2. Disconnect the fuel line at the carburetor. Plug the end of the fuel line to prevent dust entry.

3. Disconnect the choke and throttle control cables.

4. Disconnect the fuel shut-off solenoid wires.

5. Remove the carburetor retaining bolts and the carburetor. Leave the insulator on the manifold.

NOTE: *After removing the carburetor, cover the intake manifold parts to keep out foreign materials.*

THROTTLE LINKAGE ADJUSTMENT

1170 and 1237 cc Models

1. Check the gas pedal free-play (the amount of free movement before the throttle cable starts to pull the throttle valve). Adjust the free-play at the throttle cable adjusting nut (near the carburetor) so the pedal has 0.04–0.12 in. (1.0–3.0 mm) freeplay.

2. Make sure that when the accelerator pedal is fully depressed, the primary and secondary throttle valves are opened fully (contact the stops). If the secondary valve does not open fully, adjust by bending the secondary throttle valve connecting rod.

1487 and 1600 cc CVCC Models

1. Remove the air cleaner assembly to provide access.

2. Check that the cable free-play (deflection) is 0.16–0.40 in. This is measured right before the cable enters the throttle shaft bellcrank.

3. If deflection is not to specifications, rotate the cable adjusting nuts in the required direction.

4. As a final check, have a friend press the gas pedal all the way to the floor, while you look down inside the throttle bore checking that the throttle plates reach the wide open throttle (WOT) vertical position.

5. Install the air cleaner.

Throttle cable adjusting location—CVCC models

FLOAT AND FUEL LEVEL ADJUSTMENT

Poor fuel combustion, black sooty exhaust, and fuel overflow are indications of improper float level.

1170 and 1237 cc Models

1. Check the float level by looking at the sight glass on the right of the carburetor. Fuel level should align with the dot on the sight glass. If the level is above or below the dot, the carburetor must be disassembled and the float level set.

NOTE: *Try to check float level with the dot at eye level.*

2. Remove the carburetor from the engine and disconnect the air horn assembly from the carburetor body.

NOTE: *When removing the air horn, do not drop the float pin.*

3. Invert the air horn and raise the float.

4. Now lower the float carefully until the float tang just touches the needle valve stem. The valve stem is spring loaded, so do not allow the float to compress the spring during measurement. Measure the distance between the float and the air horn flange (without gasket). The distance should be 0.44 in., or 11 mm. Adjust by bending the tang.

5. Raise the float until the float stop contacts the air horn body. Measure the distance between the float tang and the needle valve stem. The distance should be 0.051–0.067 in. (1.3–1.77 mm). Adjust by bending the float stop tang.

6. When the carburetor is installed, recheck the float level by looking into the carburetor float sight glass. Fuel level should be within the range of the dot on the glass.

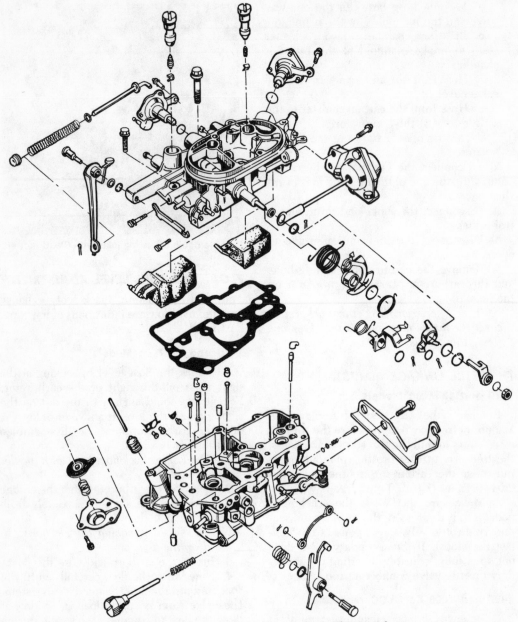

Exploded view of Keihin 3-bbl used on CVCC engines

1487 and 1600 cc CVCC Models

Due to the rather unconventional manner in which the Keihin 3-bbl carburetor float level is checked and adjusted, this is one job best left to the dealer, or someone whith Honda tool no. 07501-6570000 (which is a special float level gauge/fuel catch tray/drain bottle assembly not generally available to the public). This carburetor is adjusted while mounted on a running engine. After the auxiliary and the primary/secondary main jet covers are removed, the special float gauge apparatus is installed over the jet aperatures. With the engine running, the float level is checked against a red index line on the gauge. If adjustment proves necessary, there are adjusting screws provided for both the auxiliary and the primary/secondary circuits atop the carburetor.

FAST IDLE ADJUSTMENT

During cold engine starting and the engine warm-up period, a specially enriched fuel mixture is required. If the engine fails to run

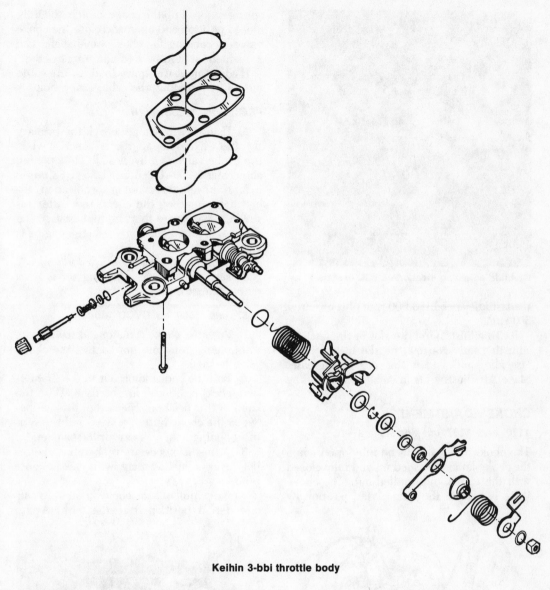

Keihin 3-bbi throttle body

properly or if the engine over-revs with the choke knob pulled out in cold weather, the fast idle system should be checked and adjusted. This is accomplished with the carburetor installed.

1170 and 1237 cc Models

1973

1. Run the engine until it reaches normal operating temperature.

2. With the engine still running, pull the choke knob out to the first detent. The idle speed should rise to 1,500 to 2,000 rpm.

3. If the idle speed is not within this range, adjust by bending the choke rod. (See "Choke Adjustment" section below for further details.)

1974–78

1. Open the primary throttle plate and insert an 0.8 mm (0.032 in.), diameter drill bit between the plate and the bore.

2. With the throttle plate opened 0.8 mm, bend the reference tab so that it is midway between the two scribed lines on the throttle control lever.

1487 and 1600 cc CVCC Models

1. Run the engine until it reaches normal operating temperature.

2. Place the choke control knob in its second detent position (two clicks out from the dash). With the coke knob in this position, run the engine for 30 seconds and check that

Fast idle adjusting location—CVCC models

the fast idle speed is 3,000 rpm plus or minus 500 rpm.

3. To adjust, bend the slot in the fast idle adjusting link. Narrow the slot to lower the fast idle, and widen the slot to increase. Make all adjustments in small increments.

CHOKE ADJUSTMENT

1170 and 1237 cc Models

The choke valve should be fully open when the choke knob is pushed in, and fully closed with the choke knob pulled out. The choke valve is held in the fully closed position by

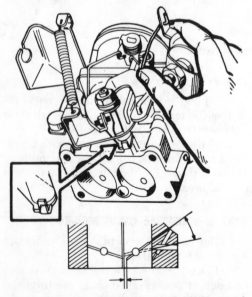

Precision choke adjustment—1170, 1237 models

spring action. Pull the choke knob to the fully closed position and open and close the choke valve by rotating the choke valve shaft. The movement should be free and unrestricted.

If adjustment is required, adjust the cable length by loosening the cable clamp bolt.

PRECISION ADJUSTMENT

1. Using a wire gauge, check the primary throttle valve opening (dimension G1) when the choke valve is fully closed. The opening should be 0.050–0.066 in. (1.28–1.68 mm).

2. If the opening is out of specification, adjust it by bending the choke rod. After installing, make sure that the highest fast idle speed is 2,500–2,800 rpm while the engine is warm.

NOTE: *When adjusting the fast idle speed, be sure the throttle adjusting screw does not contact the stop.*

1487 and 1600 cc CVCC Models

1. Push the choke actuator rod towards its diaphragm, so it does not contact the choke valve linkage.

2. Pull the choke knob out to the first detent (click) position from the dash. With the knob in this position, check the distance between the choke butterfly valve and the venturi opening with a $^3/_{16}$ in. drill (shank end).

3. Adjust as necessary by bending the relief lever adjusting tang with needle nose pliers.

4. Now, pull out the choke knob to its second detent position from the dash. Again,

1. Stop tab
2. Relief lever adjusting tang
3. Actuator rod
4. Choke opener diaphragm

Choke adjusting components—CVCC models

make sure the choke actuator rod does not contact the choke valve linkage.

5. With the choke knob in this position, check that the clearance between the butterfly valve and venturi opening is ⅛ in. using the shank end of a ⅛ in. drill.

6. Adjust as necessary by bending the stop tab for the choke butterly linkage.

CHOKE CABLE ADJUSTMENT
1974–78 1237 cc Models

NOTE: *Perform the adjustment only after the throttle plate opening has been set and referenced, as in the preceding procedure.*

1. Choke butterfly valve   2. Adjusting nut
3. Locknut

Choke cable adjustment—CVCC models

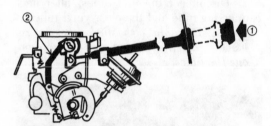

Choke cable adjustment—1974 and later 1237 cc models. Number one is the detent position, and number two is the link adjusting location

1. Make sure that the choke cable is correctly adjusted.

   a. With the choke knob in, the choke butterfly should be completely open;

   b. Slowly pull out the choke knob and check for slack in the cable. Remove any excessive free-play and recheck for full open when the knob is pushed in.

2. Check the link rod adjustment by pulling the choke knob out to the first detent. The two scribed lines on the throttle control lever should line up on either side of the reference tab. If not, adjust by bending the choke link rod.

1487 and 1600 cc CVCC Models

1. Remove the air cleaner assembly.

2. Push the choke knob all the way in at the dash. Check that the choke butterfly valve (choke plate) is fully open (vertical).

3. Next, have a friend pull out the choke knob while you observe the action of the butterfly valve. When the choke knob is pulled out to the second detent position, the butterfly valve should just close. Then, when the choke knob is pulled all the way out, the butterfly valve should remain in the closed position.

4. To adjust, loosen the choke cable lock-

nut and rotate the adjusting nut so that with the choke knob pushed flush against the dash (open position), the butterfly valve just rests against its positioning stop tab. Tighten the locknut.

5. If the choke butterfly valve is notchy in operation, or if it does not close properly, check the butterfly valve and shaft for binding. Check also the operation of the return spring.

THROTTLE VALVE OPERATION
1170 and 1237 cc Models

1. Check to see if the throttle valve opens fully when the throttle lever is moved to he fully open position. See if the valve closes fully when the lever is released.

2. Measure the clearance between the primary throttle valve and the chamber wall where the connecting rod begins to open the secondary throttle valve. The clearance should be 0.221–0.237 in. (5.63–6.03 mm).

3. If the clearance is out of specification, adjust by bending the connecting rod.

NOTE: *After adjusting, operate the throttle lever and check for any sign of binding.*

ACCELERATOR PUMP ADJUSTMENT
1170 and 1237 cc Models

Check the pump for smooth operation. See if fuel squirts out of the pump nozzle by operating the pump lever or the throttle lever. When the pump is operated slowly, fuel must squirt out until the pump comes to the end of its travel. If the pump is defective,

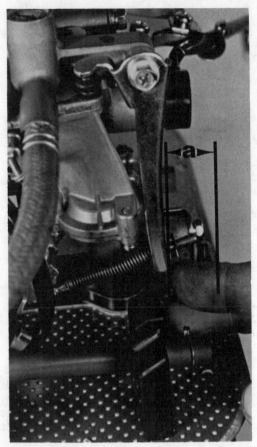

Accelerating pump travel adjustment—CVCC models. Distance "A" is 0.0311–0.0335 in.

check for clogging or a defective piston. Adjust the pump by either repositioning the end of the connecting rod arm in the pump lever, or the arm itself.

1487 and 1600 cc CVCC Models

1. Remove the air cleaner assembly.

2. Check that the distance between the tang at the end of the accelerator pump lever and the lever stop at the edge of the throttle body (distance "A") is 0.0311–0.0335 in. This corresponds to effective pump lever travel.

3. To adjust, bend the pump lever tang in the required direction.

4. Install the air cleaner.

FUEL TANK

REMOVAL AND INSTALLATION

1. Drain the tank by loosening the tank drain bolt.

NOTE: *Catch the fuel in a clean, safe container.*

2. Disconnect the fuel tubes, filler neck connecting tube and the clear vinyl tube.

NOTE: *Disconnect the fuel tubes by removing the clips, taking care not to damage the tubes.*

Filler tube location

3. Disconnect the fuel meter unit wire at its connection.

4. Remove the fuel tank by removing its attaching bolts.

5. To install, reverse the removal procedure. Be sure that all tubes and fuel lines are securely fastened by the clips.

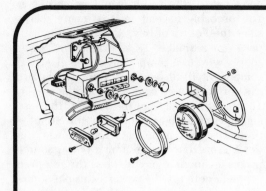

Chassis Electrical

UNDERSTANDING AND TROUBLESHOOTING ELECTRICAL SYSTEMS

For any electrical system to operate, it must make a complete circuit. This simply means that the power flow from the battery must make a complete circle. When an electrical component is operating, power flows from the battery to the component, passes through the component causing it to perform its function (lighting a light bulb), and then returns to the battery through the ground of the circuit. This ground is usually (but not always) the metal part of the car on which the electrical component is mounted.

Perhaps the easiest way to visualize this is to think of connecting a light bulb with two wires attached to it to your car battery. The battery in your car has two posts (negative and positive). If one of the two wires attached to the light bulb was attached to the negative post of the battery and the other wire was attached to the positive post of the battery, you would have a complete circuit. Current from the battery would flow out one post, through the wire attached to it and then to the light bulb, where it would pass through causing it to light. It would then leave the light bulb, travel through the other wire, and return to the other post of the battery.

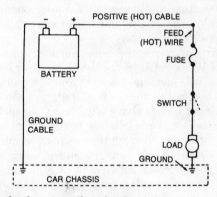

A simple automotive circuit

The normal automotive circuit differs from this simple example in two ways. First, instead of having a return wire from the bulb to the battery, the light bulb returns the current to the battery through the chassis of the vehicle. Since the negative battery cable is attached to the chassis and the chassis is made of electrically conductive metal, the chassis of the vehicle can serve as a ground wire to complete the circuit. Secondly, most automotive circuits contain switches to turn components on and off as required.

There are many types of switches, but the most common simply serves to prevent the passage of current when it is turned off. Since the switch is a part of the circle necessary for a complete circuit, it operates to leave an opening in the circuit, and thus an incomplete or open circuit, when it is turned off.

Some electrical components which require a large amount of current to operate also have a relay in their circuit. Since these circuits carry a large amount of current, the thickness of the wire in the circuit (gauge size) is also greater. If this large wire were connected from the component to the control switch on the instrument panel, and then back to the component, a voltage drop would occur in the circuit. To prevent this potential drop in voltage, an electromagnetic switch (relay) is used. The large wires in the circuit are connected from the car battery to one side of the relay, and from the opposite side of the relay to the component. The relay is normally open, preventing current from passing through the circuit. An additional, smaller, wire is connected from the relay to the control switch for the circuit. When the control switch is turned on, it grounds the smaller wire from the relay and completes the circuit. This closes the relay and allows current to flow from the battery to the component. The horn, headlight, and starter circuits are three which use relays.

Did you ever notice how your instrument panel lights get brighter the faster your car goes? This happens because your alternator (which supplies the battery) puts out more current at speeds above idle. This is normal. However, it is possible for larger surges of current to pass through the electrical system of your car. If this surge of current were to reach an electrical component, it could burn it out. To prevent this from happening, fuses are connected into the current supply wires of most of the major electrical systems of your car. The fuse serves to head off the surge at the pass. When an electrical current of excessive power passes through the component's fuse, the fuse blows out and breaks the circuit, saving it from destruction.

The fuse also protects the component from damage if the power supply wire to the component is grounded before the current reaches the component.

Let us here interject another rule to the complete circle circuit. *Every complete circuit from a power source must include a component which is using the power from the power source.* If you were to disconnect the light bulb (from the previous example of a light bulb being connected to the battery by two wires) from the wires and touch the two wires together (please take my word for this;

don't try it), the result would be shocking. You probably haven't seen so many sparks since the Fourth of July. A similar thing happens (on a smaller scale) when the power supply wire to a component or the electrical component itself becomes grounded before the normal ground connection for the circuit. To prevent damage to the system, the fuse for the circuit blows to interrupt the circuit—protecting the components from damage. Because grounding a wire from a power source makes a complete circuit—less the required component to use the power—this phenomenon is called a shirt circuit. The most common causes of short circuits are: the rubber insulation on a wire breaking or rubbing through to expose the current carrying core of the wire to a metal part of the car, or a shorted switch.

The final protective device in the chassis electrical system is a fuse link. A fuse link is a wire that acts as a fuse. It is connected between the starter relay and the main wiring harness for the car. This connection is under the hood, very near a similar fuse link which protects the engine electrical system. Since the fuse link protects all the chassis electrical components, it is the probable cause of trouble when none of the electrical components function, unless the battery is disconnected or dead.

COMMON ELECTRICAL PROBLEMS

Electrical problems generally fall into one of three areas:

1. The component that is not functioning is not receiving current.

2. The component itself is not functioning.

3. The component is not properly grounded.

Problems that fall into the first category are by far the most complicated. It is the current supply system to the component which contains all the switches, relays, fuses, etc.

The electrical system can be checked with a test light and a jumper wire. A test light is a device that looks like a pointed screwdriver with a wire attached to it. It has a light bulb in its handle. A jumper wire is a piece of insulated wire with an alligator clip attached to each end. To check the system you must follow the wiring diagrams found in this chapter. A wiring diagram is a road map of the car's electrical system.

If a light bulb is not working, you must follow a systematic plan to determine which of the three causes is the villain.

1. Turn on the switch that controls the inoperable bulb.

2. Disconnect the power supply wire from the bulb.

3. Attach the ground wire on the test light to a good metal ground.

4. Touch the probe end of the test light to the end of the power supply wire that was disconnected from the bulb. If the bulb is receiving current, the light will go on.

NOTE: *If the bulb is one which works only when the ignition key is turned on (turn signal), make sure the key is turned on.*

If the test light does not go on, then the problem is in the circuit between the battery and the bulb. As mentioned before, this includes all the switches, fuses, and relays in the system. Turn to the wiring diagram and find the bulb on the diagram. Follow the wire that runs back to the battery. The problem is an open circuit between the battery and the bulb. If the fuse is blown and, when replaced, immediately blows again, there is a short circuit in the system which must be located and repaired. If there is a switch in the system, bypass it with a jumper wire. This is done by connecting one end of the jumper wire to the power supply wire into the switch and the other end of the jumper wire to the wire coming out of the switch. Again, consult the wiring diagram. If the test light lights with the jumper wire installed, the switch or whatever was bypassed is defective.

NOTE: *Never substitute the jumper wire for the bulb, as the bulb is the component required to use the power from the power source.*

5. If the bulb in the test light goes on, then the current is getting to the bulb that is not working in the car. This eliminates the first of the three possible causes. Connect the power supply wire and connect a jumper

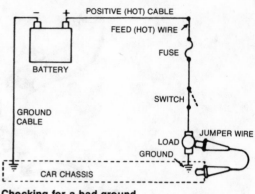
Checking for a bad ground

wire from the bulb to a good metal ground. Do this with the switch which controls the bulb turned on, and also the ignition switch turned on if it is required for the light to work. If the bulb works with the jumper wire installed, then it has a bad ground. This is usually caused by the metal area on which the bulb mounts to the car being coated with some type of foreign matter.

6. If neither test located the source of the trouble, then the light bulb itself is defective.

The above test procedure can be applied to any of the components of the chassis electrical system by substituting the component that is not working for the light bulb. Remember that for any electrical system to work, all connections must be clean and tight.

HEATER

REMOVAL AND INSTALLATION
All Except Accord

NOTE: *These procedures do not apply to cars equipped with air conditioning. On cars equipped with air conditioning, heater removal may differ from the procedures listed below. Only a trained air conditioning specialist should disassemble A/C equipped units. Air conditioning units contain pressurized Freon which can be extremely dangerous (e.g. burns and/or blindness) to the untrained.*

1. Drain the radiator.

2. Disconnect the right and left defroster hoses.

3. Disconnect the inlet and outlet water hoses at the heater assembly.

NOTE: *There will be a coolant leakage when disconnecting the hoses. Catch the coolant in a container to prevent damage to the interior.*

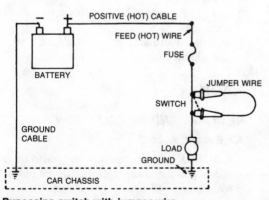
Bypassing switch with jumper wire

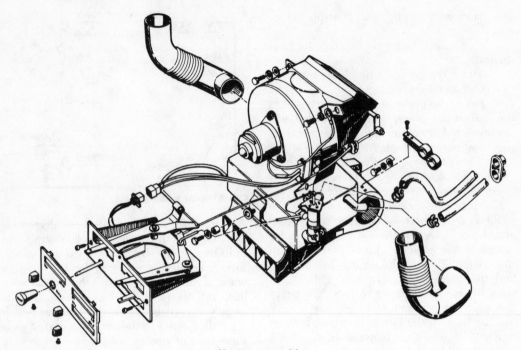

Heater assembly

4. Disconnect the following items:
   a. Fre-Rec control cable;
   b. Temperature control rod;
   c. Room/Def. control cable;
   d. Fan motor switch connector;
   e. Upper attaching bolts;
   f. Lower attaching bolts;
   g. Lower bracket.

5. Remove the heater assembly through the passenger side.

6. To install the heater assembly, reverse the removal procedure. Pay attention to the following points:
   a. When installing the heater assembly, do not forget to connect the motor ground wire to the right side of the upper bracket;
   b. Connect the inlet and outlet water hoses SECURELY;
   NOTE: *The inlet hose is a straight type, and the outlet hose is an L-type.*
   c. Install the defroster nozzles in the correct position;
   d. Connect the control cables securely. Operate the control valve and lever to check for proper operation;
   e. Be sure to bleed the cooling system (see Chapter 1).

Accord

1. The heater blower assembly can be removed by removing the glove box, the fresh air control cable, and the three bolts that hold the blower.

2. To remove the heater core, first drain the radiator.

3. Remove the instrument panel (see the instrument panel removal section later in this chapter).

4. Once the instrument panel is removed, remove the hoses from the core.

5. Remove the control cables from their clips.

6. Remove the left and right upper bolts.

7. Remove the lower bolts and remove the heater core.

8. Installation is the reverse of removal. Keep the following points in mind:
   a. Don't interchange the inlet and outlet water hoses.
   b. Make sure all the cables operate correctly.
   c. Bleed the air from the cooling system (see chapter one).

RADIO

REMOVAL AND INSTALLATION
All Except Accord

CAUTION: *Never operate the radio without a speaker; severe damage to the output transistors will result. If the speaker must be replaced, use a speaker of the correct impedance (ohms) or else the output transistors will be damaged and require replacement.*

1. Remove the screw which holds the rear radio bracket to the back tray underneath the dash. Then remove the wing nut which holds the radio to the bracket and remove the bracket.

2. Remove the control knobs, hex nuts, and trim plate from the radio control shafts.

3. Disconnect the antenna and speaker leads, the bullet type radio fuse, and the white lead connected directly over the radio opening.

4. Drop the radio out, bottom first, through the package tray.

5. To install, reverse the removal procedure. When inserting the radio through the package tray, be sure the bottom side is up and the control shafts are facing toward the engine. Otherwise, you will not be able to position the radio properly through its opening in the dash.

Accord

1. Remove the two screws which hold the center lower lid and remove the lid.

2. Remove the radio attaching screws found underneath the lid.

3. Remove the radio knobs and the faceplate.

4. Remove the heater fan switch knob and the heater lever knobs.

5. Remove the heater control bezel and the center panel. To do this, remove the three center panel screws and the ash tray. Slide the panel to the left to remove it. Unhook the cigarette lighter leads.

6. Remove the leads which are attached to the radio and remove the radio.

7. Installation is the reverse of removal.

WINDSHIELD WIPERS

Motor and Linkage
REMOVAL AND INSTALLATION

The wiper motor on all models is connected to the engine compartment wall, below the front windshield.

1. Remove the negative (−) cable from the battery.

2. Disconnect the motor leads at the connector.

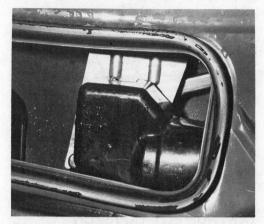

Wiper motor location

3. Remove the motor water seal cover clamp, and the seal, from the motor.

4. Remove the special nut which holds the wiper arms to the pivot shafts and remove the arms.

5. Remove the left and right pivot nuts and push the pivots down.

6. Remove the three wiper motor mounting bolts and remove the wiper/linkage assembly from the engine compartment.

7. Pull out the motor arm cotter pin and separate the linkage from the motor.

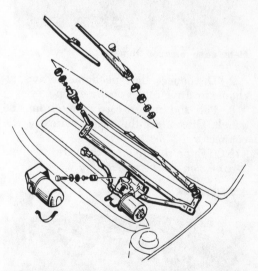

Windshield wiper motor and linkage schematic

8. Remove the three bracket bolts to remove the motor from its mounting bracket.

9. To install, reverse the removal procedure. Be sure to inspect the linkage and pivots for wear and looseness. When installing the motor, be sure it is in the "automatic stop" position.

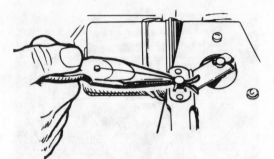

Removing the cotter pin from the motor arm linkage

INSTRUMENT CLUSTER

REMOVAL AND INSTALLATION
Meter Case Assembly

1. Remove the three meter case mounting wing nuts from the rear of the instrument panel.

Meter case removed from car

2. Disconnect the speedometer and tachometer drive cables at the engine.

3. Pull the meter case away from the panel. Disconnect the meter wires at the connectors.

NOTE: *Be sure to label the wires to avoid confusion during reassembly.*

Back of meter case showing wire connection points

4. Disconnect the speedometer and tachometer cables at the meter case and remove the case from the car.

5. To install, reverse the removal procedure.

Switch Panel

1. Loosen the four steering wheel column cover screws and remove the upper and lower covers.

2. Remove the four steering column bolts (remove the upper two bolts first) and rest the steering assembly on the floor.

3. Remove the four switch panel screws from the rear of the instrument panel.

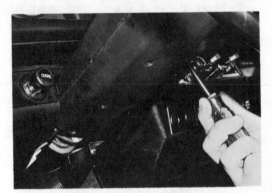

Removing steering column cover

4. To release the switch panel, remove the switches in the following manner:

a. Remove the light switch by prying the cover off the front of the knob. Pinch the retaining tabs together and pull off the knob;

b. Remove the wiper switch by pushing the knob in and turning counterclockwise. Then remove the retaining nut;

c. Remove the choke knob by loosening the set screw. Then remove the retaining nut.

5. To install, reverse the removal procedure.

Instrument Panel Assembly (Complete)
All except Accord

1. Loosen the four steering wheel column cover screws and remove the upper and lower covers.

2. Remove the four steering column bolts (remove the upper two bolts first) and rest the steering assembly on the floor.

3. Remove the screw on the outside edge of each fresh air vent and pry off the vents with a screwdriver.

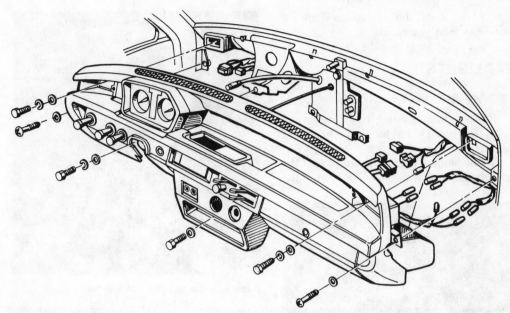

Instrument panel removal

4. Disconnect the instrument panel wiring harness from their cabin harnesses by removing the connectors and couplers.

5. Disconnect the speedometer and tachometer cables at the engine.

6. Disconnect the choke cable at the panel.

7. Remove the following switches:

a. Remove the light switch by prying the cover off the front of the knob. Pinch the retaining tabs together and pull off the knob;

b. Remove the wiper switch by pushing the knob in and turning counterclockwise. Then remove the retaining nut;

c. Remove the choke knob by loosening the set screw. Then remove the retaining nut.

8. Disconnect the three heater control cables.

9. Remove the heater fan motor wire connector.

10. Remove the six bolts which attach the panel.

11. Pull the panel out slightly and disconnect the speedometer and tachometer cables at the instruments. Then remove the instrument panel.

12. To install, reverse the removal procedure. Pay attention to the following points:

a. First, connect the speedometer and tachometer cables to the instruments. Then install the panel in place with the center pin in the panel locating hole;

b. Temporarily tighten the bolts which secure the upper, right, and left sides of the instrument panel. Make sure that the wiring harnesses are properly routed.

Accord Instrument Panel Assembly (Complete)

1. Remove the instrument cluster as outlined earlier.

2. Remove the speaker grille and then remove the clock panel and take out the clock.

3. Remove the control knobs and remove the heater control panel from the instrument panel.

4. Remove the three screws which hold the inner panel. The center panel and the heater control assembly are tightened together.

5. Remove the instrument panel left and right side covers, and remove the two bolts on either side.

6. Remove the two bolts in the center of the instrument panel.

7. Remove the bolt behind the clock panel.

8. You should now be able to remove the instrument panel.

9. Installation is the reverse of removal. Remember the following points:

a. Avoid bending the heater lever when installing the dashboard. Make sure the heater levers move freely without binding.

b. Make sure the instrument wiring harnesses aren't pinched.

HEADLIGHTS

REMOVAL AND INSTALLATION

1. Remove the retaining ring screws and remove the ring. Do not touch the headlight adjustment screws.

2. While holding the connector plug at the rear of the bulb, pull the headlight out of the

Removing the headlight connector

Retaining screw location

Removing the lower retaining screw

housing. It may be necessary to work the bulb back and forth a few times to break it loose from the connector.

3. Insert the replacement bulb into the connector and install the retaining ring and screws.

Light Bulb Specifications
Measurements given in watts except as noted

Headlights	50/40
Front Turn Signal/Parking Lights	32/3 cp
Side Marker Lights—front and rear	4 cp
Gauge Indicator Lights	1
Interior Light	5
Rear Turn/Stop/Taillight	32/32/3 cp
Back-up Lights	32 cp
License Plate Lights	4 cp

cp candle-power

FUSES AND FUSIBLE LINKS

All models are equipped with a 45 amp fusible link connected between the starter relay and the main wiring harness of the car.

The fuse box is located below the glove compartment, on the right bulkhead on Civic models. The Accord is equipped with a fuse tray which swings down from the instrument panel. It contains 8 fuses, some of which are rated at 10 amps and others at 15 amps. The rating and function of each fuse is posted inside the fuse box cap for quick reference.

Fuses can be replaced or removed simply by pulling them out of their retaining clips.

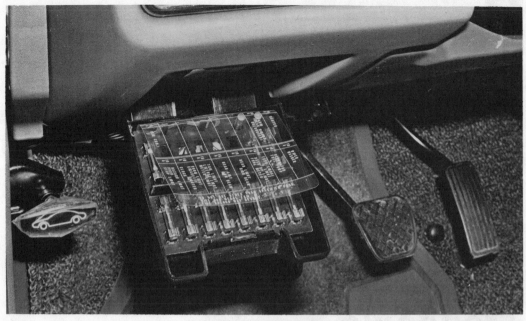

Accord fuse box location

Since each fuse protects more than one circuit, detection of a fuse blowout is an easy task of elimination.

Main circuit fusible link location

Civic fuse box location

WIRING DIAGRAMS

NOTE: *Wiring diagrams have been left out of this book. As cars have become more complex. and available with longer and longer option lists, wiring diagrams have grown in size and complexity also. It has become virtually impossible to provide a readable reproduction in a reasonable number of pages.*

6

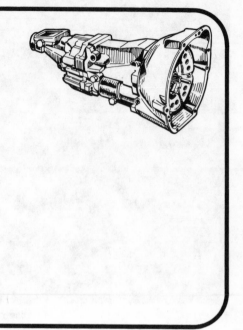

Clutch and Transaxle

DESCRIPTION

The Honda utilizes a transaxle arrangement where the transmission and the differential are contained within the same housing. Power is transmitted from the engine to the transmission, and in turn, to the differential. The front drive axle halfshafts transfer the power from the differential to the front wheels.

The Civic utilizes a standard design 4-speed, fully-synchronized transmission. The transmission is located on the right end of the engine, along with the differential. A similar 5-speed is used on Civic and Accord CVCC models.

A simple two-speed, semi-automatic transmission, Hondamatic, is also available. As in all automatic transmissions, power is transmitted from the engine to the transmission through a fluid coupling known as a torque converter. Forward gears are selected simply by moving the shift lever to the proper position—D1 (low speed range) or D2 (high speed range). The gears are engaged through the use of a complex clutch system in each gear range.

TRANSAXLE

REMOVAL AND INSTALLATION
Four and Five-Speed

1. Drain the transmission.
2. Raise the front of the car and support it with safety stands.
3. Remove the front wheels.
4. Disconnect the battery ground cable at the battery and the transmission case.
5. Remove the starter motor positive battery cable and the solenoid wire. Then remove the starter.
6. Disconnect the following cables and wires (see the "Engine Removal" section in Chapter 3 for the location of the various connections):

    a. Clutch cable at the release arm;

    b. Back-up light switch wires;

    c. TCS (Transmission Controlled Spark) switch wires (see "Emissions Controls" section in Chapter 4);

    d. Speedometer cable.

CAUTION: *When removing the speedometer cable from the transmission, it is not necessary to remove the entire cable*

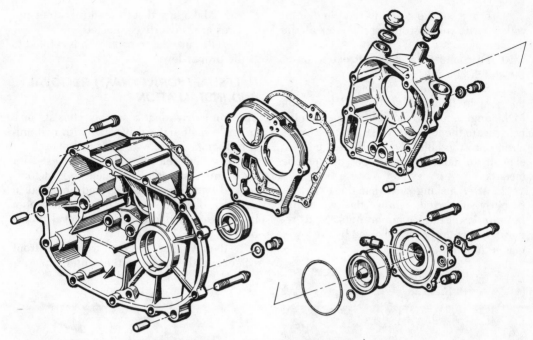

Five speed transmission housing and related parts

holder. Remove the end boot (gear holder seal), the cable retaining clip and then pull the cable out of the holder. In no way should you disturb the holder, unless it is absolutely necessary. For further details, see "Engine Removal" section in Chapter 3.

7. Disconnect the left and right lower ball joints at the knuckle, using a ball joint remover. See Chapter 8 for ball joint removal.

8. Pull on the brake disc and remove the left and right driveshafts from the differential case.

Driving out the gearshift rod pin

9. Drive out the gearshift rod pin (8 mm) with a drift and disconnect the rod at the transmission case.

10. Disconnect the gearshift extension at the clutch housing.

11. Screw in the engine hanger bolts (see the "Engine Removal" section in Chapter 3), to the engine torque rod bolt hold and to the hole just to the left of the distributor. Hook a chain onto the bolts and lift the engine just enough to take the load off the engine mounts.

12. After making sure that the engine is properly supported, remove the two center beam-to-lower engine mount nuts. Next, remove the center beam, followed by the lower engine mount.

Center engine mount nuts (arrows)

13. Reinstall the center beam (without mount) and lower the engine until it rests on the beam.

14. Place a jack under the transmission and loosen the 4 attaching bolts. Using the jack to support the transmission, slide it away from the engine and lower the jack until the transmission clears the car.

15. To install, reverse the removal procedure. Be sure to pay attention to the following points:

    a. Tighten all mounting nuts and bolts to their specified torque (see the "Engine Removal" section in Chapter 3);

    b. Use a new shift rod pin;

    c. After installing the driveshafts, attempt to move the inner joint housing in and out of the differential housing. If it moves easily, the driveshaft end clips should be replaced;

    d. Make sure that the control cables and wires are properly connected;

    e. Be sure the transmission is refilled to the proper level.

HALFSHAFT (DRIVESHAFT) REMOVAL AND INSTALLATION

The front driveshaft assembly consists of a sub-axle shaft and a driveshaft with two universal joints.

A constant velocity ball joint is used for both universal joints, which are factory-packed with special grease and enclosed in sealed rubber boots. The outer joint cannot be disassembled except for removal of the boot.

1. Remove the hubcap from the front wheel and then remove the center cap.

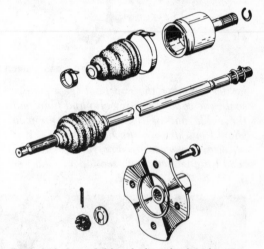

Exploded view of driveshaft and related parts

2. Pull out the 4 mm cotter pin and loosen, but do not remove, the spindle nut.

3. Raise the front of the car and support it with safety stands.

4. Remove the wheel lug nuts and then the wheel.

5. Remove the spindle nut.

6. Drain the transmission.

7. Remove the lower arm ball joints at the knuckle by using a ball joint remover.

8. To remove the driveshaft, hold the knuckle and pull it toward you. Then slide the driveshaft out of the knuckle. Pry the CV joint out about ½ in. Pull the inboard joint side of the driveshaft out of the differential case.

9. To install, reverse the removal procedure. If either the inboard or outboard joint boot bands have been removed for inspection

or disassembly of the joint (only the inboard joint can be disassembled), be sure to repack the joint with a sufficient amount of bearing grease.

CAUTION: *Make sure the CV joint sub-axle bottoms so that the spring clip may hold the sub-axle securely in the transmission.*

SHIFTER ADJUSTMENT

No external adjustment is needed or possible. However, you should check the linkage bushings for looseness and wear and replace if necessary.

CLUTCH

The clutch is a system of parts which, when engaged, connects the engine to the transmission. When the clutch is disengaged (clutch pedal pushed in), the turning motion of the engine crankshaft is separated from the transmission. Since the engine does not produce enough torque at idle to turn the rear wheels and start the car in motion, it is necessary to gradually connect the engine to the rest of the drive train to prevent the engine from stalling on acceleration. It is also much easier to shift the gears within a manual transmission when engine power is disconnected from the transmission.

The clutch unit is run directly off the flywheel. In this case, the pressure plate forces the friction disc onto the flywheel and power is then transmitted to the transmission. By depressing the clutch pedal, you allow the clutch disc to move away from the flywheel, thus isolating the engine power from the rest of the drive train.

CLUTCH TROUBLESHOOTING

The following are some symptoms that may accompany clutch troubles.
1. Excessive noise.
2. Clutch chatter or grab.
3. Clutch slip.
4. Clutch drag or failure to release.
5. Pedal pulsation.
6. Low clutch facing lift.
7. Gear lock-up or hard shifting.
8. Hard pedal.

Excessive Noise

There are 4 common sources of clutch noise:
1. Release bearing.
2. Clutch shaft pilot bearing.

3. Transmission pinion shaft bearing.
4. Transmitted engine noises.

Release Bearing

Release bearing noises vary with the degree of bearing failure. A dry or damaged bearing usually makes a shrill or scraping sound when depressing the clutch pedal to the point of release finger-to-bearing contact. This means that the noise should be audible at the lower end of clutch pedal free-play. Continued use of a car, with the release bearing in this condition, is damaging to the clutch release fingers.

Usual cause of release bearing failure is overwork—caused by riding the clutch. Other causes are not enough pedal freeplay, lack of lubricant in the bearing, clutch release fingers worn or out of true.

Pilot Bearing

Clutch shaft pilot bearing noises can be heard only when the bearing is in operation. This is at any time crankshaft speed is different from that of the clutch shaft (clutch disengaged with transmission in gear).

This is a high-pitched squeal, caused by a dry bearing and requires replacement.

Transmission Pinion Shaft Bearing

A rough, or otherwise damaged, transmission pinion (input) shaft bearing noise can be heard only when the clutch is engaged, with the transmission in any shift position. The noise is usually quite noticeable with the gears in Neutral. This noise should diminish and completely disappear as the transmission pinion gear slows down and stops after clutch release. This noise is easily distinguished from release bearing noise because of the opposite conditions of encounter.

Transmitted Engine Noises

Assuming that the clutch pedal has the required amount of free-play, there should be no objectionable amount of engine noise transmitted to the passenger area via the clutch. Some engine noises are transmitted through the positive pressure of the clutch release bearing and fingers to the clutch housing. Here they are amplified by the shape of the clutch housing and heard in the passenger compartment in the guise of clutch or transmission trouble. Engine noise transmission can usually be modified through clutch pedal manipulation.

Clutch Chatter or Grab

Usually the cause of clutch chatter or grab can be located within the clutch assembly. To correct the trouble will require the removal of the clutch. However, symptoms resembling clutch trouble may be misleading and originate in other areas.

In order to isolate the cause of the problem, we suggest that the following items be checked in this order.

1. Be sure that the clutch linkage is in adjustment and not binding. If necessary, lubricate, align, and adjust the linkage.

2. Check for worn or loose engine or transmission mounts. If necessary, tighten or replace the mounts.

3. Check for wear, looseness, or misalignment of the universal joints. Check the attaching bolts on the clutch pressure plate, transmission, and clutch housing. Tighten, align, or replace as necessary.

4. Check the freedom of movement of the clutch release bearing on its sleeve. Free up or replace as necessary.

5. Check for oil or grease on the flywheel, friction disc, or pressure plate.

6. Check for trueness of the friction disc, and that the disc hub is not binding on the splines of the transmission input shaft (clutch shaft).

7. Be sure that the disc or the pressure plate is not broken.

8. Examine clutch pressure plate and cover plate assembly for cracks or heat discoloration.

Clutch Slippage

Clutch slippage is usually most noticeable when pulling away, and during acceleration from a standing start. A severe, but positive, test for slippage is to start the engine, set the parking brake, and apply the service brakes; shift the transmission into high gear and release the clutch pedal while accelerating the engine. A clutch in good condition should hold and stall the engine. If the clutch slips, the cause may be one or more of the following:

1. Improper linkage adjustment (not enough free-play).

2. Broken or disconnected parts.

3. Clutch linkage or lever mechanism binding or broken, not allowing full pressure plate application.

4. Friction disc oil-saturated or excessively worn.

5. Pressure plate worn, springs weak from temper loss or failure (damaging heat will usually cause parts to appear blue).

Clutch Drag or Failure to Release

There are many reasons for clutch drag (spin) or failure to release. The following conditions, therefore, apply to unmodified versions of standard vehicles. Changing the driven plate mass (replacing the standard driven plate with a heavy-duty unit), changing transmission oil viscosity, etc., may influence clutch spin-time. Three seconds is a good, typical, spin-time for the standard transmission and clutch, driven under normal conditions, in temperate zone climates.

The friction disc and some of the transmission gears spin briefly after clutch disengagement, so normal clutch action should not be confused with a dragging clutch.

Clutch drag, failure to release, or abnormal spin-time may be caused by one or more of the following:

1. Improper clutch linkage adjustment.

2. Clutch plate hub binding on the transmission input (pinion) shaft.

3. A warped or bent friction disc or pressure plate; or loose friction material on the driven disc.

4. The transmission input shaft may be binding or sticking in the pilot bearing.

5. Misalignment of the transmission to the engine.

6. Transmission lubricant low or not heavy enough.

Pedal Pulsation

This condition can be felt by applying light foot pressure to the clutch pedal with the engine idling. It may be caused by any of the following:

1. Bent or uneven clutch release finger adjustment.

2. Excessive flywheel run-out due to bent wheel or crankshaft flange, or flywheel not properly seated on crankshaft flange.

3. Release bearing cocked on transmission bearing retainer.

4. Poor alignment of transmission with the engine.

Low Clutch Facing Life

This sort of complaint warrants a close study of the operator's driving habits. Poor clutch facing wear may be caused by any of the following:

1. Riding the clutch.

2. Drag strip type operation.

3. Continuous overloading, or the hauling of heavy trailers or other equipment.

4. Holding the car from drifting backward on a grade by slipping the clutch instead of using the brakes.

5. Improper pedal linkage adjustment (free-play and pedal height).

6. Rough surface on the flywheel or pressure plate.

7. Presence of oil or water on the clutch facing.

8. Weak pressure plate springs, causing clutch creep or slip.

Gear Lock Up or Hard Shifting

This trouble is so closely related to "Clutch Drag or Failure to Release" that diagnosis should be conducted in the same way as given under that heading. If, after checking the items listed and finding that the transmission still locks up or is hard to shift, the trouble probably lies in the transmission cover or shifter assembly, or in the transmission proper. In that case, transmission work is needed.

Hard Pedal

A stiff clutch pedal or a clutch release that requires abnormal pedal pressure may result from one or more of the following:

1. Dry and binding clutch linkage.

2. Linkage out of alignment.

3. Wrong type clutch assembly (heavy-duty) being used.

CLUTCH REMOVAL AND INSTALLATION

1. Follow Steps 1 through 14 of the transaxle removal procedure, previously given in this chapter. Matchmark the flywheel and clutch for reassembly.

2. Hold the flywheel ring gear with a large screwdriver or other fabricated tool (see illustration), remove the retaining bolts and remove the pressure plate and clutch disc.

NOTE: *Loosen the retaining bolts two turns at a time in a circular pattern. Removing one bolt while the rest are tight may warp the diaphragm spring.*

3. The flywheel can now be removed, if it needs repairing or replacing.

4. To separate the pressure plate from the diaphragm spring, remove the 4 retracting clips.

5. To remove the release, or throw-out, bearing, first straighten the locking tab and remove the 8 mm bolt, followed by the re-

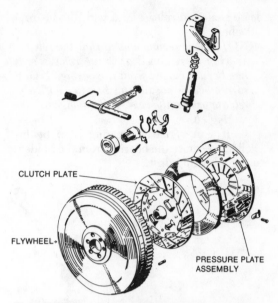

CLUTCH PLATE

FLYWHEEL

PRESSURE PLATE
ASSEMBLY

Civic CVCC clutch, flywheel, and related parts

Clutch disc

Pressure plate

lease shaft and release arm with the bearing attached.

NOTE: *It is recommended that the release bearing be removed after the release arm has been removed from the casing. Trying to remove or install the bearing with the release arm in the case, will damage the retaining clip.*

6. If a new release bearing is to be installed, separate the bearing from the holder, using a bearing drift.

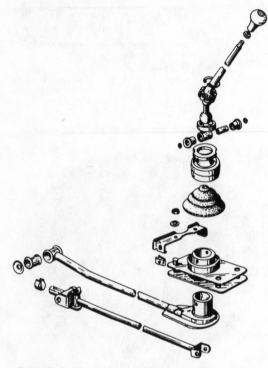

Exploded view of gearshift mechanism and related parts

7. To assemble and install the clutch, reverse the removal procedure. Be sure to pay attention to the following points:

a. Make sure that the flywheel and the end of the crankshaft are clean before assembling;

b. When installing the pressure plate, align the mark on the outer edge of the flywheel with the alignment mark on the pressure plate. Failure to align these marks will result in imbalance;

c. When tightening the pressure plate bolts, use a pilot shaft to center the friction disc. The pilot shaft can be bought at any large auto supply store or fabricated from a wooden dowel. After centering the disc, tighten the bolts two turns at a time, in a circular pattern to avoid warping the diaphragm spring;

d. When installing the release shaft and arm, place a lock tab washer under the retaining bolt;

e. When installing the transmission, make sure that the mainshaft is properly aligned with the disc spline and the aligning pins are in place, before tightening the case bolts.

PEDAL HEIGHT ADJUSTMENT

Check the clutch pedal height and if necessary, adjust the upper stop, so that the clutch and brake pedals rest at approximately the same height from the floor. First, be sure that the brake pedal freeplay is properly adjusted.

FREE PLAY ADJUSTMENT

Adjust the clutch release lever so that it has 0.12–0.16 in. (3–4 mm) of play when you move the clutch release lever at the transmission with your hand. This adjustment is made at the outer cable housing adjuster, near the release lever on non-CVCC models. Less than ⅛ in. of free-play may lead to clutch slippage, while more than ⅛ in. clearance may cause difficult shifting.

CAUTION: *Make sure that the upper and lower adjusting nuts are tightened after adjustment.*

On CVCC models, the free-play adjustment is made on the cable at the firewall. Remove the C-clip and then rotate the threaded control cable housing until there is 0.12–0.16 in. free-play at the release lever.

Accord slave cylinder (arrow)

Closeup of Accord slave cylinder showing lock nut and adjusting nut

On Accord models, adjustment is made at the slave cylinder. Simply loosen the lock nut and turn the adjusting nut until the correct free play is obtained. Free play at the clutch pedal should not exceed ½ in.

PEDAL RELEASE HEIGHT

You will probably need two people to perform this measurement; one to start and run the car, and the other to observe and measure.

To check the pedal release height:

a. Raise the front wheels off the ground and support the car with safety stands;

b. Place the transmission in Fourth gear;

c. Depress the clutch pedal and start the engine;

d. Release the clutch pedal until the front wheels begin to turn and measure the pedal height at this point, from the floor mat to the center of the pedal. The height should be over 1.18 in. (30 mm). If free-play and pedal height are properly adjusted, but the release height is not within specifications, then clutch components are damaged.

Clutch Master Cylinder

REMOVAL AND INSTALLATION

Accord CVCC

1. The clutch master cylinder is located on the firewall.

2. After locating the master cylinder, remove the hydraulic line to the slave cylinder. Either plug the port to prevent fluid escaping, or remove the brake fluid from the reservoir prior to this step.

3. Remove the pin which attaches the master cylinder rod to the clutch pedal arm. The rod is located under the instrument panel.

4. Remove the two bolts which retain the master cylinder to the firewall or the power booster.

5. Remove the master cylinder.

6. Installation is the reverse of removal.

OVERHAUL

1. Remove the snap ring which retains the stopper plate.

2. Once the snap ring is removed, use compressed air to remove the piston assembly. Note the order of all components. The piston assembly is in two parts—the piston itself and the spring assembly.

3. Check the inside of the cylinder bore for rust, pitting, or scratching. Light scores or scratches can be removed with a brake cylinder hone. If the bore won't clean up with a few passes of the hone, the entire cylinder will have to be replaced.

4. Replace the interior components with new ones. Overhaul kits will simply be two pieces—a new piston and a new spring assembly. Reassemble them in the correct order. Coat the inside of the cylinder with brake fluid before installing the parts.

5. Install the cylinder and bleed the system.

Clutch Slave Cylinder

REMOVAL AND INSTALLATION

The slave cylinder is retained by two bolts. To remove the cylinder, simply disconnect the hydraulic line, remove the return spring and remove the bolts. Installation is the reverse of removal. Bleed the system after installation.

OVERHAUL

1. There is little you can do to the slave cylinder other than replace the piston and seal inside the cylinder.

2. Blow the piston out of the cylinder with compressed air. The seal will probably come out with it.

3. Once the piston and seal are removed, check the inside of the cylinder bore for pit-

ting, rust or scratching. The bore can be honed, but it's probably not worth the effort. A new slave cylinder would make more sense.

AUTOMATIC TRANSMISSION

Understanding Automatic Transmissions

The automatic transmission allows engine torque and power to be transmitted to the rear wheels within a narrow range of engine operating speeds. The transmission will allow the engine to turn fast enough to produce plenty of power and torque at very low speeds, while keeping it at a sensible rpm at high vehicle speeds. The transmission performs this job entirely without driver assistance. The transmission uses a light fluid as the medium for the transmission of power. This fluid also works in the operation of various hydraulic control circuits and as a lubricant. Because the transmission fluid performs all of these three functions, trouble within the unit can easily travel from one part to another. For this reason, and because of the complexity and unusual operating principles of the transmission, a very sound understanding of the basic principles of operation will simplify troubleshooting.

THE TORQUE CONVERTER

The torque converter replaces the conventional clutch. It has three functions:

1. It allows the engine to idle with the vehicle at a standstill—even with the transmission in gear.

2. It allows the transmission to shift from range to range smoothly, without requiring that the driver close the throttle during the shift.

3. It multiplies engine torque to an increasing extent as vehicle speed drops and throttle opening is increased. This has the effect of making the transmission more responsive and reduces the amount of shifting required.

The torque converter is a metal case which is shaped like a sphere that has been flattened on opposite sides. It is bolted to the rear end of the engine's crankshaft. Generally, the entire metal case rotates at engine speed and serves as the engine's flywheel.

The case contains three sets of blades. One set is attached directly to the case. This set

forms the torus or pump. Another set is directly connected to the output shaft, and forms the turbine. The third set is mounted on a hub which, in turn, is mounted on a stationary shaft through a one-way clutch. This third set is known as the stator.

A pump, which is driven by the converter hub at engine speed, keeps the torque converter full of transmission fluid at all times. Fluid flows continuously through the unit to provide cooling.

Under low-speed acceleration, the torque converter functions as follows:

The torus is turning faster than the turbine. It picks up fluid at the center of the converter and, through centrifugal force, slings it outward. Since the outer edge of the converter moves faster than the portions at the center, the fluid picks up speed.

The fluid then enters the outer edge of the turbine blades. It then travels back toward the center of the converter case along the turbine blades. In impinging upon the turbine blades, the fluid loses the energy picked up in the torus.

If the fluid were now to immediately be returned directly into the torus, both halves of the converter would have to turn at approximately the same speed at all times, and torque input and output would both be the same.

In flowing through the torus and turbine, the fluid picks up two types of flow, or flow in two separate directions. It flows through the turbine blades, and it spins with the engine. The stator, whose blades are stationary when the vehicle is being accelerated at low speeds, converts one type of flow into another. Instead of allowing the fluid to flow straight back into the torus, the stator's curved blades turn the fluid almost 90° toward the direction of rotation of the engine. Thus the fluid does not flow as fast toward the torus, but is already spinning when the torus picks it up. This has the effect of allowing the torus to turn much faster than the turbine. This difference in speed may be compared to the difference in speed between the smaller and larger gears in any gear train. The result is that engine power output is higher, and engine torque is multiplied.

As the speed of the turbine increases, the fluid spins faster and faster in the direction of engine rotation. As a result, the ability of the stator to redirect the fluid flow is reduced. Under cruising conditions, the stator is eventually forced to rotate on its one-way clutch in the direction of engine rotation. Under these conditions, the torque converter begins to behave almost like a solid shaft, with the torus and turbine speeds being almost equal.

THE PLANETARY GEARBOX

The ability of the torque converter to multiply engine torque is limited. Also, the unit tends to be more efficient when the turbine is rotating at relatively high speeds. Therefore, a planetary gearbox is used to carry the power output the turbine to the driveshaft to make the most efficient use of the converter.

Planetary gears function very similarly to conventional transmission gears. However, their construction is different in that three elements make up one gear system, and in that all three elements are different from one another. The three elements are: an outer gear that is shaped like a hoop, with teeth cut into the inner surface; a sun gear, mounted on a shaft and located at the very center of the outer gear; and a set of three planet gears, held by pins in a ring-like planet carrier and meshing with both the sun gear and the outer gear. Either the outer gear or the sun gear may be held stationary, providing more than one possible torque multiplication factor for each set of gears. Also, if all three gears are forced to rotate at the same speed, the gearset forms, in effect, a solid shaft.

Most modern automatics use the planetary gears to provide either a single reduction ratio of about 1.8:1, and an intermediate of about 1.5:1. Bands and clutches are used to hold various portions of the gearsets to the transmission case or to the shaft on which they are mounted. Shifting is accomplished, then, by changing the portion of each planetary gearset which is held to the transmission case or to the shaft.

THE SERVOS AND ACCUMULATORS

The servos are hydraulic pistons and cylinders. They resemble the hydraulic actuators used on many familiar machines, such as bulldozers. Hydraulic fluid enters the cylinder, under pressure, and forces the piston to move to engage the band or clutches.

The accumulators are used to cushion the engagement of the servos. The transmission fluid must pass through the accumulator on the way to the servo. The accumulator housing contains a thin piston which is sprung away from the discharge passage of the accumulator. When fluid passes through the

accumulator on the way to the servo, it must move the piston against spring pressure, and this action smooths out the action of the servo.

THE HYDRAULIC CONTROL SYSTEM

The hydraulic pressure used to operate the servos comes from the main transmission oil pump. This fluid is channeled to the various servos through the shift valves. There is generally a manual shift valve which is operated by the transmission selector lever and an automatic shift valve for each automatic upshift the transmission provides: i.e., two-speed automatics have a low-high shift valve, while three-speeds will have a 1–2 valve, and a 2–3 valve.

There are two pressures which effect the operation of these valves. One is the governor pressure which is affected by vehicle speed. The other is the modulator pressure which is affected by intake manifold vacuum or throttle position. Governor pressure rises with an increase in vehicle speed, and modulator pressure rises as the throttle is opened wider. By responding to these two pressures, the shift valves cause the upshift points to be delayed with increased throttle opening to make the best use of the engine's power output.

Most transmissions also make use of an auxiliary circuit for downshifting. This circuit may be actuated by the throttle linkage or the vacuum line which actuates the modulator, or by a cable or solenoid. It applies pressure to a special downshift surface on the shift valve or valves.

The transmission modulator also governs the line pressure, used to actuate the servos. In this way, the clutches and bands will be actuated with a force matching the torque output of the engine.

Automatic Transmission Troubleshooting

FAILURE TO UPSHIFT

Low fluid level
Incorrect linkage adjustment
Faulty or sticking governor
Leaking valve body
Leak in vacuum lines to vacuum modulator
Faulty modulator
Stuck shift valve, detent cable, or downshift solenoid
Faulty clutches, ervos, or oil pump

FAILURE TO DOWNSHIFT (KICK-DOWN)

Improperly adjusted throttle linkage
Sticking downshift linkage or cable
Faulty modulator
Stuck shift valve
Faulty downshift solenoid or wiring
Faulty detent valve
Faulty clutches or servos

HIGH LINE PRESSURE

Vacuum leak or modulator leak or malfunction

FAULTY PRESSURE REGULATOR

Improper pressure regulator adjustment
Faulty valve body

LOW LINE PRESSURE

Low fluid level
Faulty modulator
Faulty oil pump
Clogged strainer
Faulty seals in accumulators or clutches
Faulty transmission case

SLIPPAGE

Low oil level
Low line pressure (see above)
Faulty accumulator seals
Faulty servo piston seals
Clutch plates worn or burned
Incorrect shift linkage adjustment

NOISE

Low oil level
Clogged strainer
Faulty oil pump
Water in oil
Valve body malfunction (buzzing)

HONDAMATIC

Shift Lever

INSPECTION

1. Pull up fully on the parking brake lever and run the engine at idle speed, while depressing the brake pedal.
CAUTION: *Be sure to check continually for car movement.*
2. By moving the shift selector lever

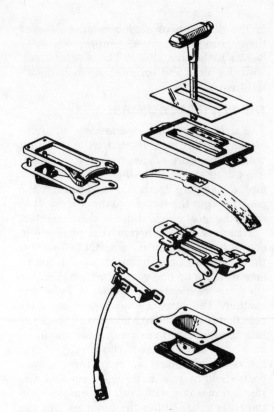

Exploded view of automatic transmission shift lever control

slowly forward and backward from the "N" position, make sure that the distance between the "N" and the points where the D clutch is engaged for the "2" and "R" positions are the same. The D clutch engaging point is just before the slight response is felt. The reverse gears will make a noise when the clutch engages. If the distances are not the same, then adjustment is necessary.

ADJUSTMENT

1. Remove the center console retaining screws, and pull away the console to expose the shift control cable and turnbuckle.
2. Adjust the length of the control cable by turning the turnbuckle, located at the front bottom of the shift lever assembly. After adjustment, the cable and turnbuckle should twist toward the left (driver's) side of the car when shifted toward the "2" position and toward the right-side when shifted into the R position.

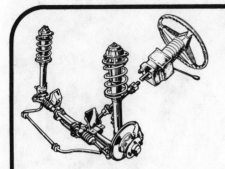

7

Suspension and Steering

FRONT SUSPENSION

All models use a MacPherson strut type front suspension. Each steering knuckle is suspended by a lower control arm at the bottom and a combined coil spring/shock absorber unit at the top. A front stabilizer bar, mounted between each lower control arm and the body, doubles as a locating rod for the suspension. Caster and camber are not adjustable and are fixed by the location of the strut assemblies in their respective sheet metal towers.

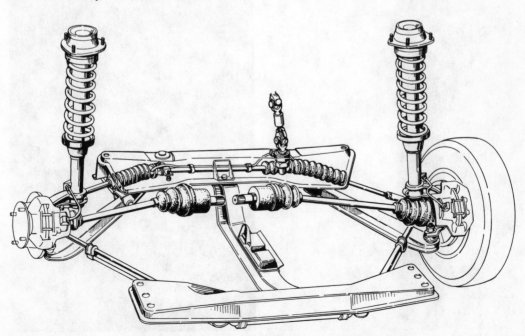

Assembled view of front suspension and steering assemblies

Front Strut Assembly

REMOVAL AND INSTALLATION

1. Raise the front of the car and support it with safety stands. Remove the front wheels.

2. Disconnect the brake pipe at the strut and remove the brake hose retaining clip.

3. Loosen the bolt on the knuckle that retains the lower end of the shock absorber. Push down firmly while tapping it with a hammer until the knuckle is free of the strut.

4. Remove the three nuts retaining the

Upper strut removal points

Front strut

Lower strut retaining bolt (arrow)

upper end of the strut and remove the strut from the car.

5. To install, reverse the removal procedure. Be sure to properly match the mating surface of the strut and the knuckle notch.

DISASSEMBLY

1. Disassemble the strut according to the procedure given in the rear strut disassembly section.

2. Remove the rubber cover and remove the center retaining nuts.

3. Slowly release the compressor and remove the spring.

4. Remove the upper mounting cap, washers, thrust plates, bearings and bushing.

NOTE: *Before discarding any parts, check a parts list to determine which parts are available as replacements.*

5. To reassemble, first pull the strut shaft all the way out, hold it in this position and slide the rubber bumper down the shaft to the strut body. This should hold the shaft in the extended position.

6. Install the spring and its top plate. Make sure the spring seats properly.

7. Install the partially assembled strut in the compressor. Compress the strut until the shaft protrudes through the top plate about 1 in.

8. Now install the bushings, thrust plates, top mounting cap washers and retaining nuts in the reverse order of removal.

9. Once the retaining nut is installed, release the tension on the compressor and loosen the thumbscrew on the bottom plate. Separate the bottom plates and remove the compressor.

INSPECTION

1. Check for wear or damage to bushings and needle bearings.

2. Check for oil leaks from the struts.

3. Check all rubber parts for wear or damage.

4. Bounce the car to check shock absorbing effectiveness. The car should continue to bounce for no more than two cycles.

Lower Ball Joints
INSPECTION

Check ball joint play as follows:

a. Raise the front of the car and support it with safety stands;

b. Clamp a dial indicator onto the lower

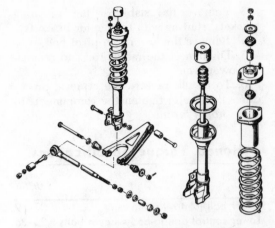

Exploded view of lower control arm assembly

control arm and place the indicator tip on the knuckle, near the ball joint;

c. Place a pry bar between the lower control arm and the knuckle. Replace the ball joint if the play exceeds 0.020 in.

REMOVAL AND INSTALLATION

1. Raise the car and support it with safety stands.

2. Remove the front wheel.

3. Pull out the cotter pin holding the ball joint castle nut and remove the nut.

4. Remove the ball joint from the knuckle using a ball joint remover. This is done by hitting the end of the long wedge, thus forcing the ball joint down and out.

5. To install, reverse the removal procedure. Tighten the ball joint nut to 29–35 ft lbs of torque. Be sure to grease the ball joint.

LUBRICATION

1. Remove the screw plug from the bottom of the ball joint and install a grease nipple.

2. Lubricate the ball joint with NLGI No. 2 multipurpose type grease.

3. Remove the nipple and reinstall the screw plug.

4. Repeat for the other ball joint.

Lower Control Arm and Stabilizer Bar
REMOVAL AND INSTALLATION

1. Raise the front of the car and support it with safety stands. Remove the front wheels.

2. Disconnect the lower arm ball joint as described above. Be careful not to damage the seal.

3. Remove the stabilizer bar retaining brackets, starting with the center brackets.

4. Remove the lower arm pivot bolt.

5. Disconnect the radius rod and remove the lower arm.

6. To install, reverse the removal procedure. Be sure to tighten the components to their proper torque.

Honda Torque Specifications

Part(s)	Torque (ft lbs)
Lower ball joint retaining nut	22–29
Lower control arm-to-body mount bolts	25–36
Front radius rod-to-knuckle bolt	25–36
Rear radius rod-to-carrier bolt	40–54
Rear radius rod-to-body bolt	25–36
Front stabilizer mount bolts	5–9
Strut center nut (front and rear)	40–50
Strut to body retaining bolts (front and rear)	7–12
Front strut-to-knuckle retaining bolt	36–43
Rear strut-to-carrier mount bolts	26–35
Rear strut-to-control arm bolt	36–47

Steering Knuckles

REMOVAL AND INSTALLATION

1. Raise the front of the car and support it with safety stands. Remove the front wheel.

2. Remove the spindle nut cotter pin and the spindle nut.

3. Remove the two bolts retaining the brake caliper and remove the caliper from the knuckle. Do not let the caliper hang by the brake hose, support it with a length of wire.

NOTE: *In case it is necessary to remove the disc, hub, bearings and/or outer dust seal, use Steps 4 and 5 given below. You will need a hydraulic press for this (see Chapter 9). If this is unnecessary, omit Steps 4 and 5.*

4. Install a hub puller attachment against the hub with the lug nuts.

5. Attach a slide hammer in the center hole of the attachment and pull out the hub, with the disc attached, from the knuckle.

6. Remove the tie-rod from the knuckle using the ball joint remover. Use care not to damage the ball joint seals.

7. Remove the lower arm from the knuckle using the ball joint remover.

8. Loosen the lockbolt which retains the strut in the knuckle. Tap the top of the knuckle with a hammer and slide it off the shock.

9. Remove the knuckle and hub, if still attached, by sliding the driveshaft out of the hub.

10. To install, reverse the removal procedure. If the hub was removed, refer to Chapter 9 (Brake Disc Removal), for procedures with the dydraulic press. Be sure to visually check the knuckle for visible signs of wear or damage and to check the condition of the inner bearing dust seals.

Wheel Alignment

Front wheel alignment (also known as front end geometry) is the position of the front wheels relative to each other and to the vehicle. Correct alignment must be maintained to provide safe, accurate steering, vehicle stability, and minimum tire wear. The factors which determine wheel alignment are interdependent. Therefore, when one of the factors is adjusted, the others must be adjusted to compensate.

CASTER ANGLE

Caster angle is the number of degrees that a line, drawn through the center of the upper and lower ball joints and viewed from the side, can be tilted forward or backward. Positive caster means that the top of the upper ball joint is tilted toward the rear of the car, and negative caster means that it is tilted toward the front. A car with a slightly positive caster setting will have its lower ball joint pivot slightly ahead of the tire's center. This will assist the directional stability of the car by causing a drag at the bottom center of the wheel when it turns, thereby resisting the turn and tending to hold the wheel steady in whatever direction the car is pointed. Therefore, the car is less susceptible to crosswinds and road surface deviations. A car with too much (positive) caster will be hard to steer and shimmy at low speeds. A car with insufficient (negative) caster may tend to be unstable at high speeds and may respond erratically when the brakes are applied.

CAMBER ANGLE

Camber angle is the number of degrees that the wheel itself is tilted from a vertical line when viewed from the front. Positive camber means that the top of the wheel is slanted

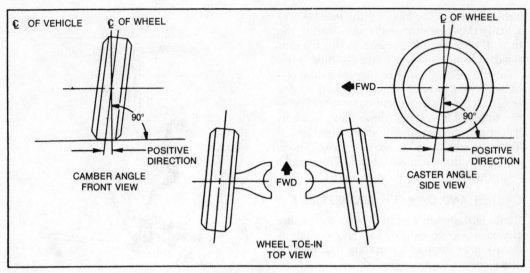

Caster, camber, and toe-in

away from the car, while negative camber means that it is tilted toward the car. Ordinarily, a car will have a slight positive camber when unloaded. Then, when the car is loaded and rolling down the road, the wheels will just about be vertical. If you started with no camber at all, then loading the car would produce a negative camber. Excessive camber (either positive or negative) will produce rapid tire wear, since one side of the tire will be more heavily loaded than the other side.

STEERING AXIS INCLINATION

Steering axis inclination is the number of degrees that a line drawn through the upper and lower ball joints and viewed from the front, is tilted to the left or the right. This, in combination with caster, is responsible for the directional stability and self-centering of the steering. As the steering knuckle swings from lock to lock, the spindle generates an arc, causing the car to be raised when it is turned from the straight-ahead position. The reason the car body must rise is straightforward: since the wheel is in contact with the ground, it cannot move down. However, when it is swung away from the straight-ahead position, it must move either up or down (due to the arc generated by the steering knuckle). Not being able to move down, it must move up. Then, the weight of the car acts against this lift, and attempts to return the spindle to the straight-ahead position when the steering wheel is released.

TOE-IN

Toe-in is the difference (in inches) between the front and the rear of the front tires. On a car with toe-in, the distance between the front wheels is less at the front than at the rear. Toe-in is normally only a few fractions of an inch, and is necessary to ensure parallel rolling of the front wheels and to prevent excessive tire wear. As the car is driven at increasingly faster speeds, the steering linkage has a tendency to expand slightly, thereby allowing the front wheels to turn out and away from each other. Therefore, initially setting the front wheels so that they are pointing slightly inward (toe-in), allows them to turn straight ahead when the car is underway.

INCLUDED ANGLE

The included angle is the sum of the steering axis inclination and the camber angle. Included angle determines the point of intersection of the wheel and the steering axis center lines. This is important because this determines, in turn, whether the wheel will toe out or toe in. When the point of intersection is below the road surface, the wheel will toe out. When the intersection point is above the road surface, the wheel tends to toe in.

TOE-OUT (DURING TURNS)

The steering is designed so that the inner wheel turns more sharply toward the center of the turn than the outer wheel turns. This compensates for the fact that the inner wheel actually travels a shorter distance during the turn. Designing the steering in this manner avoids having the front wheels fight each other, thus improving tire life and aiding stability. Where toe-out is to be checked, angles are given for the inner and outer wheel relative to travel in a straight line. Thus, in a left-hand turn, the left (inner) wheel might be 24° from straight ahead, and the right (outer) wheel 20° from straight ahead. For a right turn, the figures would be reversed.

CASTER AND CAMBER ADJUSTMENT

Caster and camber cannot be adjusted on any Honda. If caster, camber or kingpin angle is incorrect or front end parts are damaged or worn, they must be replaced.

TOE-IN ADJUSTMENT

Toe-in (or toe-out) can be adjusted on all Hondas by loosening the locknuts at each end of the tie-rods. To increase toe-out, turn the right tie-rod in the direction of forward wheel rotation and turn the left tie-rod in the opposite direction. Turn both tie-rods an equal amount until toe-out becomes 0.039 in. (1 mm).

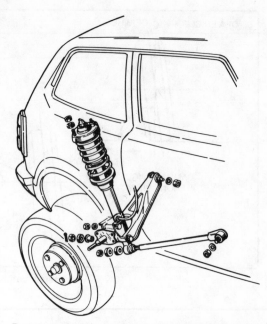

Rear suspension—sedan and hatchback models

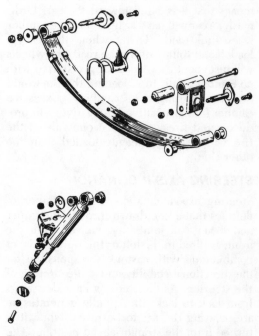

Front Wheel Alignment

Year	Model	Caster Pref Setting ± ½° (deg)	Camber Pref Setting ± ½° (deg)	Toe-Out (in.)	Steering Axle Inclination (deg)
1973–78	Sedan	1¾P	½P	0.039	8.9
1975–78	Station Wagon	2P*	½P	0.039	9.3
1976–78	Accord	2P	½P	0.039	12.10

* 1976 models—1P; 1977–78 models—½P

Exploded view of rear suspension—station wagon models

REAR SUSPENSION

All Civic sedan and hatchback models utilize an independent MacPherson strut arrangement for each rear wheel. Each suspension unit consits of a combined coil spring/shock absorber strut, a lower control arm, and a radius rod.

Station wagon models use a more conventional leaf spring rear supension with a solid rear axle. The springs are three-leaf, semi-elliptic types located longitudinally with a pair of telescopic shock absorbers to control rebound. The solid axle and leaf springs allow for a greater load carrying capacity for the wagon over the sedan.

Strut Assembly

REMOVAL AND INSTALLATION

1. Raise the rear of the car and support it with safety stands.

2. Remove the rear wheel.

3. Disconnect the brake line at the shock absorber. Remove the retaining clip and separate the brake hose from the shock absorber.

4. Disconnect the parking brake cable at the backing plate lever.

5. Remove the lower strut retaining bolt and hub carrier pivot bolt. To remove the pivot bolt, you first have to remove the castle nut and its cotter pin.

6. Remove the two upper strut retaining nuts and remove the strut from the car.

7. To install, reverse the removal procedure. Be sure to install the top of the strut in the body first. After installation, bleed the brake lines (see Chapter 9).

DISASSEMBLY

1. Use a coil spring compressor to disassemble the strut. When assembling the compressor onto the strut, the long studs should be installed so that they are flush with the bottom plate and also flush with the retaining nut on the top end. The adjustable plate in the center cup should be screwed all the way in.

2. Insert the strut in the compressor and compress the strut about 2 in. Then remove the center retaining nut.

3. Loosen the compressor and remove the strut.

4. Remove the top plate, rubber protector, spring and rubber bumper.

5. To assemble, reverse the removal procedure after checking the shock for oil leaks and all rubber parts for damage, wear or deterioration.

Rear Control Arm

REMOVAL AND INSTALLATION

All Except Wagon

1. Remove the control arm outboard and inboard pivot bolts.

2. Pull the inboard side of the arm down until it clears the body.

3. Slide the arm towards the center of the car until it is free of the hub carrier.

4. To install, reverse the removal procedure. Be sure to check the bushings at each

Rear control arm

end of the control arm and the control arm for damage and wear.

REAR WHEEL ALIGNMENT

Toe-in is adjustable on the rear wheels of all models except the station wagon. On the

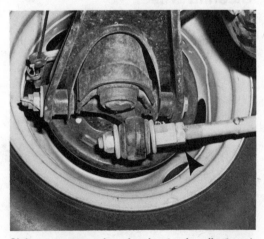

Civic rear suspension showing toe-in adjustment point (arrow)

Rear toe-in adjustment point on Accord (arrow)

Civic, toe-in is adjusted by means of a threaded radius rod. On the Accord, a cam-type adjuster is used. Toe-in is held to zero on the Civic, and 1 mm (0.039 in.) on the Accord.

STEERING

All Hondas are equipped with rack and pinion steering. Movement of the steering wheel is transmitted through the linkage to the input shaft, which in turn is connected to the pinion gear. The pinion gear engages the rack, and rotation of the pinion, transmitted from the input shaft, causes the rack to move laterally.

Steering Wheel
REMOVAL AND INSTALLATION

1. Remove the steering wheel pad by lifting it off.

2. Remove the steering wheel retaining nut. Gently hit the backside of each of the steering wheel spokes with equal force from the palms of your hands.

CAUTION: *Avoid hitting the wheel or the shaft with excessive force. Damage to the shaft could result.*

3. Intallation is the reverse of the removal procedure. Be sure to tighten the steering wheel nut to the specified torque.

Turn Signal Switch
REMOVAL AND INSTALLATION

1. Remove the steering wheel.

2. Disconnect the column wiring harness and coupler.

3. Remove the four attaching bolts (remove the upper two bolts first), holding the steering column to the instrument panel and lower the column.

CAUTION: *Be careful not to damage the steering column or shaft.*

4. Remove the upper and lower column covers.

5. Loosen the screw on the turn signal switch cam nut and lightly tap its head to per-

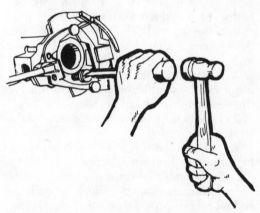

Loosening the turn signal cam nut screw

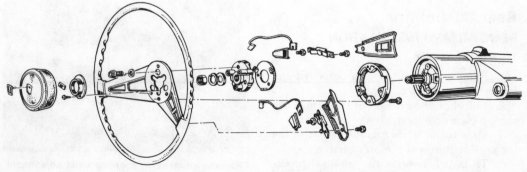

Exploded view of steering wheel and related parts

mit the cam nut to loosen. Then remove the turn signal switch assembly and the steering shaft upper bushing.

6. To assemble and install, reverse the above procedure. When installing the turn signal switch assembly, engage the locating tab on the switch with the notch in the steering column. The steering shaft upper bushing should be installed with the flat side facing the upper side of the column. The alignment notch for the turn signal switch will be centered on the flat side of the bushing.

NOTE: *If the cam nut has been removed, be sure to install it with the small end up.*

Ignition Switch

REMOVAL AND INSTALLATION

1. Remove the steering shaft hanger retaining bolts and lower the steering shaft from the instrument panel to expose the ignition switch.

2. Remove the steering column housing upper and lower covers.

3. Disconnect the ignition switch wiring at the couplers.

4. The ignition switch assembly is held onto the column by two shear bolts. Remove these bolts, using a drill, to separate and remove the ignition switch.

5. To install, reverse the removal procedure. You will have to replace the shear bolts with new ones.

Steering Gear

TESTING

1. Remove the dust seal ellows retaining bands and slide the dust seals off the left and right side of the gearbox housing.

2. Turn the front wheels full left and, using your hand, attempt to move the steering rack in an up-down direction.

3. Repeat with the wheel turned full right.

4. If any movement is felt, the steering gearbox must be adjusted.

ADJUSTMENT

1. Make sure that the rack is well lubricated.

2. Loosen the rack guide adjusting locknut.

3. Tighten the adjusting screw just to the point where the front wheels cannot be turned by hand.

4. Back off the adjusting screw 45 degrees

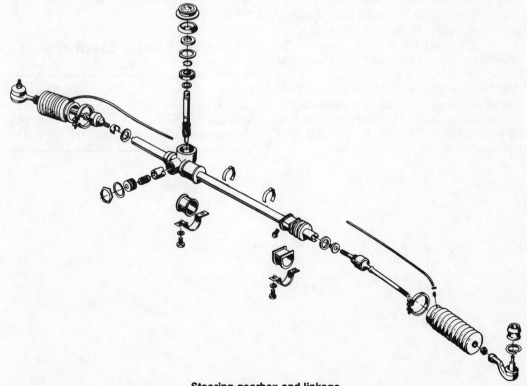

Steering gearbox and linkage

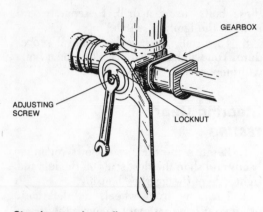

Steering gearbox adjustment

and hold it in that position while adjusting the locknut.

5. Recheck the play, and then move the wheels lock-to-lock, to make sure that the rack moves freely.

6. Check the steering force by first raising the front wheels and then placing them in a straight-ahead position. Turn the steering wheel with a spring scale to check the steering force. Steering force should be no more than 3.3 lbs.

Tie-Rods

REMOVAL AND INSTALLATION

1. Raise the front of the car and support it with safety stands. Remove the front wheels.

2. Use a special ball joint remover. To remove the tie-rod from the knuckle on the Civic:

3. Remove the tie-rod dust seal bellows clamps and move the rubber bellows on the tie-rod and rack joints. On the Civic, you first have to disconnect the air tube at the dust seal joint.

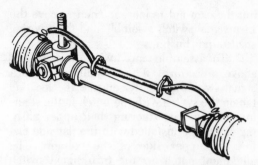

Separate the air tube from the dust seal bellows

4. Straighten the tie-rod lockwasher tabs at the tie-rod-to-rack joint and remove the tie-rod by turning it with a wrench.

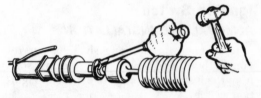

Tie-rod lockwasher removal

5. To install, reverse the removal procedure. Always use a new tie-rod lockwasher during reassembly. Fit the locating lugs into the slots on the rack and bend the outer edge of the washer over the flat part of the rod, after the tie-rod nut has been properly tightened.

Steering Torque Specifications
(ft lbs)

Tie-rod end locknut	29.0–35.0
Tie-rod ball joint nut	29.0–35.0
Bask guide locknut	29.0–36.0
Steering wheel retaining nut(s)	22.0–33.0

8

Brakes

BRAKE SYSTEM

Understanding the Brakes

HYDRAULIC SYSTEM

The brake pedal operates a hydraulic system that is used for 2 reasons. First, fluid under pressure can be carried to all parts of the car by small hoses or metal lines without taking up a lot of room or causing routing problems. Second, the hydraulic fluid offers a great mechanical advantage—little foot pressure is required on the pedal, but a great deal of pressure is generated at the wheels.

The brake pedal is linked to a piston in the brake master cylinder, which is filled with hydraulic brake fluid. The master cylinder consists of a cylinder, containing a small piston, and a fluid reservoir.

Modern master cylinders are actually 2 separate cylinders. These systems are called a dual circuit, because the front cylinder is connected to the front brakes and the rear cylinder to the rear brakes. (Some cars are connected diagonally.) The 2 cylinders are actually separated, allowing for emergency stopping power should one part of the system fail.

The entire hydraulic system from the master cylinder to the wheels is full of hydraulic brake fluid. When the brake pedal is depressed, the pistons in the master cylinder

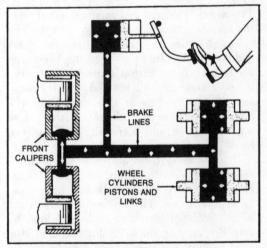

Hydraulic system schematic

are forced to move, exerting tremendous force on the fluid in the lines. The fluid has nowhere to go, and forces the wheel cylinder piston (drum brakes) or caliper pistons (disc brakes) to exert pressure on the brake shoes or pads. The resulting friction between the brake shoe and wheel drum or the brake pad and disc slows the car down and eventually stops it.

Also attached to the brake pedal is a switch which lights the brake lights as the pedal is depressed. The lights stay on until the brake pedal is released and returns to its normal position.

Each wheel cylinder in a drum brake system contains 2 pistons, one at either end, which push outward in opposite directions. In disc brake systems, the wheel cylinders are part of the caliper (there can be as many as 4 or as few as 1). Whether disc or drum type, all pistons use some type of rubber seal to prevent leakage around the piston, and a rubber dust boot seals the outer ends of the wheel cylinders against dirt and moisture.

When the brake pedal is released, a spring pushes the master cylinder pistons back to their normal position. Check valves in the master cylinder piston allow fluid to flow toward the wheel cylinders or calipers as the piston returns. Then as the brake shoe return springs pull the brake shoes back to the released position, excess fluid returns to the master cylinder through compensating ports, which have been uncovered as the pistons move back. Any fluid that has leaked from the system will also be replaced through the compensating ports.

All dual circuit brake systems use a switch to activate a light, warning of brake failure. The switch is located in a valve mounted near the master cylinder. A piston in the valve receives pressure on each end from the front and rear brake circuits. When the pressures are balanced, the piston remains stationary, but when one circuit has a leak, greater pressure during the application of the brakes will force the piston to one side or the other, closing the switch and activating the warning light.

Disc brake systems also have a metering valve to prevent the front disc brakes from engaging before the rear brakes have contacted the drums. This ensures that the front brakes will not normally be used alone to stop the car. Approportioning valve is also used to limit pressure to the rear brakes to prevent rear wheel lock-up during hard braking.

DRUM BRAKES

Drum brakes use two brake shoes mounted on a stationary backing plate. These shoes are positioned inside a circular cast iron drum which rotates with the wheel assembly. The shoes are held in place by springs; this allows them to slide toward the drums (when they are applied) while keeping the linings and drums in alignment. The shoes are actuated by a wheel cylinder which is usually mounted at the top of the backing plate. When the

brakes are applied, hydraulic pressure forces the wheel cylinder's two actuating links outward. Since these links bear directly against the top of the brake shoes, the tops of the shoes are then forced outward against the inner side of the drum. This action forces the bottoms of the two shoes to contact the brake drum by rotating the entire assembly slightly (known as servo action). When pressure within the wheel cylinder is relieved, return springs pull the shoes back away from the drum.

Most modern drum brakes are designed to self-adjust during application when the vehicle is moving in reverse. This motion causes both shoes to rotate very slightly with the drum, rocking an adjusting lever. The self-adjusters are only intended to compensate for normal wear. Although the adjustment is "automatic," there is a definite method to actuate the self-adjuster, which is done during normal driving. Driving the car in reverse and applying the brakes usually activates the automatic adjusters. If the brake pedal was low, you should be able to feel an increase in the height of the brake pedal.

DISC BRAKES

Instead of the traditional expanding brakes that press outward against a circular drum, disc brake systems utilize a cast iron disc with brake pads positioned on either side of it. Braking effect is achieved in a manner similar to the way you would squeeze a spinning disc between your fingers. The disc (rotor) is a one-piece casting with cooling fins between the two braking surfaces. This enables air to circulate between the braking surfaces making them less sensitive to heat buildup and more resistant to fade. Dirt and water do not affect braking action since contaminants are thrown off by the centrifugal action of the rotor or scraped off by the pads. Also, the equal clamping action of the two brake pads tends to ensure uniform, straightline stops. All disc brakes are inherently self-adjusting.

There are three general types of disc brake:

1) A fixed caliper, four-piston type.
2) A floating caliper, single piston type.
3) A sliding caliper, single piston type.

The fixed caliper design uses two pistons mounted on either side of the rotor (in each side of the caliper). The caliper is mounted rigidly and does not move.

The sliding and floating designs are quite

similar and often considered as one. The pad on the inside of the rotor is moved into contact with the rotor by hydraulic force. The caliper, which is not held in a fixed position, moves slightly, bringing the outside pad into contact with the rotor. There are various methods of attaching floating calipers; some pivot at the bottom or top, and some slide on mounting bolts.

POWER BRAKE BOOSTERS

Power brakes operate just as standard brake systems except in the actuation of the master cylinder pistons. A vacuum diaphragm is located behind the master cylinder and assists the driver in applying the brakes, reducing both the effort and travel he must put into moving the brake pedal.

The vacuum diaphragm housing is connected to the intake manifold by a vacuum hose. A check valve at the point where the hose enters the diaphragm housing, ensures that during periods of low manifold vacuum brake assist vacuum will not be lost.

Depressing the brake pedal closes off the vacuum source and allows atmospheric pressure to enter on one side of the diaphragm. This causes the master cylinder pistons to move and apply the brakes. When the brake pedal is released, vacuum is applied to both sides of the diaphragm, and return springs return the diaphragm and master cylinder pistons to the released position. If the vacuum fails, the brake pedal rod will butt against the end of the master cylinder actuating rod, and direct mechanical application will occur as the pedal is depressed.

The hydraulic and mechanical problems that apply to conventional brake systems also apply to power brakes.

Honda uses a dual hydraulic system, with the brakes connected diagonally. In other words, the right front and left rear brakes are on the same hydraulic line and the left front and right rear are on the other line. This has the added advantage of front disc emergency braking, should either of the hydraulic systems fail. The diagonal rear brake serves to counteract the sway from single front disc braking.

A leading/trailing drum brake is used for the rear brakes, with disc brakes for the front. All Hondas are equipped with a brake warning light, which is activated when a defect in the brake system occurs.

Adjustments
BRAKE PEDAL FREE-PLAY

Free-play is the distance the pedal travels from the stop (brake light switch) until the pushrod actuates the master cylinder.

To check free-play, first measure the distance (with the carpet removed) from the floor to the brake pedal. Then disconnect the return spring and again measure the distance from the floor to the brake pedal. The difference between the two measurements is the pedal free-play. The specified free-play is 0.04–0.20 in. Free-play adjustment is made by loosening the locknut on the brake light switch and rotating the switch body until the specified clearance is obtained.

CAUTION: *If there is no free-play, the master cylinder pistons will not return to their stops. This can block the compensating ports, which will prevent the brake pads and linings from returning fully when the pedal is released. This will result in rapid brake burn-up. Free-play provides a safety factor against normal rubber swell and expansion or deflection of body parts and pedal linkage.*

REAR DRUM BRAKE ADJUSTMENT

1. Block the front wheels, release the parking brake and raise the rear of the car, supporting it with safety stands.
2. Depress the brake pedal two or three times and release.
3. The adjuster is located on the inboard

Drum brake adjustment

side, underneath the control arm. Turn the adjuster clockwise until the wheel no longer turns.

4. Back off the adjuster two (2) clicks and turn the wheel to see if the brake shoes are dragging. If they are dragging, back off the adjuster one more click.

FRONT DISC BRAKES

Front disc brakes require no adjustment, as hydraulic pressure maintains the proper brake pad-to-disc contact at all times.

NOTE: *Because of this, the brake fluid level should be checked regularly (see Chapter 1).*

HYDRAULIC SYSTEM

The hydraulic system is composed of the master cylinder and brake booster, the brake lines, the brake pressure differential valve(s), and the wheel cylinders (drum brakes) and calipers (disc brakes).

The master cylinder serves as a brake fluid reservoir and (along with the booster) as a hydraulic pump. Brake fluid is stored in the

Brake Troubleshooting

Problem & Possible Causes	Solution
Uneven braking	
1. Improper inflation of tire	Inflate properly
2. Water or oil on the brake pad surface or disc	Clean or replace
3. Worn or damaged (stain, rust) disc and drum	Correct by machining or replace
4. Poor contact of pad surface	Correct or replace
5. Carbonized or faulty pad	Replace
6. Loose caliper mounting bolt	Retighten
7. Malfunction of brake cylinder	Check and replace, if necessary
8. Improper tightening of wheel bearing	Retighten
9. Different pad material used on the left and right wheels	Replace
10. Improperly aligned front wheel	Realign
11. Clogged fluid pressure system	Clean
12. Improper action of caliper yoke	Clean and apply brake grease

Problem & Possible Causes	Solution
Dragging of one or both wheels	
1. No pedal play	Adjust
2. Weak or broken brake pedal return spring	Replace
3. Malfunction of pedal link system	Adjust
4. Clogged master cylinder return port	Repair
5. Poor action of caliper yoke	Apply brake grease
6. Loose wheel bearing	Retighten
7. Clogged fluid pressure system	Clean

Problem & Possible Causes	Solution
Excessive vibration or large pedal stroke	
1. Air present in fluid pressure system	Bleed brakes
2. Oil leakage from fluid pressure system	Repair
3. Faulty master cylinder piston, cup and seal	Replace
4. Insufficient brake oil	Replenish and bleed air
5. Worn front brake pad	Replace
6. Uneven worn front brake pad	Repair or replace
7. Malfunction of pedal link system	Adjust
8. Excessive run-out of brake disc	Adjust

Brake Troubleshooting

Problem & Possible Causes	Solution
Squealing noise	
1. Dragging of brake	Refer to the section on dragging
2. Worn brake pad	Replace
3. Deteriorated brake lining surface	Replace
4. Improperly installed shim	Correct
5. Foreign particles deposited on the fraction area of disc	Clean
6. Run-out or damaged disc	Correct by machining
7. Disc surfaces not parallel	Correct by machining or replace

Problem & Possible Causes	Solution
Insufficient braking force	
1. Worn brake pad	Replace
2. Water and oil on the brake pad contact area	Clean or replace
3. Insufficient brake fluid	Replenish
4. Air mixed into brake fluid	Bleed air
5. Oil leakage from the fluid pressure system	Check and repair
6. Oil leakage from master cylinder and caliper body seal	Check and replace
7. Incorrect brake pad	Replace with correct part
8. Deteriorated pad and poor contact	Repair or replace
9. Improper action of caliper yoke	Clean and apply brake grease
10. Clogged fluid pressure system	Check and clean

two sections of the master cylinder. Each section corresponds to each part of the dual braking system. This tandem master cylinder is required by Federal law as a safety device.

When the brake pedal is depressed, it moves a piston mounted in the bottom of the master cylinder. The movement of this piston creates hydraulic pressure in the master cylinder. This pressure is carried to the wheel cylinders or the calipers by brake lines, passing through the pressure differential or proportioning valve.

When the hydraulic pressure reaches the wheels, after the pedal has been depressed, it enters the wheel cylinders or calipers. Here it comes into contact with a piston or pistons. The hydraulic pressure causes the piston(s) to move, which moves the brake shoes or pads (disc brakes), causing them to come into contact with the drums or rotors (disc brakes). Friction between the brake shoes and the drums causes the car to slow down. There is a relationship between the amount of pressure that is applied to the brake pedal and the amount of force which moves the brake shoes against the drums. Therefore, the harder the brake pedal is depressed, the quicker the car will stop.

Since a hydraulic system is one which operates on fluids, air is a natural enemy of the brake system. Air in the hydraulic system retards the passage of hydraulic pressure from the master cylinder to the wheels. Anytime a hydraulic component below the master cylinder is opened or removed, the system must be bled of air to ensure proper operation. Air trapped in the hydraulic system can also cause the brake warning light to come on, even though the system has not failed. This is especially true after repairs have been performed on the system.

Master Cylinder
REMOVAL AND INSTALLATION

CAUTION: *Before removing the master cylinder, cover the body surfaces with fender covers and rags to prevent damage to painted surfaces by brake fluid.*

1. Disconnect the brake lines at the master cylinder.

2. Remove the master cylinder-to-vacuum booster attaching bolts and remove the master cylinder from the car.

3. To install, reverse the removal procedure. Before operating the car, you must bleed the brake system (see below).

DISASSEMBLY AND OVERHAUL

1. Remove the fluid reservoir caps and floats, and drain the reservoirs.

2. Loosen the retaining clamps and remove the reservoirs.

3. Remove the primary piston stop bolt.

4. Remove the piston retaining clip and washer, and remove the primary piston.

5. Wrap a rag around the end of the master cylinder, so that it blocks the bore. Hold your finger over the stop bolt hole and direct a small amount of compressed air into the primary outlet. This should slide the primary piston to the end of the master cylinder bore, so that it can be removed.

Removing retaining clip

Disassembled master cylinder

Piston removal

Closeup of master cylinder stop bolt

6. Remove the two union caps, washers, check valves and springs.

7. For overhaul, check the following:

    a. Clogged orifices in the pistons and cylinder;

    b. Damage to the reservoir attaching surface;

    c. Damage to the check valves;

    d. Wear or damage to the piston cups;

    e. The clearance between the master cylinder bore and the pistons. The clearance should be 0.0008–0.0050 in.

8. Assembly of the master cylinder is the reverse of the disassembly procedures. Be sure to check the following:

    a. The check valves and piston cups should be replaced when the master cylinder is assembled, regardless of their condition;

    b. Apply a thin coat of brake fluid to the pistons before installing. When installing the pistons, push in while rotating to prevent damage to the piston cups;

    c. Tighten the union cap and stop bolts securely.

BLEEDING

When it is necessary to flush the brake hydraulic system because of parts replacement or fluid contamination, the following procedure should be observed:

1. Loosen the wheel cylinder bleeder screw. Drain the brake fluid by pumping the brake pedal. Pump the pedal until all of the old fluid has been pumped out and replaced by new fluid.

2. The flushing procedure should be performed in the following sequence:

    a. Bleed the left front brake;

    b. Bleed the right rear brake;

    c. Bleed the right front brake;

    d. Bleed the left rear brake.

3. Bleed the back of the master cylinder before the front, through the two bleed valves. Fasten one end of a plastic tube onto the bleed valve and immerse the other end in a clear jar filled with brake fluid. When air bubbles cease to emerge from the end of the tubing, the bleeding is completed. Be sure to keep the fluid reservoir filled at all times during the bleeding process so air does not enter the system.

CAUTION: *Brake fluid is adversely affected by contamination from dirt, automative petroleum products and water. Contaminants can plug parts of the hydraulic system, causing rapid wear or swelling of rubber parts and lower the boiling point of the fluid. KEEP FLUID CLEAN.*

Bleeding the rear brakes

Vacuum Booster

INSPECTION

A preliminary check of the vacuum booster can be made as follows:

    a. Depress the brake pedal several times using normal pressure. Make sure that the pedal height does not vary;

    b. Hold the pedal in the depressed position and start the engine. The pedal should drop slightly;

    c. Hold the pedal in the above position and stop the engine. The pedal should stay in the depressed position for approximately 30 seconds;

    d. If the pedal does not drop when the engine is started or rises after the engine is stopped, the booster is not functioning properly.

REMOVAL AND INSTALLATION

1. Disconnect the vacuum hose at the booster.

2. Disconnect the brake lines at the master cylinder.

3. Remove the brake pedal-to-booster link pin and the four nuts retaining the booster. The pushrod and nuts are located inside the

Closeup of front bleeder

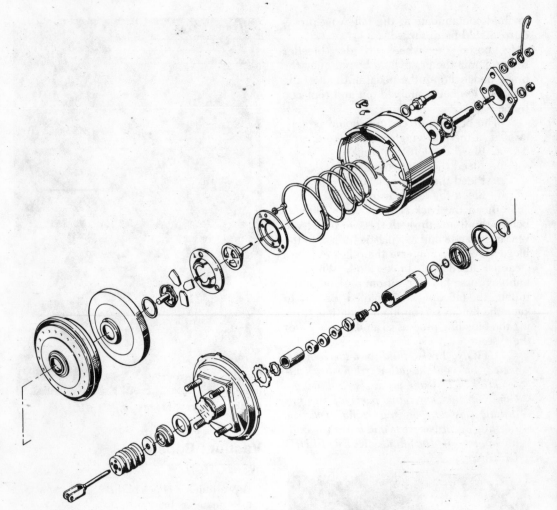

Exploded view of the vacuum booster

car on the passenger side, under the dash-board.

4. Remove the booster with the master cylinder attached.

5. To install, reverse the removal procedure. Don't forget to bleed the brake system before operating the car.

FRONT DISC BRAKES

The major components of the disc brake system are the brake pads, the caliper, and the rotor (disc). The caliper is similar in function to the wheel cylinder used with drum brakes, and the rotor is similar to the brake drum used in drum brakes.

The major difference between drum brakes and disc brakes is that with drum brakes, the wheel cylinder forces the brake shoes *out* against the brake drum to stop the

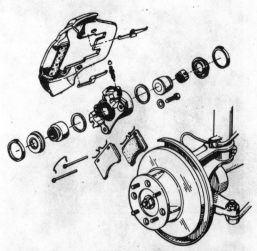

Exploded view of the disc brake components

car, while with disc brakes, the caliper forces the brake pads *in*ward to squeeze the rotor and stop the car. The biggest advantage of disc brakes over drum brakes is that the caliper and brake pads enclose only a small portion of the rotor, leaving the rest of it exposed to outside air. This aids in rapid heat dissipation, reducing brake fade, and throws off water fast, too.

Disc Brake Pads
REMOVAL AND INSTALLATION
All Models

1. After removing the wheel, remove the pad retaining clip which is fitted in the holes of the pad retaining pins.

2. Remove the two retaining pins and fitting springs with pliers. When removing

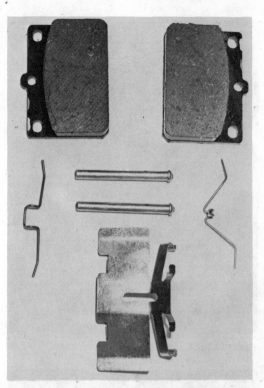
Disc brake pads, springs and pins

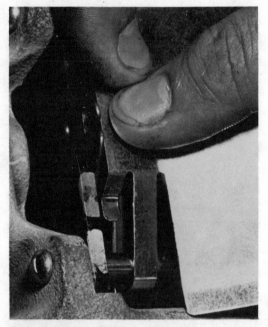
Removing the pad retaining clip

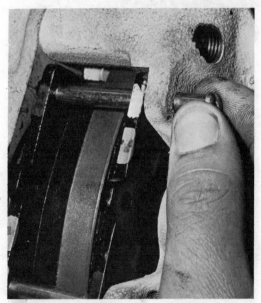
Retaining pin removal

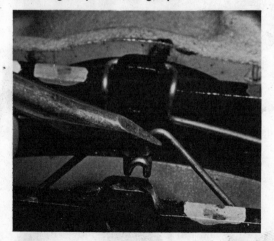
Removing the retaining pin springs

them, care must be taken to prevent the springs from flying apart.

3. The front brake pad can be removed, together with the shim, after removing the springs and pins. If the pads are difficult to remove, open the bleeder valve and move the caliper in the direction of the piston. The

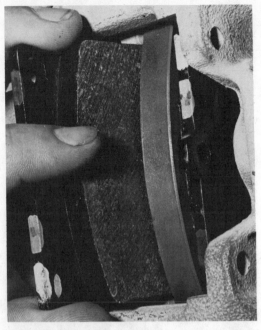

Removing the pads

Closeup showing retaining pins

pads will become loose and can be easily re-moved.

NOTE: *After the pads are removed, the brake pedal must not be touched.*

The disc pads should be replaced when approximately 0.08 in. lining thickness remains (thickness of lining material only).

To provide space for installing the pad, loosen the bleed valve and push the inner piston back into the cylinder. Also push back the outer piston by applying pressure to the caliper. After providing space for the pads, close the bleed valve and insert the pad. Insert a shim behind each pad with the arrow on the shim pointing up. Incorrect installation of the shims can cause squealing brakes.

Disc Brake Calipers
REMOVAL AND INSTALLATION
All Models

1. Raise the front of the car and support it with safety stands. Remove the front wheels.

Caliper housing removal

2. Loosen the brake line at the wheel cylinder.

3. The caliper housing is mounted to the knuckle with two bolts located behind the cylinder. Remove these bolts and the caliper.

To install, reverse the removal procedure. Be sure to inspect all parts before installing and bleed the brake system before operating the car.

INSPECTION AND OVERHAUL

NOTE: *Wash all parts in brake fluid. Do not use cleaning solvent or gasoline.*

1. Remove the inner and outer pad springs and pin clips. Then remove the pins and pads.

NOTE: *The springs are different, so note the location and method of installation before removing.*

2. Push the yoke toward the rear (inboard side) of the cylinder, until it is free to separate the yoke from the cylinder. You may have to tap lightly with a plastic hammer (where the mounting bolts are located) to remove the cylinder. Exercise extreme care to avoid damaging the cylinder body. If only the cylinder body moves, without the outer piston, a gentle tap on the piston should loosen it.

Retaining ring removal

Piston removal

3. To dismantle the cylinder, first remove the retaining rings at both ends of the cylinder with a screwdriver, being careful not to damage the rubber boot.

4. Both pistons can be removed from the cylinder body either by pushing through one end with a wooden rod or by blowing compressed air into the cylinder inlet port.

NOTE: *If the wheel cylinder pistons are removed for any reason, the piston seals must be replaced.*

Piston seal

5. Remove the piston seals, installed on the inside of the cylinder at both ends, with a screwdriver.

6. Inspect the caliper operation. If the lining wear differs greatly between the inner and outer pads, the caliper may be unable to move properly due to rust and dirt on the

Note the discoloration in the caliper. If it cannot be cleaned up easily, it will have to be replaced

sliding surfaces. Clean the sliding part of the caliper and apply brake grease.

NOTE: *All brake parts are critical items. If there is any question as to the serviceability of any brake part—replace it.*

7. Check the piston-to-cylinder clearance. The specified clearance is 0.0008–0.005 in. Also check the pistons and cylinder bore for scuffing and scratching.

Installing piston in caliper

8. Check the dust covers, retaining rings, nylon retainers and all other parts for wear or damage.

9. To reassemble the caliper, reverse the removal procedure. Bleed the brake system.

Brake Disc

REMOVAL AND INSTALLATION

NOTE: *The following procedure for the brake disc removal necessitates the use of a hydraulic press. You will have to go to a machine or auto shop equipped with a press. Do not attempt this procedure without a press.*

1. Raise the front of the car and support it with safety stands. Remove the front wheels.

2. Remove the center spindle nuts.

3. Remove the caliper assembly. Do not let the caliper assembly hang by the brake hose.

4. Use a slide hammer with a hub puller attachment, or a conventional hub puller, to extract the hub with the disc attached.

5. Remove the four bolts and separate the hub and disc.

6. Remove the knuckle from the car (see Chapter 8).

7. Remove the wheel bearings from the knuckle (see below).

NOTE: *If, for any reason, the hub is removed, the front wheel bearings must be replaced.*

8. To install the disc, you have to use a hydraulic press for both the bearings and the hub. After installing the bearings (see below), install the front hub using the special base (tool no. 07965-6340300) and drifts (tool no. 07965-6340100 and 07965-6340200). Position the hub with the knuckle underneath on the base and press it down through the base.

INSPECTION

1. The brake disc develops circular scores after long or even short usage when there is frequent braking. Excessive scoring not only causes a squealing brake, but also shortens the service life of the brake pads. However, light scoring of the disc surface, not exceeding 0.015 in. in depth, will result from normal use and is not detrimental to brake operation.

NOTE: *Differences in the left and right disc surfaces can result in uneven braking.*

2. Disc run-out is the movement of the disc from side-to-side. Place a dial indicator

Checking disc runout

in the middle of the pad wear area and turn the disc, while checking the indicator. If disc run-out exceeds 0.006 in., replace the disc.

3. Disc parallelism is the measurement of variations in disc thickness at several locations on the disc circumference. To measure parallelism, place a mark on the disc and measure the disc thickness with a micrometer. Repeat this measurement at eight (8) equal increments on the circumference of the disc. If the measurements vary more than 0.0028 in., replace the disc.

NOTE: *Only the outer portion of the disc can be checked while installed on the car. If the installed parallelism check is within specifications, but you have reason to suspect that parallelism is the problem, then remove the disc and repeat the check using the center of pad wear for a checking point.*

Wheel Bearings

REMOVAL AND INSTALLATION

NOTE: *The following procedure for the Honda wheel bearing removal and installation necessitates the use of an hydraulic press. You will have to go to a machine or auto shop equipped with a press. Do not attempt this procedure without a press.*

1. Raise the front of the car and support it with safety stands. Remove the front wheel.

2. Remove the caliper assembly from the brake disc and separate the tie-rod ball joint and lower ball joint from the knuckle (see Chapter 8).

3. Loosen the lockbolt which retains the front strut in the knuckle. Tap the top of the knuckle with a hammer and slide it off the shock. Remove the knuckle and hub by sliding the driveshaft out of the hub.

4. Remove the wheel bearing dust cover on the inboard side of the knuckle.

5. Remove the four bolts which hold the brake disc onto the hub. Remove the splashguard by removing the three retaining screws.

6. Remove the outer bearing retainer.

7. Remove the wheel bearings by supporting the knuckle in a hydraulic press, using two support plates (or special tool no. 07965-6340300). Make sure that the plates do not overlap the outer bearing race. Now use a proper sized driver (or tool no. 07947-6340400) and handle (tool no. 07949-6110000) to remove the bearings.

NOTE: *Whenever the wheel bearings are removed, always replace with a new set of bearings and outer dust seal.*

8. Pack each bearing with grease before installing (see below).

9. To install the bearings, press them into the knuckle using the same support plates as above, plus the installing base (tool no. 07965-634040). Use the same driver and handle you used to remove the bearing.

NOTE: *The front wheel bearings are the angular contact type. It is important that they be installed with the manufacturer's markings facing inward.*

10. Use the press to install the front hub (see above).

11. The rest of installation is the reverse of the removal procedure.

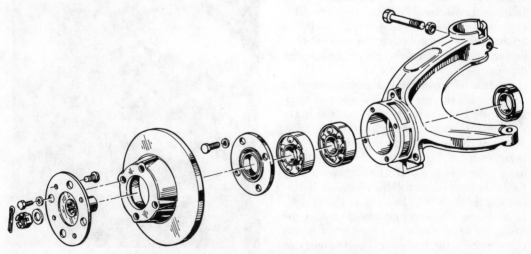

Exploded view of front wheel bearings, rotor, and related parts

CLEANING AND REPACKING

1. Clean all old grease from the driveshafts spindles on the car.

2. Remove all old grease from the hub and knuckle and thoroughly dry and wipe clean all components.

3. When fitting new bearings, you must pack them with wheel bearing grease. To do this, place a glob of grease in your left palm, then, holding one of the bearings in your right hand, drag the face of the bearing heavily through the grease. This must be done to work as much grease as possible through the ball bearings and the cage. Turn the bearing and continue to pull it through the grease, until the grease is thoroughly packed between the bearing balls and the cage, all around the bearing. Repeat this operation until all of the bearings are packed with grease.

4. Pack the inside of the rotor and knuckle hub with a moderate amount of grease. Do not overload the hub with grease.

5. Apply a small amount of grease to the spindle and to the lip of the inner seal before installing.

6. To install the bearings, check the above procedures.

7. See Chapter 1 for adjustment and spindle nut torque.

REAR DRUM BRAKES

All Hondas employ a leading/trailing type of drum brake, in which there are two curved brake shoes supported by an anchor plate and wheel cylinder. When the brake pedal is depressed and hydraulic pressure is delivered to the wheel cylinder, the wheel cylinder expands to force the shoes against the drum.

Friction between the brake shoes and the drum causes the car to slow down and stop. When the brake pedal is released, the brake shoe return springs move the brakes away from the drum. If the lining on the brakes becomes contaminated or if the lining or drum becomes grooved, the engagement of the brakes and drum will become very harsh, causing the brakes to lock up and/or squeal. If the brake shoes on one wheel contact the drum before the same action occurs in the other wheels, the brakes will pull to one side when applied.

Brake Drums

REMOVAL AND INSTALLATION

All Models

1. Raise the rear of the car and support it with safety stands. Remove the rear wheels. Make sure that the parking brake is *off*.

2. Remove the bearing cap and the castle nut.

3. Pull off the rear brake drum. If the drum is difficult to remove, use a brake drum puller, or a front hub puller and slide hammer.

4. To install, reverse the removal procedures.

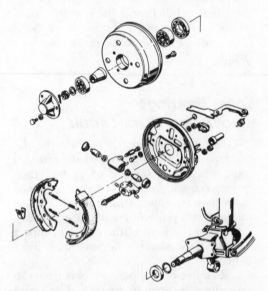

Exploded view of rear drum brake assembly—Civic sedan and hatchback

Bearing cap removal on the Civic

Cotter pin removal

Castle nut removal

Tighten the rear hub nut to 83 ft lbs on the Civic. On the Accord, which has a tapered roller bearing, use the following procedure:

1. Tighten the hub nut to 18 ft lbs.
2. Rotate the drum by hand several times and then loosen the nut.
3. Torque the nut to 3.6 ft lbs.
4. If the spindle nut is not aligned with the hole in spindle, tighten the nut just enough to align the nut and the hole.

Bearing cap removal on the Accord

Removing the rear drum with a slide hammer

5. Insert the cotter pin holder and a new cotter pin.

INSPECTION

Check the drum for cracks and the inner surface of the shoe for excessive wear and damage. The inner diameter (I.D.) of the drum should be no more than specifications, nor should the drum be more than 0.004 in. out-of-round.

Brake Shoes
REMOVAL AND INSTALLATION
All Models

1. Remove the brake drum (see above).
2. Remove the tension pin clips and the

Inspecting the drum for cracks

Rear brake shoes

two brake return springs. Then remove the shoes. If you are installing new shoes, back off the adjusters.

CAUTION: *The upper and lower brake shoe return springs on the sedan are different and should not be interchanged. The upper spring is designed so that the spring coils are located on the outboard side of the shoe, while the lower spring is designed so that its coils are located on the inboard side*

Closeup of brake shoe retaining clip

Torquing the rear hub nut on the Civic

of the shoe with the crossbar facing downward.

3. To install, reverse the removal procedure. Be sure to check the brake lining thickness before assembly. If the thickness is less than 0.08 in., replace the lining.

Wheel Cylinders
REMOVAL AND INSTALLATION
All Models

1. Remove the brake drum and shoes (see above).

2. Disconnect the parking brake cable and brake lines at the backing plate. Be sure to have a drip pan to catch the brake fluid.

3. Remove the two wheel cylinder retaining nuts on the inboard side of the backing plate and remove the wheel cylinder.

4. To install, reverse the removal procedure. When assembling, apply a thin coat of grease to the grooves of the wheel cylinder piston and the sliding surfaces of the backing plate.

OVERHAUL

Remove the wheel cylinder dust seals from the grooves to permit the removal of the cylinder pistons.

Disassembled wheel cylinder

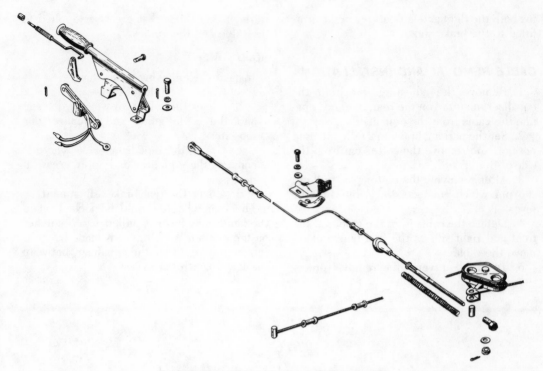

Exploded view of parking brake components

Wash all parts in fresh brake fluid and check the cylinder bore and pistons for scratches and other damage, replacing where necessary. Check the clearance between the piston and the cylinder bore, by taking the difference between the piston diameter and the bore diameter. The specified clearance is 0.0008–0.004 in.

When assembling the wheel cylinder, apply a coat of brake fluid to the pistons, piston cups and cylinder walls.

HANDBRAKE (PARKING BRAKE)

The parking brake is a mechanical type which applies braking force to the rear wheels, through the rear brake shoes. The cable, which is attached to the tail end of the parking brake lever, extends to the equalizer and to the right and left rear brakes. When the lever is pulled, the cable becomes taut, pull-

Brake Specifications
(All measurements given in inches)

Year	Model	Rear Drum ID		Minimum Disc Thickness	Front Pad Thickness		Rear Shoe Thickness	
		New	Max Allow-able		New	Min Allow-able	New	Min Allow-able
1973–78	Sedan	7.087–7.126	7.146	0.354	0.4055	0.063	0.197	0.079
1975–78	Wagon	7.874–7.913	7.933	0.449	0.5510	0.300	0.236	0.118
1976–78	Accord	7.08	7.15	0.437	0.381	0.060	0.197	0.079

ing both the right and left parking brake arms fitted to the brake shoes.

CABLE REMOVAL AND INSTALLATION

1. Remove the adjusting nut from the equalizer mounted on the rear axle and separate the cable from the equalizer.

2. Set the parking brake to a fully released position and remove the cotter pin from the side of the brake lever.

3. After removing the cotter pin, pull out the pin which connects the cable and the lever.

4. Detach the cable from the guides at the front and right side of the fuel tank and remove the cable.

5. To install, reverse the removal procedure, making sure that grease is applied to the cable and the guides.

ADJUSTMENT

Inspect the following items:

a. Check the ratchet for wear;

b. Check the cables for wear or damage and the cable guide and equalizer for looseness;

c. Check the equalizer cable where it contacts the equalizer and apply grease if necessary;

d. Check the rear brake adjustment.

The rear wheels should be locked when the handbrake lever is pulled 1 to 5 notches on the ratchet. Adjustment is made by turning the nut located at the equalizer, between the lower control arms.

9

Body

The list of tools and equipment you may need to fix minor body damage ranges from very basic hand tools to a wide assortment of specialized body tools. Most minor scratches, dings and rust holes can be fixed using an electric drill, wire wheel or grinder attachment, half-round plastic file, sanding block, various grades of sandpaper (#120, which is coarse through #600, which is fine, in both wet and dry types), auto body plastic, primer, touch-up paint, spreaders, newspaper and masking tape. If you intend to try straightening any dents, you'll probably also need a slide hammer (dent puller).

Most auto body repair kits contain all the materials you need to do the job right in the kit. So, if you have a small rust spot or dent you want to fix, check the contents of the kit before you run out and buy any additional tools.

ALIGNING BODY PANELS

Doors

There are several methods of adjusting doors. Your vehicle will probably use one of those illustrated.

Whenever a door is removed and is to be reinstalled, you should matchmark the posi-tion of the hinges on the door pillars. The holes of the hinges and/or the hinge attaching points are usually oversize to permit alignment of doors. The striker plate is also moveable, through oversize holes, permitting up-and-down, in-and-out and fore-and-aft movement. Fore-and-aft movement is made by adding or subtracting shims from behind the striker and pillar post. The striker should be adjusted so that the door closes fully and remains closed, yet enters the lock freely.

DOOR HINGES

Don't try to cover up poor door adjustment with a striker plate adjustment. The gap on each side of the door should be equal and uniform and there should be no metal-to-metal contact as the door is opened or closed.

1. Determine which hinge bolts must be loosened to move the door in the desired direction.

2. Loosen the hinge bolt(s) just enough to allow the door to be moved with a padded pry bar.

3. Move the door a small amount and check the fit, after tightening the bolts. Be sure that there is no bind or interference with adjacent panels.

4. Repeat this until the door is properly positioned, and tighten all the bolts securely.

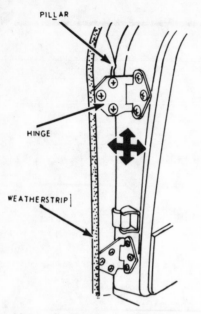

Door hinge adjustment

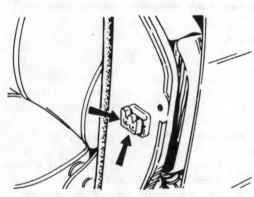

Move the door striker as indicated by arrows

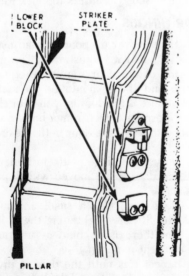

Striker plate and lower block

Hood, Trunk or Tailgate

As with doors, the outline of hinges should be scribed before removal. The hood and trunk can be aligned by loosening the hinge bolts in their slotted mounting holes and moving the hood or trunk lid as necessary. The hood and trunk have adjustable catch locations to regulate lock engagement bumpers at the front and/or rear of the hood provide a vertical adjustment and the hood lockpin can be adjusted for proper engagement.

The tailgate on the station wagon can be adjusted by loosening the hinge bolts in their slotted mounting holes and moving the tailgate on its hinges. The latchplate and

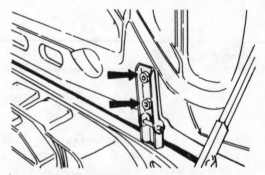

Loosen the hinge boots to permit fore-and-aft and horizontal adjustment

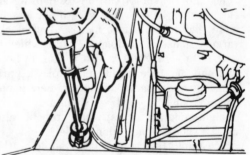

The hood is adjusted vertically by stop-screws at the front and/or rear

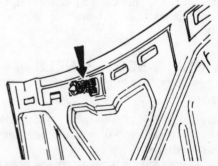

The hood pin can be adjusted for proper lock engagement

latch striker at the bottom of the tailgate opening can be adjusted to stop rattle. An adjustable bumper is located on each side.

RUST, UNDERCOATING, AND RUSTPROOFING

Rust

About the only technical information the average backyard mechanic needs to know about rust is that it is an electro-chemical process that works from **the inside out** on unprotected ferrous metals such as steel and iron. Salt, pollution, humidity—these things and more create and promote the formation of rust. You can't stop rust once it starts. Once rust has started on a fender or a body panel, the only sure way to stop it is to replace the part.

It's a lot easier to prevent rust than to remove it, especially if you have a new car and most late model cars are pretty well rustproofed when the leave the factory. In the early seventies, it seemed like cars were rusting out faster than you could pay them off and Detroit (and the imports) realized that this is not exactly the way you build customer loyalty.

Undercoating

Contrary to what most people think, the primary purpose of undercoating is not to prevent rust, but to deaden noise that might otherwise be transmitted to the car's interior. Since cars are pretty quiet these days anyway, dealers are only too willing to promote undercoating as a rust preventative. Undercoating will of course, prevent some rust, but only if applied when the car is brand-new. In any case, undercoating doesn't provide the protection that a good rustproofing does. If you do decide to undercoat your car and it's not brand-new, you have a big clean-up job ahead of you. It's a good idea to have the underside of the car professionally steam-cleaned and save yourself a lot of work. Spraying undercoat on dirty or rusty parts is only going to make things worse, since the undercoat will trap any rust causing agents.

Rustproofing

The best thing you can do for a new or nearly new car is to have it properly rust-proofed. There are two ways you can go about this. You can do it yourself, or you can have one of the big rustproofing companies do it for you. Naturally, it's going to cost you a lot more to have a big company do it, but it's worth it if your car is new or nearly new. If you own an older car that you plan to hang onto for a while, then doing it yourself might be the best idea. Professional rust-proofing isn't cheap ($100–$250), but it's definitely worth it if your car is new. The rustproofing companies won't guarantee their jobs on cars that are over three months old or have more than about 3000 miles on them because they feel the corrosion process may have already begun.

If you have an older car that hasn't started to rust yet, the best idea might be to purchase one of the do-it-yourself rustproofing kits that are available, and do the job yourself.

Drain Holes

Rusty rocker panels are a common problem on nearly every car, but they can be prevented by simply drilling some holes in your rocker panels to let the water out, or keeping the ones that are already there clean and unclogged. Most cars these days have a series of holes in the rocker panels to prevent moisture collection there, but they frequently become clogged up. Just use a small screwdriver or penknife to keep them clean. If your car doesn't have drain holes, it's a simple matter to drill a couple of holes in each panel.

Repairing Minor Body Damage

Unless your car just rolled off the showroom floor, chances are it has a few minor scratches or dings in it somewhere, or a small rust spot you've been meaning to fix. You just haven't been able to decide whether or not you can really do the job. Well, if the damage is anything like that presented here, there are a number of auto body repair kits that contain everything you need to repair minor scratches, dents, and rust spots. Even rust holes can be repaired if you use the correct kit. If you're unsure of your ability, start out with a small scratch. Once you've mastered small scratches and dings, you can work your way up to the more complicated repairs. When doing rust repairs, remember that unless all the rust is removed, it's going to come back in a year or less. Just sanding the rust down and applying some paint won't work.

Repairing Minor Surface Rust and Scratches

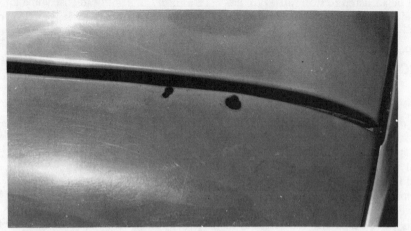

1. Just about everybody has a minor rust spot or scratches on their car. Spots such as these can be easily repaired in an hour or two. You'll need some sandpaper, masking tape, primer, and a can of touch-up paint.

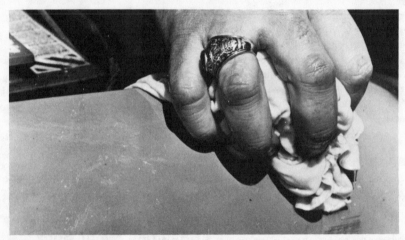

2. The first step is to wash the area down to remove all traces of dirt and road grime. If the car has been frequently waxed, you should wipe it with thinner or some other wax remover so that the paint will stick.

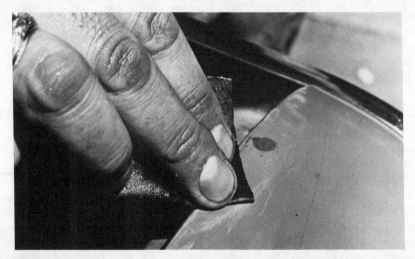

3. Small rust spots and scratches like these will only require light hand sanding. For a job like this, you can start with about grade 320 sandpaper and then use a 400 grit for the final sanding.

4. Once you've sanded the area with 320 paper, wet a piece of 400 paper and sand it lightly. Wet sanding will feather the edges of the surrounding paint into the area to be painted. For large areas, you could use a sanding block, but it's not really necessary for a small job like this.

5. The area should look like this once you're finished sanding. Wipe off any water and run the palm of your hand over the sanded area with your eyes closed. You shouldn't be able to feel any bumps or ridges anywhere. Make sure you have sanded a couple of inches back in each direction so you'll get good paint adhesion.

6. Once you have the area sanded to your satisfaction, mask the surrounding area with masking tape and newspaper. Be sure to cover any chrome or trim that might get sprayed. You'll have to mask far enough back from the damaged area to allow for overspray. If you mask right around the sanded spots, you'll end up with a series of lines marking the painted area.

7. You can avoid a lot of excess overspray by cutting a hole in a piece of cardboard that approximately matches the area you are going to paint. Hold the cardboard steady over the area as you spray the primer on. If you haven't painted before, it's a good idea to practice on something before you try painting your car. Don't hold the paint can in one spot. Keep it moving and you'll avoid runs and sags.

8. The primered area should look like this when you have finished. It's better to spray several light coats than one heavy coat. Let the primer dry for several minutes between coats. Make sure you've covered all the bare metal.

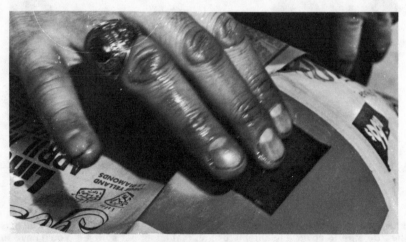

9. After the primer has dried, sand the area with wet 400 paper, wash it off and let it dry. Your final coat goes on next, so make sure the area is clean and dry.

10. Spray the touch-up paint on using the cardboard again. Make the first coat a very light coat (known as a fog coat). Remember to keep the paint can moving smoothly at about 8–12 inches from the surface.

11. Once you've finished painting, let the paint dry for about 15 minutes before you remove the masking tape and newspaper.

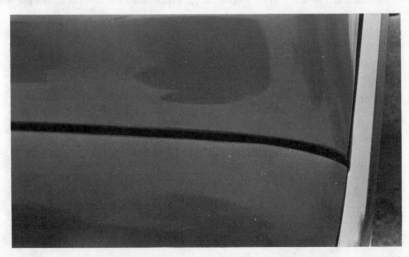

12. Let the paint dry for several days before you rub it out lightly with rubbing compound, and the finished job should be indistinguishable from the rest of the car. Don't rub hard or you'll cut through the paint.

Repairing Rust Holes With Fiberglass

1. The job we've picked here isn't an easy one mainly because of the location. The compound curves make the work trickier than if the surface were flat.

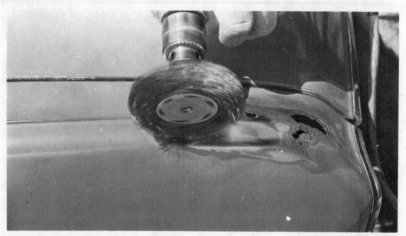

2. You'll need a drill and a wire brush for the first step, which is the removal of all the paint and rust from the rusted-out area.

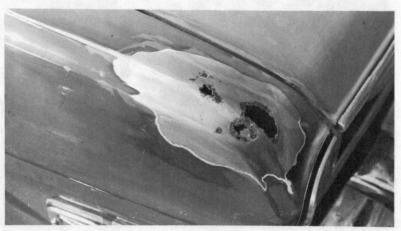

3. When you've finished grinding, the area to be repaired should look like this. Grind the paint back several inches in each direction to ensure that the patch will adhere to the metal. Remove all the damaged metal or the rust will return.

4. Tap the edges of the holes inward with a ballpeen hammer to allow for the thickness of the fiberglass material. Tap lightly so that you don't destroy any contours.

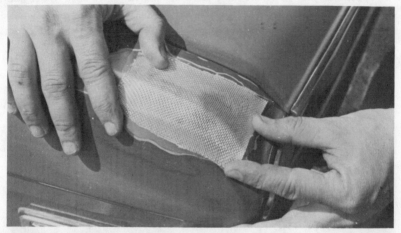

5. Follow the directions of the kit you purchase carefully. With fiberglass repair kits, the first step is generally to cut one or two pieces of fiberglass to cover the hole. Quite often, the procedure is to cut one patch the size of the prepared area and one patch the size of the hole.

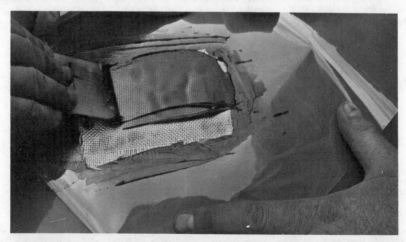

6. Mix the fiberglass material and the patching compound together following the directions supplied with the kit. With this particular kit, a layer type process is used, with the entire mixture being prepared on a piece of plastic film known as a release sheet. Keep in mind that not all kits work this way. Be careful when you mix the catalyst with the resin, as too much catalyst will harden the mixture before you can apply it.

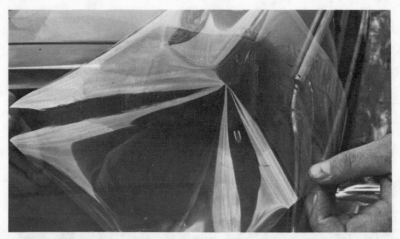

7. Spread the material on the damaged area using the release sheet. This process is essentially meant for smooth flat areas, and as a result, the release sheet would not adhere to the surface properly on our test car. If this happens to you, you'll probably have to remove the release sheet and spread the fiberglass compound out with your fingers or a small spreader.

8. This is what the fiberglass mixture looked like on our car after it had hardened. Because of the contours, we found it nearly impossible to smooth the mixture with a spreader, so we used our fingers. Unfortunately, it makes for a messy job that requires a lot of sanding. If you're working on a flat surface, you won't have this problem.

9. After the patch has hardened, sand it down to a smooth surface. You'll probably have to start with about grade 100 sandpaper and work your way up to 400 wet paper. If you have a particularly rough surface, you could start with a half-round plastic file.

10. This is what the finished product should look like before you apply paint. Many of the kits come with glazing compound to fill in small imperfections left after the initial sanding. You'll probably need some. We did. The entire sanding operation took about an hour. Feather the edges of the repaired area into the surrounding paint carefully. As in any other body job, your hand is the best indicator of what's smooth and what isn't. It doesn't matter if it looks smooth. It's got to feel smooth. Take your time with this step and it will come out right.

11. Once you've smoothed out the repair, mask the entire area carefully, and spray the repair with primer. Keep the spray can moving in steady even strokes, overlap every stroke, and keep the spray can about 8–12 inches from the surface. Apply several coats of primer, letting the primer dry between coats.

12. The finished product (in primer) looks like this. If you were going to just spot paint this area, the next step would be to spray the correct color on the repaired area. This particular car is waiting for a complete paint job.

Appendix

General Conversion Table

Multiply by	To convert	To	
2.54	Inches	Centimeters	.3937
30.48	Feet	Centimeters	.0328
.914	Yards	Meters	1.094
1.609	Miles	Kilometers	.621
.645	Square inches	Square cm.	.155
.836	Square yards	Square meters	1.196
16.39	Cubic inches	Cubic cm.	.061
28.3	Cubic feet	Liters	.0353
.4536	Pounds	Kilograms	2.2045
4.226	Gallons	Liters	.264
.068	Lbs./sq. in. (psi)	Atmospheres	14.7
.138	Foot pounds	Kg. m.	7.23
1.014	H.P. (DIN)	H.P. (SAE)	.9861
—	To obtain	From	Multiply by

Note: 1 cm. equals 10 mm.; 1 mm. equals .0394″.

Conversion—Common Fractions to Decimals and Millimeters

Common Fractions	Decimal Fractions	Millimeters (approx.)	Common Fractions	Decimal Fractions	Millimeters (approx.)	Common Fractions	Decimal Fractions	Millimeters (approx.)
1/128	.008	0.20	11/32	.344	8.73	43/64	.672	17.07
1/64	.016	0.40	23/64	.359	9.13	11/16	.688	17.46
1/32	.031	0.79	3/8	.375	9.53	45/64	.703	17.86
3/64	.047	1.19	25/64	.391	9.92	23/32	.719	18.26
1/16	.063	1.59	13/32	.406	10.32	47/64	.734	18.65
5/64	.078	1.98	27/64	.422	10.72	3/4	.750	19.05
3/32	.094	2.38	7/16	.438	11.11	49/64	.766	19.45
7/64	.109	2.78	29/64	.453	11.51	25/32	.781	19.84
1/8	.125	3.18	15/32	.469	11.91	51/64	.797	20.24
9/64	.141	3.57	31/64	.484	12.30	13/16	.813	20.64
5/32	.156	3.97	1/2	.500	12.70	53/64	.828	21.03
11/64	.172	4.37	33/64	.516	13.10	27/32	.844	21.43
3/16	.188	4.76	17/32	.531	13.49	55/64	.859	21.83
13/64	.203	5.16	35/64	.547	13.89	7/8	.875	22.23
7/32	.219	5.56	9/16	.563	14.29	57/64	.891	22.62
15/64	.234	5.95	37/64	.578	14.68	29/32	.906	23.02
1/4	.250	6.35	19/32	.594	15.08	59/64	.922	23.42
17/64	.266	6.75	39/64	.609	15.48	15/16	.938	23.81
9/32	.281	7.14	5/8	.625	15.88	61/64	.953	24.21
19/64	.297	7.54	41/64	.641	16.27	31/32	.969	24.61
5/16	.313	7.94	21/32	.656	16.67	63/64	.984	25.00
21/64	.328	8.33						

Conversion—Millimeters to Decimal Inches

mm	inches	mm	inches	mm	inches	mm	inches	mm	inches
1	.039 370	31	1.220 470	61	2.401 570	91	3.582 670	210	8.267 700
2	.078 740	32	1.259 840	62	2.440 940	92	3.622 040	220	8.661 400
3	.118 110	33	1.299 210	63	2.480 310	93	3.661 410	230	9.055 100
4	.157 480	34	1.338 580	64	2.519 680	94	3.700 780	240	9.448 800
5	.196 850	35	1.377 949	65	2.559 050	95	3.740 150	250	9.842 500
6	.236 220	36	1.417 319	66	2.598 420	96	3.779 520	260	10.236 200
7	.275 590	37	1.456 689	67	2.637 790	97	3.818 890	270	10.629 900
8	.314 960	38	1.496 050	68	2.677 160	98	3.858 260	280	11.032 600
9	.354 330	39	1.535 430	69	2.716 530	99	3.897 630	290	11.417 300
10	.393 700	40	1.574 800	70	2.755 900	100	3.937 000	300	11.811 000
11	.433 070	41	1.614 170	71	2.795 270	105	4.133 848	310	12.204 700
12	.472 440	42	1.653 540	72	2.834 640	110	4.330 700	320	12.598 400
13	.511 810	43	1.692 910	73	2.874 010	115	4.527 550	330	12.992 100
14	.551 180	44	1.732 280	74	2.913 380	120	4.724 400	340	13.385 800
15	.590 550	45	1.771 650	75	2.952 750	125	4.921 250	350	13.779 500
16	.629 920	46	1.811 020	76	2.992 120	130	5.118 100	360	14.173 200
17	.669 290	47	1.850 390	77	3.031 490	135	5.314 950	370	14.566 900
18	.708 660	48	1.889 760	78	3.070 860	140	5.511 800	380	14.960 600
19	.748 030	49	1.929 130	79	3.110 230	145	5.708 650	390	15.354 300
20	.787 400	50	1.968 500	80	3.149 600	150	5.905 500	400	15.748 000
21	.826 770	51	2.007 870	81	3.188 970	155	6.102 350	500	19.685 000
22	.866 140	52	2.047 240	82	3.228 340	160	6.299 200	600	23.622 000
23	.905 510	53	2.086 610	83	3.267 710	165	6.496 050	700	27.559 000
24	.944 880	54	2.125 980	84	3.307 080	170	6.692 900	800	31.496 000
25	.984 250	55	2.165 350	85	3.346 450	175	6.889 750	900	35.433 000
26	1.023 620	56	2.204 720	86	3.385 820	180	7.086 600	1000	39.370 000
27	1.062 990	57	2.244 090	87	3.425 190	185	7.283 450	2000	78.740 000
28	1.102 360	58	2.283 460	88	3.464 560	190	7.480 300	3000	118.110 000
29	1.141 730	59	2.322 830	89	3.503 903	195	7.677 150	4000	157.480 000
30	1.181 100	60	2.362 200	90	3.543 300	200	7.874 000	5000	196.850 000

To change decimal millimeters to decimal inches, position the decimal point where desired on either side of the millimeter measurement shown and reset the inches decimal by the same number of digits in the same direction. For example, to convert 0.001 mm to decimal inches, reset the decimal behind the 1 mm (shown on the chart) to 0.001; change the decimal inch equivalent (0.039″ shown) to 0.000039″.

Tap Drill Sizes

Screw & Tap Size	National Fine or S.A.E. Threads Per Inch	Use Drill Number
No. 5	44	37
No. 6	40	33
No. 8	36	29
No. 10	32	21
No. 12	28	15
1/4	28	3
5/16	24	1
3/8	24	Q
7/16	20	W
1/2	20	29/64
9/16	18	33/64
5/8	18	37/64
3/4	16	11/16
7/8	14	13/16
1 1/8	12	1 3/64
1 1/4	12	1 11/64
1 1/2	12	1 27/64

Tap Drill Sizes

Screw & Tap Size	National Coarse or U.S.S. Threads Per Inch	Use Drill Number
No. 5	40	39
No. 6	32	36
No. 8	32	29
No. 10	24	25
No. 12	24	17
1/4	20	8
5/16	18	F
3/8	16	5/16
7/16	14	U
1/2	13	27/64
9/16	12	31/64
5/8	11	17/32
3/4	10	21/32
7/8	9	49/64
1	8	7/8
1 1/8	7	63/64
1 1/4	7	1 7/64
1 1/2	6	1 11/32

Decimal Equivalent Size of the Number Drills

Drill No.	Decimal Equivalent	Drill No.	Decimal Equivalent	Drill No.	Decimal Equivalent
80	.0135	53	.0595	26	.1470
79	.0145	52	.0635	25	.1495
78	.0160	51	.0670	24	.1520
77	.0180	50	.0700	23	.1540
76	.0200	49	.0730	22	.1570
75	.0210	48	.0760	21	.1590
74	.0225	47	.0785	20	.1610
73	.0240	46	.0810	19	.1660
72	.0250	45	.0820	18	.1695
71	.0260	44	.0860	17	.1730
70	.0280	43	.0890	16	.1770
69	.0292	42	.0935	15	.1800
68	.0310	41	.0960	14	.1820
67	.0320	40	.0980	13	.1850
66	.0330	39	.0995	12	.1890
65	.0350	38	.1015	11	.1910
64	.0360	37	.1040	10	.1935
63	.0370	36	.1065	9	.1960
62	.0380	35	.1100	8	.1990
61	.0390	34	.1110	7	.2010
60	.0400	33	.1130	6	.2040
59	.0410	32	.1160	5	.2055
58	.0420	31	.1200	4	.2090
57	.0430	30	.1285	3	.2130
56	.0465	29	.1360	2	.2210
55	.0520	28	.1405	1	.2280
54	.0550	27	.1440		

Decimal Equivalent Size of the Letter Drills

Letter Drill	Decimal Equivalent	Letter Drill	Decimal Equivalent	Letter Drill	Decimal Equivalent
A	.234	J	.277	S	.348
B	.238	K	.281	T	.358
C	.242	L	.290	U	.368
D	.246	M	.295	V	.377
E	.250	N	.302	W	.386
F	.257	O	.316	X	.397
G	.261	P	.323	Y	.404
H	.266	Q	.332	Z	.413
I	.272	R	.339		

Anti-Freeze Chart

Temperatures Shown in Degrees Fahrenheit +32 is Freezing

Cooling System Capacity Quarts	Quarts of ETHYLENE GLYCOL Needed for Protection to Temperatures Shown Below													
	1	2	3	4	5	6	7	8	9	10	11	12	13	14
10	+24°	+16°	+ 4°	−12°	−34°	−62°								
11	+25	+18	+ 8	− 6	−23	−47								
12	+26	+19	+10	0	−15	−34	−57°							
13	+27	+21	+13	+ 3	− 9	−25	−45							
14			+15	+ 6	− 5	−18	−34							
15			+16	+ 8	0	−12	−26							
16			+17	+10	+ 2	− 8	−19	−34	−52°					
17			+18	+12	+ 5	− 4	−14	−27	−42					
18			+19	+14	+ 7	0	−10	−21	−34	−50°				
19			+20	+15	+ 9	+ 2	− 7	−16	−28	−42				
20				+16	+10	+ 4	− 3	−12	−22	−34	−48°			
21				+17	+12	+ 6	0	− 9	−17	−28	−41			
22				+18	+13	+ 8	+ 2	− 6	−14	−23	−34	−47°		
23				+19	+14	+ 9	+ 4	− 3	−10	−19	−29	−40		
24				+19	+15	+10	+ 5	0	− 8	−15	−23	−34	−46°	
25				+20	+16	+12	+ 7	+ 1	− 5	−12	−20	−29	−40	−50°
26					+17	+13	+ 8	+ 3	− 3	− 9	−16	−25	−34	−44
27					+18	+14	+ 9	+ 5	− 1	− 7	−13	−21	−29	−39
28					+18	+15	+10	+ 6	+ 1	− 5	−11	−18	−25	−34
29					+19	+16	+12	+ 7	+ 2	− 3	− 8	−15	−22	−29
30					+20	+17	+13	+ 8	+ 4	− 1	− 6	−12	−18	−25

For capacities over 30 quarts divide true capacity by 3. Find quarts Anti-Freeze for the ⅓ and multiply by 3 for quarts to add.

For capacities under 10 quarts multiply true capacity by 3. Find quarts Anti-Freeze for the tripled volume and divide by 3 for quarts to add.

To Increase the Freezing Protection of Anti-Freeze Solutions Already Installed

Cooling System Capacity Quarts	Number of Quarts of ETHYLENE GLYCOL Anti-Freeze Required to Increase Protection													
	From +20° F. to					From +10° F. to					From 0° F. to			
	0°	−10°	−20°	−30°	−40°	0°	−10°	−20°	−30°	−40°	−10°	−20°	−30°	−40°
10	1¾	2¼	3	3½	3¾	¾	1½	2¼	2¾	3¼	¾	1½	2	2½
12	2	2¾	3½	4	4½	1	1¾	2½	3¼	3¾	1	1¾	2½	3¼
14	2¼	3¼	4	4¾	5½	1¼	2	3	3¾	4½	1	2	3	3½
16	2½	3½	4½	5¼	6	1¼	2½	3½	4¼	5¼	1¼	2¼	3¼	4
18	3	4	5	6	7	1½	2¾	4	5	5¾	1½	2½	3¾	4¾
20	3¼	4½	5¾	6¾	7½	1¾	3	4¼	5½	6½	1½	2¾	4¼	5¼
22	3½	5	6¼	7¼	8¼	1¾	3¼	4¾	6	7¼	1¾	3¼	4½	5½
24	4	5½	7	8	9	2	3½	5	6½	7½	1¾	3½	5	6
26	4¼	6	7½	8¾	10	2	4	5½	7	8¼	2	3¾	5½	6¾
28	4½	6¼	8	9½	10½	2¼	4¼	6	7½	9	2	4	5¾	7¼
30	5	6¾	8½	10	11½	2½	4½	6½	8	9½	2¼	4¼	6¼	7¾

Test radiator solution with proper hydrometer. Determine from the table the number of quarts of solution to be drawn off from a full cooling system and replace with undiluted anti-freeze, to give the desired increased protection. For example, to increase protection of a 22-quart cooling system containing Ethylene Glycol (permanent type) anti-freeze, from +20° F. to −20° F. will require the replacement of 6¼ quarts of solution with undiluted anti-freeze.

Index

Gear, 147
Wheel, 146

T

Thermostat, 80
Tie-rod, 148
Tires, 11
Towing, 16
Transmission
  Automatic, 136
  Manual, 128
Troubleshooting, 34
Tune-up, 18
  Procedures, 18
  Specifications, 20
Turn signal switch, 146

V

Valves
  Adjustment, 30
Vehicle identification, 2

W

Water pump, 80
Wheels, 11
Wheel alignment, 144
Wheel bearings, 161
Wheel cylinders, 164
Windshield wipers, 123
  Linkage, 123
  Motor, 123

25 Ways

TO BETTER GAS MILEAGE

The Federal government's goal is to cut gasoline consumption 10% by 1985. In addition to intelligent purchase of a new vehicle and efficient driving habits, there are other ways to increase gas mileage with your present car or truck.

Tests have shown that almost ¾ of all vehicles on the road need maintenance in areas that directly effect fuel economy. Using this book for regular maintenance and tune-ups can increase fuel economy as much as 10%, depending on your vehicle.

1. **Replace spark plugs regularly.** New plugs alone can increase fuel economy by 3%.

2. **Be sure the plugs are the correct type and properly gapped.**

3. **Set the ignition timing to specifications.**

4. If your vehicle does not have electronic ignition, **check the points, rotor and cap as specified.**

5. **Replace the air filter regularly.** A dirty air filter richens the air/fuel mixture and can increase fuel consumption as much as 10%. Tests show ⅓ of all vehicles have air filters in need of replacement.

6. **Replace the fuel filter** at least as often as recommended.

7. **Be sure the idle speed and carburetor fuel mixture are set to specifications.**

8. **Check the automatic choke.** A sticking or malfunctioning choke wastes gas.

9. **Change the oil and filter as recommended.** Dirty oil is thick and causes extra friction between the moving parts, cutting efficiency and increasing wear.

10. **Replace the PCV valve** at regular intervals.

11. **Service the cooling system** at regular recommended intervals.

12. **Be sure the thermostat is operating properly.** A thermostat that is stuck open delays engine warm-up, and a cold engine uses twice as much fuel as a warm engine.

13. **Be sure the tires are properly inflated.** Under-inflated tires can cost as much as 1 mpg. Better mileage can be achieved by over-inflating the tires (never exceed the maximum inflation pressure on the side of the tire), but the tires will wear faster.

14. **Be sure the drive belts (especially the fan belt) are in good condition** and properly adjusted.

15. **Be sure the battery is fully charged for fast starts.**

16. **Use the recommended viscosity motor oil to reduce friction.**

17. **Use the recommended viscosity fluids in the rear axle and transmission.**

18. **Be sure the wheels are properly balanced.**

19. **Be sure the front end is correctly aligned.** A misaligned front end actually has wheels going in different directions, creating additional drag.

20. **Correctly adjust the wheel bearing.** Wheel bearings adjusted too tight increase rolling resistance.

21. **Be sure the brakes are properly adjusted and not dragging.**

22. **If possible, install radial tires.** Radial tires deliver as much as ½ mpg more than bias belted tires.

23. **Install a flex-type fan** if you don't have a clutch fan. Flex fans push more air at low speeds when more cooling is needed. At high speeds the blades flatten out for less resistance.

24. **Check the radiator cap for a cracked or worn gasket.** If the cap doesn't seal properly, the cooling system will not function properly.

25. **Check the spark plug wires for bad cracks, burned or broken insulation.** Cracked wires decrease fuel efficiency by failing to deliver full voltage to the spark plugs.